A Penguin Special
Beating the Terrorists?

N

Peter Taylor was born in Yorkshire in 1942 and was educated
at Scarborough High School for Boys and Pembroke College,
Cambridge, where he graduated in Classics and Modern
History. After a brief flirtation with teaching, he joined
ITV's 'This Week' programme as a researcher in 1967. From
1969 to 1971 he reported for Thames TV's local 'Today'
programme, and then returned to 'This Week' as a reporter in
1972, where he worked until 1978 before joining Thames
TV's 'TV Eye'. One of his first assignments was 'Bloody
Sunday', which was also his introduction to the violent
politics of Northern Ireland. Since then he has made over
thirty documentaries on the Irish conflict, three of which were
banned: one on IRA fund-raising in America, another on the
Queen's visit to Northern Ireland and a third on the Amnesty
report on police brutality during interrogation. In fact, it was
Peter Taylor's controversial investigation into the Castlereagh
Interrogation Centre that triggered off the Amnesty mission.
In recent years much of his work has been concerned with the
administration of justice in Northern Ireland, such as the
operation of the Diplock courts and the conditions in the
H Blocks. He has also reported on conflicts in Africa, the
Middle East and Vietnam, and is a regular contributor to the
New Statesman, the *Listener* and other publications. He now
reports for BBC TV's 'Panorama' programme.

Peter Taylor is married to Sue McConachy, who is an
Associate Producer in television. They have one son, Ben
Jonathan.

Peter Taylor

Beating the Terrorists?

Interrogation at Omagh, Gough and Castlereagh

 Penguin Books

Penguin Books Ltd, Harmondsworth,
Middlesex, England
Penguin Books, 625 Madison Avenue,
New York, New York 10022, U.S.A.
Penguin Books Australia Ltd, Ringwood,
Victoria, Australia
Penguin Books Canada Ltd, 2801 John Street,
Markham, Ontario, Canada L3R 1B4
Penguin Books (N.Z.) Ltd, 182–190 Wairau Road,
Auckland 10, New Zealand

First published 1980

Copyright © Peter Taylor, 1980
All rights reserved

Filmset, printed and bound in Great Britain
by Hazell Watson & Viney Ltd,
Aylesbury, Bucks
Set in Times

To Susan and B.J.

Contents

Appendices:

Acknowledgements

There are many I wish to thank without whose assistance and trust I could never have written this book. To mention them by name, however, might in many cases jeopardize jobs and careers. They include members of the RUC at all levels, politicians and civil servants on both sides of the water, many members of the legal profession, and in particular the doctors of Northern Ireland. I only hope they feel that their trust has not been misplaced.

The reason for writing this book is to place on the record for public scrutiny the abuses of the police interrogation system which shocked many of those mentioned above and which were consistently denied by those in authority as they tried to cover them up, in particular by attacking those who sought to expose them. The ordeal of Bernard O'Connor, awarded £5,000 'exemplary' damages against the Chief Constable for brutality suffered during his interrogation at Castlereagh in January 1977, is but one case in point. Only by attempting to tell the full story can judgements be made. I have endeavoured to unearth as much of that story as possible to try to set the record straight lest such a critical period in Northern Ireland's history be conveniently buried in the political sand.

Surprisingly, given the sensitive nature of the subject, there were few individuals or bodies who refused to talk to me. Of all those most intimately concerned with events at the time, only Roy Mason, the then Secretary of State for Northern Ireland, declined assistance. Mr Mason said that most of what I would want from him could be found in his speeches in Northern Ireland and Westminster. The Prime Minister at the time, James Callaghan, also declined to discuss the subject owing to his heavy commitments.

To avoid the pitfalls of the Amnesty report, whose cases were dismissed in some quarters because they were anonymous, I have named names in my casebook. Wherever possible I have obtained the permission of those concerned either directly or through their relatives and solicitors, where such cases were not already a matter of court record. In a few instances I preserve anonymity at the request of those concerned.

It would be impossible to thank everyone who helped me in my work, not because there is risk attached to the publication of their names, but because the list is so long. They all have my gratitude.

There are, however, certain individuals and bodies whom I must thank: in particular Sir Kenneth Newman, then Chief Constable of the RUC, who afforded me many privileged facilities; all members of the RUC who provided, directly and indirectly, answers to what must have seemed an unending stream of questions, and the RUC's Press Office, who co-ordinated everything so patiently and efficiently; Professor Kevin Boyle and Michael O'Boyle, who led me skilfully through the legal jungle of Emergency legislation and Strasbourg; Heather Laughton, whose skill and typewriter transformed a maze of words into an illuminated manuscript; all my colleagues at Thames Television who supported me in the work I did; my literary agent, Julian Friedman and Penguin Editor, Neil Middleton, who gave me every encouragement and guidance; and finally, my wife Susan whose support, patience and editorial assistance made this book possible.

Introduction: The Reason Why

> 'No one shall be subjected to torture or to inhuman or degrading treatment or punishment.'
>
> Article 3 of the European Convention on Human Rights

By its very nature the subject matter of this book is bound to arouse strong feelings. There are two parties involved in the interrogation process. On the one side stand detectives of the RUC, who perhaps as much as any branch of the hard-pressed and courageous force, daily place their lives in jeopardy by interviewing terrorist suspects and then – named and identified – give evidence in open court in order to secure their conviction and imprisonment. Since the Emergency began in 1969, 130 policemen have been killed and over 3,500 injured in defence of the state which the IRA seeks to destroy. These detectives in particular and the RUC in general have undoubtedly been the targets of a propaganda campaign, mounted most notably by the Provisional IRA, to undermine the RUC and, especially in the period covered by this book, to destroy the Interrogation Centres whose success was undermining them. No doubt, in furtherance of that campaign, some prisoners did self-inflict their injuries, not only to discredit their interrogators and to try to get off in court by pleading that their statements were beaten out of them and therefore inadmissible as evidence, but also to protect themselves from a possible bullet in the kneecap or head, administered by their own terrorist organization, in retribution for information they may have given to the RUC under interrogation.

On the other side stand members and sympathizers of terrorist organizations like the Provisional IRA, which has been responsible for some of the most appalling atrocities – the La Mon restaurant bombing and the assassination of Lord Mountbatten are perhaps the most shocking – of the past ten years of war in Northern Ireland.[1]

With such disparities in mind, writing a book on such an emotive subject has not been easy. However difficult the task, my motive has been to provide as accurate, detailed and documented a description as possible of a most important period in the recent history of the state of Northern Ireland.

A few days after the assassination of Lord Mountbatten and the killing of eighteen soldiers at Warrenpoint, I received a letter from someone of importance who had agreed to meet and talk to me in confidence about his involvement in the events with which this book is concerned. It was an angry letter: he said that he no longer wished to discuss the matter with me and felt that in the light of 'the very terrible events of the 27th August', there was need for 'a united front against terrorism'. He clearly implied that my investigations were likely to undermine that front. I replied and said that I could not agree.

No doubt the sentiments that person expressed may be echoed by some readers of this book and, almost certainly, by some politicians and members of the security forces. However, I know that not all of them would agree. In the course of my investigations, I spoke to police officers who believed that what had happened at Castlereagh and elsewhere had not only given the I R A a powerful propaganda weapon but had undermined that public confidence in the police which they had worked so hard to establish. Without that confidence there can be no return to the 'normality' which successive British governments have sought and failed to achieve in the province. In British political terms, the prerequisite of that normality is a return to normal policing such as that exercised throughout the rest of the United Kingdom. But Northern Ireland is not

1. Civilians were also killed by the security forces, most notably on 'Bloody Sunday'.

like the rest of the UK, where traditionally the police have been affectionately regarded as 'bobbies on the beat'. Since the foundation of the state of Northern Ireland in 1920, a significant minority of its citizens have no more accepted the police than the political institutions they defend. Repression of one kind or another has always been an inherent part of its existence. For the fifty years that followed the partition of Ireland, the RUC, and in particular its paramilitary wing the B-Specials, were seen by the Catholic minority as the military arm of the Unionist government whose survival depended on keeping the nationalist minority under control. When the civil rights movement seemed to threaten the stability of the Protestant state in 1968, it was the police who were ordered to suppress it. Scenes of Protestant policemen batoning Catholic demonstrators simply confirmed what the nationalist population had always believed, that the RUC was the military arm of a one-party state. Northern Ireland was, in the words of an ex-Labour Minister, a police state.

When the state erupted in 1969, the British quickly realized that the RUC would have to be reformed and reorganized if the slide into anarchy was to be avoided. In their report to the British government in 1969, Lord Hunt and Robert Mark concluded that law and order could only be effectively restored when the police was seen by the public to be civilian, impartial and accountable to it.[1] More than a decade later, in my opinion those conditions have yet to be achieved. Old images of the force which successive British governments and Chief Constables have sought to dispel still remain as powerful as ever in the minds of many Catholics whose support the security forces need if the IRA is to be defeated. Evidence of police ill-treatment and the repeated denials of it by those in authority has convinced many Catholics, even those who might have wished to think otherwise, that the RUC has not changed its spots. Castlereagh has perpetuated an image of the

1. Hunt Report (Report of the Advisory Committee on Police in Northern Ireland, Cmd 535), paras. 175–6, p. 43.

R U C which ought to have faded long ago, given the efforts made to change it. But in Ireland old myths die hard, especially where the police and the army are concerned.

What makes this a disturbing story is that it mirrors almost exactly events at the beginning of the decade when suspects were ill-treated in police custody in the months that followed internment. Although at that time too the allegations were denied and dismissed as terrorist propaganda, the British government subsequently paid out over half a million pounds in compensation for injuries received, and was taken to Strasbourg by the Irish government for violations of Article 3 of the European Convention on Human Rights. In a case that dragged on for five years, and cost as much as the compensation, Britain was found guilty of torture, inhuman and degrading treatment by the European Commission of Human Rights, a verdict which was later modified on appeal to the European Court of Human Rights, when the 'torture' count was dropped. This at least gave the British press the opportunity to print the satisfying if misleading headline 'Britain acquitted of torture'. The words cleared the conscience; the niceties of torture as opposed to inhuman and degrading treatment were of little concern to the British public, which read what it wanted to believe and, relieved, sank back as if nothing had happened. However, the most significant finding at Strasbourg, by both Commission and Court, was that the ill-treatment had constituted an 'administrative practice': that is to say, the authorities knew about and condoned it. Ironically, the European Commission and Court published their findings in 1976 and 1978 respectively, when the British government was trying to stem the tide of fresh allegations.

A final question deserves to be answered. Who cares if suspects are beaten up when they palpably belong to organizations responsible for atrocities such as the La Mon bombing and the assassination of Airey Neave and Lord Mountbatten? Even in Northern Ireland's emergency, a man is innocent until he is proved guilty. Ill-treatment is not only illegal but politically counter-productive because it destroys confidence in the police without which law and order can never be effectively restored. Further, on the purely practical level, dangerous men may have gone free because they were beaten up in police custody and their statements therefore rejected in court. Finally, even if the end were to justify the means, the end has not been achieved. The IRA has not been defeated.

Reviewing interrogation techniques used in 1971, the ex-Lord Chancellor Lord Gardiner wrote:

I do not believe that, whether in peace time for the purpose of obtaining information relating to men like the Richardson gang or the Kray gang, or in emergency terrorist conditions, or even in a war against a ruthless enemy, such procedures are morally justifiable against those suspected of having information of importance to the police or army, even in the light of any marginal advantages which may therefore be obtained.[1]

Pursuing the argument that if such methods are necessary to obtain results, they should be legalized, Lord Gardiner concludes:

The only logical limit to the degree of ill treatment to be legalized would appear to be whatever degree of ill treatment proves to be necessary to get the information out of him, which would include, if necessary, extreme torture. I cannot think that Parliament should, or would, legislate.

Such is the conundrum. In Northern Ireland it has been avoided by denying that ill-treatment existed.

1. Parker Report (Committee of Privy Counsellors Appointed to Consider Authorized Procedures for the Interrogation of Persons Suspected of Terrorism), Cmnd 4901, March 1972, S.20(1), p. 20.

Part One

1. Blueprint for Success

> 'Quite a large number of those held in custody at Palace Barracks were subjected to violence by members of the RUC.'
>
> Judgement of European Court of Human Rights in 1978 on interrogation practices in autumn 1971

The roots of the events described in this book lie back in the spring of 1971, when Northern Ireland's first Interrogation Centres were planned. In April there was a secret meeting in Belfast between senior British Intelligence officers and members of the RUC's Special Branch. The purpose of the seminar was to discuss the most effective way of obtaining vital intelligence on the IRA which the RUC had failed to gather using their traditional methods. Special Branch files on suspected IRA members were old and out of date, most of them based on information from the IRA's last campaign in 1956–62. It had been a border campaign, fought in the country areas, and the intelligence that survived it largely concerned families that had had IRA connections in the country districts in the late fifties. Although in the spring of 1971 the Provisionals' command structure contained many veterans of that campaign, many of the Volunteers who formed the Active Service Units (ASUs) at the time were the young unemployed from the streets of Belfast and Derry, and intelligence on them was in short supply. There was growing political pressure for results. Two months before the secret intelligence seminar in Belfast, the Provisionals had machine-gunned Gunner Robert Curtis, the first British soldier to be killed by the IRA in Ireland for nearly fifty years. A few weeks later two policemen were shot dead in the Ardoyne and three off-duty soldiers – aged seventeen, eighteen and twenty-three – were found murdered in a country lane just outside

Belfast. Internment, the measure that had always contained the IRA in the past – partly because the Republic had used it simultaneously – was inevitable. At the time the then Home Secretary Reginald Maudling said, 'internment is a very ugly thing but political murder is even uglier'. But to the men who attended the secret Belfast seminar, internment was also a means to the end of gathering intelligence.

The British officers present at that meeting were from the English Intelligence Centre, a top-secret establishment then situated on the edge of the Ashdown Forest near Maresfield in Sussex. The planning of the internment/intelligence operation was probably one of its last assignments before the Centre moved to Ashford in Kent. The English Intelligence Centre was the storehouse of the experience the British had gained in counterinsurgency operations in her colonies in the post-war years.

The interrogation techniques which the army had used against insurgents in the colonies which fought for their independence – Kenya, Malaya, Cyprus and Aden – were never published or even written down. It was the English Intelligence Centre which received and transmitted them orally to others. The 'Five Techniques' of interrogation taught at the Centre consisted of hooding the suspect, subjecting him to a high-pitched noise, making him stand against the wall, and depriving him of sleep and proper diet – all classic techniques of sensory deprivation pioneered by the KGB. Now in the province closest to home it was the RUC's turn to be taught the methods that had proved so successful in further outposts of Empire.

But in fact in the political storm that followed their use, the 'Five Techniques' were a red herring. They attracted most of the publicity because they were dramatic, although only fourteen men, the 'guinea pigs', were subjected to them.[1] There was a limit to how many rounds of ammunition, pounds of explosives and piles of weapons fourteen

1. EHRR (European Human Rights Reports), January 1979, published by European Law Centre, p. 59.

men could reveal, especially when some had only the slightest IRA connections. But the 'guinea pigs' were only fourteen of the 3,000 suspects interrogated by the RUC in the year that followed internment. Most of them were interrogated at Palace Barracks, Holywood. Here suspects were detained under Regulation 10 of the draconian Special Powers Act[1] of 1922, which authorized 'detention for a period of not more than 48 hours of any person for the purpose of interrogation'. Palace Barracks was Northern Ireland's first Interrogation Centre, and the blueprint for Castlereagh.

Palace Barracks was run jointly by the army and the RUC. Army Intelligence officers supervised, while RUC Special Branch detectives interrogated. These Special Branch officers were independent of the uniformed branch of the RUC and came under the control of a Special Branch Inspector, who had been present at the secret seminar the previous April.

Faced with the tide of allegations that flowed from Palace Barracks and the currency they were given by newspapers like the *Sunday Times*, the Conservative government of the day had little choice but to order an inquiry. The Ombudsman, Sir Edmund Compton, and a senior doctor and lawyer were appointed to report on 'allegations against the security forces of physical brutality'. Its terms of reference were limited to arrests made on one day, 9 August, the day of internment, which meant that the report was concerned almost exclusively with the application of the 'Five Techniques' and had little concern with systematic interrogation at Palace Barracks. There were other limitations. No complainants gave evidence as they felt that the terms of reference were too narrow. No evidence was given under oath; and there was no cross-examination of witnesses. In short, critics felt that a British government which had sanctioned the techniques was hardly likely to leave itself open to attack by setting up an inquiry which

1. Civil Authorities (Special Powers) Act (NI) 1922.

would have got at the truth. There were fears that Compton would be a whitewash.

The conclusion of the Compton Report was hamstrung by its own definition of what constituted 'physical brutality':

We consider that brutality is an inhuman or savage form of cruelty, and that cruelty implies a disposition to inflict suffering coupled with indifference to, or pleasure in, the victim's pain.

It was a subjective definition that astonished Lord Gardiner, who, as a member of the Parker Committee appointed a few months later to review interrogation procedures, said:

Lest by silence I should be thought to have accepted this remarkable definition, I must say that I cannot agree with it. Under this definition, which some of our witnesses thought came from the Inquisition, if an interrogator believed, to his great regret, that it was necessary for him to cut off the fingers of a detainee one by one to get the required information out of him for the sole purpose of saving life, this would not be cruel and, because not cruel, not brutal.[1]

But Compton's particular definition of 'physical brutality' did enable him to reach the conclusion that most people wanted to hear and believe – that none of the forty complainants whose allegations the committee had investigated 'suffered physical brutality as we understand the term'.

The fact that the Report *did* state that there had been instances of ill-treatment was lost in the political sigh of relief his conclusion produced. The Compton Report produced a heated and inconclusive debate in the House of Commons, and a call from Amnesty International for a commission of inquiry into 'serious and apparently substantiated allegations of ill-treatment of internees in Northern Ireland'. The Dublin government announced it was

1. Parker Report, March 1972, Cmd 4901, para. 7(d), in Gardiner's minority submission.

taking the British government to Strasbourg for its violations of the European Convention on Human Rights.

The European Commission heard the evidence. Few
tribunals could have been more independent or thorough
in their investigations. The Commission consists of sixteen
members, drawn from each of the sixteen states who have
ratified the European Convention on Human Rights:
Austria, Belgium, Cyprus, Denmark, Federal Republic of
Germany, Greece, Iceland, Ireland, Italy, Luxembourg,
Malta, the Netherlands, Norway, Sweden, Turkey and the
United Kingdom. (At the time of these hearings, France
and Switzerland had still to ratify the Convention.) The
Commission's delegates are elected for a period of six
years and sit as 'individuals' to make sure they remain
independent of public and political pressures from home.
In proceedings before the delegates, witnesses are cross-
examined on oath by defence and prosecuting counsel as
in a court of law. Over a period of sixteen months the
Commission's delegates heard 119 witnesses give oral
evidence which is reproduced in fourteen volumes of
verbatim record, running to 4,500 pages. One hundred
witnesses testified on the allegations of torture under
Article 3. The 560-page Report was testimony to a massive
investigation.

Unlike Compton, the Commission was concerned with
more than just those arrests made on the morning of
internment and the 'Five Techniques'. It tried to establish
whether ill-treatment had been an instrument of policy in
the months that followed. The British had no reason to
facilitate an investigation which was designed not only to
get at the truth of the allegations, but to identify those
responsible. The wrangles were interminable, particularly
when it came to the conditions on which the British would
allow their police and army witnesses to give evidence. The
British sent a security expert from the Ministry of Defence
to check out the Strasbourg Human Rights building where
the hearings were scheduled to be heard. He decided it
was not safe. Eventually the Norwegian Commissioner

resolved the deadlock by offering the somewhat spartan facilities of a disused military air base at Sola near Stavanger in Norway. The Norwegian government agreed to provide the security, on the grounds that it was good practice for their army and a change from keeping an eye on the Russians. It was, as some cynics observed, as if the Provisional IRA had suddenly acquired intercontinental ballistic missiles.

Sola was a joyless place, especially in January, when the snows had set in and the temperatures were below zero. The Irish party found it even less hospitable when they discovered they had been booked into a 'dry' hotel. The perimeter of the air base – which later became a centre for North Sea oil exploration – was constantly patrolled by the Norwegian army, while the hearings were held in the centre in what were described as 'up-market Nissen huts'. The British had agreed to provide witnesses only on condition that they remained anonymous. They gave evidence behind a screen, visible only to the Commission's delegates and the defence and prosecuting counsels. The members of the Irish team were not allowed to see the witnesses, presumably because the British thought the Irish a security risk.

To confuse the Irish even more, the British security force witnesses were given letters and numbers as codes. So obsessive were the British about security that one witness on entering the country caused a scene at Customs by insisting on giving the Norwegian officials his code number, not his name. Often the same witness would be given a different code for a different incident. For example, it transpired that witness coded PO17B – the Special Branch Inspector responsible for Palace Barracks – was also referred to as PO12B and PO13G.[1] at no time did any witness admit that he had done, seen or heard anything wrong.

Only one security-force witness came even remotely

1. For the best accounts of the coding of the British witnesses see Jack Holland, 'Strasbourg: The Men Behind the Torture', *Hibernia*, 8 October 1976, and 'The Torturers' Who's Who', *The Leveller*, December 1976.

close to conceding that there might have been anything wrong at Palace Barracks. He was witness PO4A, a Special Branch Inspector who was stationed in Omagh, County Tyrone. No complainant ever alleged that he had been beaten by him. The Commission said that 'he seemed to be more concerned about the allegations than most others'.

The Inspector made it clear that he did not wish to be associated with Palace Barracks. When the delegates questioned him about the possibility of others being responsible for the beatings, he was vague. When asked if the rules for normal police interrogation applied, he replied that as far as he was concerned they did. He said that he was aware of the allegations but made sure that when he was around nothing untoward happened. He was also asked, as were many of the security-force witnesses, why it was that prisoners had to be brought from all over Northern Ireland to Palace Barracks for interrogation. The standard police reply was that facilities in local police stations were inadequate, but this Inspector admitted that the presence of more experienced interrogators at Palace Barracks must have been one of the reasons. He promptly added that there was also a lack of local facilities.

The Inspector, coded witness PO4A, was forty-seven-year-old Detective Inspector Peter Flanagan, Head of the Special Branch in Omagh. On Friday, 23 August 1974, he was shot dead by the Provisionals while drinking in a pub in the town. He died three months after giving evidence before the Commission's delegates at the Sola air force base.

In regard to Palace Barracks, the European Commission and Court concluded:

Quite a large number of those held in custody at Palace Barracks were subjected to violence by members of the RUC. It also led to intense suffering and to physical injury which on occasions was substantial[1] . . . No member of the security forces who was heard by the Delegates admitted that he had beaten the

1. EHRR, Part I, Vol. 2, January 1979, p. 81, para. 174.

men or knew that they had been beaten up . . . Those in command at Palace Barracks at the relevant time could not have been ignorant of the acts involved.[1]

Those in command at Palace Barracks were police officers coded PO17B and PO4B. The Special Branch officer coded PO17B had been present at the secret intelligence seminar in Belfast in April 1971. Both denied there had been any ill-treatment at Palace Barracks. PO4B admitted he sometimes shouted, but only to deaf people. Both officers were later believed to have been promoted and gone on to work at Castlereagh.

In June 1972 the Palace Barracks Interrogation Centre was closed down. Speaking in the House of Commons the Prime Minister, Edward Heath, said:

I must explain that interrogation in depth will continue but that these techniques [i.e. the 'Five Techniques'] will not be used. It is important that interrogation should continue. The statement that I have made covers all future circumstances. If a Government did decide – on whatever grounds I would not like to foresee – that additional techniques were required for interrogation . . . they would probably have to come to the House and ask for the powers to do it.[2]

No such request was ever made.

At Strasbourg, in the hope that the Commission would view 1971 as an unfortunate 'aberration', the British government laid great emphasis on the Directives it had subsequently issued to the security forces as evidence of its determination to see that such incidents should never happen again. The Attorney-General issued a directive:

I have told the police and army that interrogation, whether under ordinary police powers or under the Special Powers Act, must only be conducted in accordance with the law . . . I have

1. ECHR (European Commission of Human Rights), application no. 5310/71, Ireland Against the United Kingdom, pp. 418, 465.
2. *Hansard*, 2 March 1972.

warned that in no circumstances shall any person in custody be assaulted or intimidated and that if any person, whosoever he may be, were to assault a person in custody, he would be liable to immediate prosecution. I have moreover made it clear that if these instructions are broken and any form of physical ill-treatment is reported, the Director of Public Prosecutions will prosecute.

The army too issued a directive, which in addition to prohibiting the 'Five Techniques' said:

No form of coercion is to be inflicted on persons being interrogated. Persons who refuse to answer questions are not to be threatened, insulted or exposed to other forms of ill-treatment.

And there was a third directive issued to the army and RUC:

It is recognized that persons arrested or detained in internal security operations are likely to be valuable sources of intelligence and that interrogation is the only way of gaining it urgently. Prisoners however must be properly treated . . . Prisoners are at all times to be treated humanely. They must not be threatened, insulted, or subjected to torture or cruel, inhuman or degrading treatment.

Before these new directives were issued both the RUC and the army had regulations which expressly forbade ill-treatment of persons in custody. At Strasbourg the Irish government argued that they had not been worth the paper they were written on, as they had not prevented ill-treatment. The RUC code had stated:

Prisoners in police custody are to be treated with the most humane consideration . . . no harshness or unnecessary restraint is to be used against them.

In addition the RUC's Disciplinary Regulations stated:

Any member commits an offence against discipline if he is guilty of unlawful or unnecessary exercise of authority, that is to say, if he uses any unnecessary violence or harshness to any prisoner . . . in the execution of his duty or knowingly allows such violence to be used.

Both these regulations were in force at the time of Palace Barracks. They made little difference.

By the summer of 1972 the British government could hardly have stated more clearly its determination to stop any further ill-treatment of suspects. The new directives on interrogation and the closure of Palace Barracks were meant to mark the end of the chapter. Further, the concept of the centralized Interrogation Centre seems to have been buried for the time being. Interrogation was now decentralized and suspects were questioned in police stations and 'holding centres', invariably located at the back of police stations where suspects were questioned jointly by the police and the army.

There had always been a police station at Castlereagh, the predominantly Protestant district two miles from the centre of Belfast to the east of the River Lagan. When the army moved into Belfast in 1969, police stations were a natural billet for the troops. Castlereagh was no exception, and became the base for the local army unit. After the closure of Palace Barracks, Castlereagh Holding Centre took over some of its workload. It was only a few miles down the road. A few huts that the army had been using in the courtyard at the back of the police station became interview rooms, and the Castlereagh Holding Centre was born.

The Provisionals were not impressed by the change of location or the change of name. Within weeks of Palace Barracks closing down, the Provisionals blew up half the new Holding Centre at Castlereagh police station.

2. Laying the Foundations

'We consider that the detailed technical rules and practice as to the "admissibility" of inculpatory statements by the accused are hampering the course of justice in the case of terrorist crimes.'

Diplock Report, para. 87

Interrogation at Palace Barracks had served two purposes. It produced the scraps of intelligence on the basis of which a suspect could be interned, and confessions or statements made by the suspect during interrogation, which could be used as evidence against him in the normal courts of law. Most of the results were in the former category, as few suspects made confessions, which, to be acceptable as evidence in a court of law, had to pass the common law test of admissibility. This means that to accept the statement, the court has to be convinced that it has been given voluntarily by the suspect and not as the result of any threat or inducement made by his interrogators. As long as internment existed the reluctance of suspects to make statements, and the difficulties interrogators had in obtaining them, were no great handicap as suspects could be locked up on suspicion, not evidence. But the government realized that internment, which was both politically and morally unacceptable, could not last forever. But if internment was to be ended, other ways had to be found of locking up the paramilitaries. Clearly, the existing judicial system, which was indistinguishable from that in the rest of the UK, with its juries, witnesses and rules of evidence, was, as it stood, an ineffective alternative.

If internment was to be ended, then the rules had to be changed. Lord Diplock was appointed to review the situation. One of the incidents that illustrated the difficulties under which the normal judicial process operated happened several months before Lord Diplock started work.

At 11 am on 14 October 1971, Sidney Agnew was sitting in his Belfast Corporation double-decker bus at the terminus in Cregagh Road. A man wearing sun-glasses boarded the bus and produced a 9-mm Luger automatic pistol. He said he was taking over the bus. Two men who had been sitting in a blue Ford Corsair parked near by joined the gunman, poured petrol over the upper and lower decks, set the bus alight and made off in the car towards the city centre. A witness saw what happened and phoned the police at Castlereagh, the local police station. There was a chase that ended in Ormeau Park, when three men were captured and detained. The Luger pistol was found in a clump of bushes near by. Sidney Agnew later identified it as the gun held by his assailant. There were seven rounds in the chamber and one in the breech. Agnew also identified the sun-glasses found on Gerald Rooney, one of the three men detained, as 'similar' to those worn by the man with the gun. Some of the men arrested later admitted that they were members of the Provisional IRA.

On Tuesday, 18 January 1972, the RUC Inspector in charge of the case called on Sidney Agnew at 8.20 in the evening to ask him if he would be prepared to appear in court the following morning to give evidence in the case against the three men. He said he would. Twenty minutes later, there was another knock on the door. One of his children answered it. Two youths were on the doorstep and asked the child if his father was in. Sidney Agnew, who was sitting in the front room, heard the conversation and came to the front door. One of the youths asked him if he worked 'on the buses'. He said he did. One of them pulled out a gun. Sidney Agnew turned to put his son in the living room and shouted to his wife to get the children out of the house by the back door. Three shots were fired and Sidney Agnew staggered into the living room, where he fell dead.

The prosecution's key witness had been eliminated. As it happened, the police had already taken a statement from him which the judge admitted as evidence. The judge, Mr Justice McGonigal, sentenced Rooney to ten years and his two accomplices to eight years each. The killers of Sidney Agnew were never found.

Lord Diplock referred to this 'dreadful case' in his Report to illustrate the difficulties of relying on witnesses to give evidence and concluded that the minimum requirements of the judicial process – that witnesses be able to give evidence in a court of law without risk to their lives – could not apply in Northern Ireland.

Unless the State can ensure their safety, then it would be unreasonable to expect them to testify voluntarily and morally wrong to try to compel them to do so.[1]

But in the climate of Northern Ireland not only witnesses but juries too were liable to be intimidated. There were also problems in selecting them. If an IRA suspect was being tried, it was not easy to swear in members of a jury who lived in areas where the organization had its roots. As Lord Diplock remarked, 'a frightened juror was a bad juror'. Members of the jury had to be sought elsewhere and in Belfast, given the sectarian divisions of the city, that meant in Protestant areas. Juries were already loaded in the Protestants' favour. Because Protestants made up two-thirds of Belfast's population and were more likely to have the necessary property qualification (since abolished) anyway, juries trying Republicans were invariably predominantly Protestant. In view of such apparent disadvantages, Lord Diplock recommended that juries should be abolished and cases involving terrorist suspects should in future be heard before a single judge. Trial by jury, with all its inbuilt safeguards, recognized to be the cornerstone of the English judicial system, was therefore to be abolished. But Lord Diplock also recommended another fundamental and far-

1. Report of the Commission to Consider Legal Procedures to Deal with Terrorist Activities in Northern Ireland, Cmnd 5185, para. 15.

reaching change. This concerned the admissibility of state-ments or confessions made in police custody. As Lord Diplock observed:

To the ordinary man it would seem that the most cogent evidence that a person had done that which he was accused of doing, was his own admission that he had done it, unless there were some reason to suppose that he was inculpating himself falsely. All over the world courts act on this assumption daily when they convict the accused upon his own plea of guilty.[1]

In normal circumstances, few would question the assess-ment. Evidence produced as a result of interviews with accused persons forms the basic evidence offered in all criminal trials throughout the United Kingdom. However there are important safeguards which exist to ensure that such statements are made by the accused as a result of his own free will and not the result of undue police pressure. Again these safeguards apply throughout the United Kingdom. The first is the common law principle that statements should be 'voluntary', which means exactly what it says – that all statements should be made of the suspect's own free will. The second and most important safeguard involves the Judges Rules. These are not laws but guidelines which judges over the years have laid down for the police to follow in interviewing suspects in their custody:

. . . it is a fundamental condition of the admissibility in evidence against any person, equally of any oral answer given by that person to a question put by a police officer and of any statement made by that person, that it shall have been voluntary in the sense that it has not been obtained from him by fear of prejudice or hope of advantage, exercised or held out by a person in authority or by oppression . . . Non-conformity with these Rules

1. Diplock Report, para. 74.

may render answers and statements liable to be excluded from evidence in subsequent criminal proceedings.[1]

As Diplock observed, guilty men, if left to themselves, prefer to remain silent. In Northern Ireland the Judges Rules had been applied to the letter. In a famous case in the Court of Criminal Appeal the Lord Chief Justice ruled inadmissible statements made to the R U C Special Branch at the Palace Barracks Interrogation Centre, saying that they were not voluntary because of the 'oppressive circumstances' in which they were obtained. He said:

The interrogation set up was officially organized and operated in order to obtain information and in the case of these two men effectively did induce towards the obtaining of information from persons who would otherwise have been less willing to give it.[2]

Lord Diplock evidently thought the ruling absurd: he certainly did not regard the Rules as a 'statutory requirement from which no departure is permissible'. His view of the conditions necessary for successful interrogation were exactly those that the Northern Ireland Court of Criminal Appeal had ruled out:

The whole technique of skilled interrogation is to build up an atmosphere in which the initial desire to remain silent is replaced by an urge to confide in the questioner.[3]

It could have been the motto over Castlereagh's door. In a blunt attack on the way in which the Judges Rules were interpreted in Northern Ireland, Lord Diplock virtually blamed them for internment:

The detailed technical rules and practice as to the 'admissibility' of inculpatory statements by the accused as they are currently applied in Northern Ireland are hampering the course of justice in the case of terrorist crimes and compelling the authorities

1. Judges Rules and Administrative Directions to the Police, 1978 – (e), p. 6.
2. *R.* v. *Flynn and Leonard*, 24 May 1972.
3. Diplock Report, para. 84.

responsible for public order and safety to resort to detention in a significant number of cases which could otherwise be dealt with both effectively and fairly by trial in a court of law.[1]

Lord Diplock therefore recommended the abolition of the common law test of admissibility and suggested that statements or confessions should be accepted as evidence, provided the court was satisfied, on the balance of probabilities, that they had not been obtained by subjecting the accused to torture or to inhuman or degrading treatment. In other words, any methods short of those in that category – and the definition of torture, inhuman and degrading treatment was left to the judiciary, not the police – were acceptable to get suspects to confess to their crimes. The notion of 'voluntary' confessions in the sense in which it had been strictly applied was thrown out of the window. Despite this, the assumption that such confessions *were* voluntary was still maintained. All statements made at Castlereagh and elsewhere contained the lines, prior to signature by the accused:

I have read the above statement and have been told that I can correct, alter or add anything I wish. This statement is true. I have made it of my own free will.

How 'free' the suspect's will now was under the changed circumstances was a matter of some doubt. But theoretically the Judges Rules still continued as the main safeguard for suspects during interrogation.

Lord Diplock showed the government the way out of their internment dilemma. He raised the threshold of 'admissibility', thereby giving the green light for Castlereagh. The government accepted his recommendations and incorporated them in the Emergency Provisions Act,[2] the body of legislation that made the administration of justice in Northern Ireland totally different from that of the rest

1. Diplock Report, para. 87.
2. NI (Emergency Provisions) Act 1973. The sections of the Act referred to in this book are those of the 1973 Act, not of the consolidated version of 1978.

of the United Kingdom. The nature of the emergency was the reason given by the Labour government for suspending liberties that had taken centuries to consolidate.

Section 6 of the new Act recognized the new test of 'admissibility' recommended by Lord Diplock and said that statements made by the accused could be given in evidence by the prosecution provided the court was satisfied that they had not been obtained by subjecting the accused to torture, inhuman or degrading treatment. The standard of proof required was 'beyond reasonable doubt'. There were no definitions or qualifications. Some lawyers, however, were unhappy at the latitude that Section 6 appeared to give the RUC's interrogators, and wished to see the words 'the use or threat of physical violence' – words which Lord Diplock himself used in his Report[1] – included to avoid any misunderstanding as to what the police could and could not do. But this important qualification was never added. The exact meaning of Section 6 remained, perhaps deliberately, vague.

The new legislation also extended police powers to detain and question which were the prerequisite of successful interrogation. Under the 1922 Special Powers Act which this legislation replaced, a suspect could be held for only forty-eight hours, which had been long enough for Palace Barracks to operate successfully. But Section 10 of the new Act gave the police an extra day in which to obtain statements and intelligence:

Any constable may arrest without warrant any person he suspects of being a terrorist . . . a person shall not be detained for more than 72 hours after his arrest.

At the time great emphasis was laid on the 'temporary' nature of the legislation, and it was stressed that the Act would remain on the statute books only until the situation in Northern Ireland improved. It was argued that the Act itself would help bring about the return to normality which would make such legislation unnecessary.

1. Diplock Report, para. 91.

The Emergency Provisions Act became law in 1973. A year later, following the bombing of two Birmingham pubs by the Provisional IRA in which nineteen people died, Parliament gave the police even greater powers, this time on both sides of the water. Introducing the Prevention of Terrorism Bill on 25 November 1974, the Home Secretary, Roy Jenkins, said:

These powers are draconian. In combination they are unprecedented in peace time. I believe they are fully justified to meet the clear and present danger.

The Prevention of Terrorism Act gave the Home Secretary the power to exclude a citizen of one part of the United Kingdom from the rest, if he believed him to be concerned in the commission, preparation or instigation of acts of terrorism. Like its forerunner, the Emergency Provisions Act, the Prevention of Terrorism Act was to be renewed every six months. Both Acts remained in force for the rest of the decade. Few MPs bothered to turn up for the six-monthly renewals.[1]

But the Prevention of Terrorism Act also gave the police even greater powers to detain and question. Section 12 enabled them to detain any person they

reasonably suspected of being concerned or having been concerned in the commission, preparation and instigation of acts of terrorism.

Initially that person could be detained for forty-eight hours, but should the police feel it necessary they could apply to the Secretary of State (in England the Home Secretary) for authority to detain the suspect for a further five days' interrogation.

The RUC used Section 10 for general arrests, as they

1. For example, there were never more than three dozen MPs present – except for the division – at any stage during the EPA renewal debate on 2 July 1979, which came three weeks after the General Election and the assassination of Airey Neave. For most of the debate, there was only a handful of MPs on either side of the house.

could usually get the information or statements they wanted in the first two days. They reserved Section 12 for the 'hard men'.

By 1975 the new legal and judicial framework had been built. Internment could be ended as there was now an alternative way to lock up the paramilitaries. Suspected terrorists could be arrested, detained, questioned, tried and sentenced by what appeared to be, and was certainly loudly proclaimed to be, due process of law. Because the rules had been changed, the government was also able to change the public perception of the war they were fighting. As long as internment had existed, with its Nissen huts and barbed-wire fences, reminiscent of POW camps in the Second World War, it was difficult to counter the Provision-als' propaganda that they were prisoners of war, an impression that the Conservative government reinforced in 1972 when William Whitelaw granted the imprisoned paramilitaries of both sides 'Special Category' status. 'Special Category' was political status in everything but name. William Whitelaw later called it the greatest mistake of his political career.

On 5 December 1975 Merlyn Rees released the last internees from Long Kesh. The slate was wiped clean. Special Category status was abolished and all prisoners sentenced by the new Diplock courts were regarded as ordinary criminals. The fact that the new legislation which made all this possible conceded the political nature of their crimes was conveniently overlooked. Section 31 of the Emergency Provisions Act defined terrorism as 'the use of violence for *political* ends'.

The Provisionals had always claimed that their actions were politically motivated, their aim being to drive the British out of the Six Counties of the North and reunify Ireland. The ending of Special Category status, which recognized the 'special' nature of this category of prisoner, caused bitter resentment, especially among the ranks of the Provisionals. In protest they refused to wear the prison uniform, which they regarded as a symbol of the criminal status the government now sought to impose on them. As a gesture of defiance, they took to wearing only a prison blanket. The seeds of their 'blanket' protest were sown when the new judicial system replaced internment.

This fundamental change in British government policy occurred at the beginning of 1976. Broadly speaking, there was to be a change in direction and emphasis. The change in direction was a recognition of the fact that a political solution was out of the question for the next few years. The Labour government now made the defeat of the Provisional IRA its priority in the hope that, with the Provisionals at least muted, the climate for political action would improve. The change in emphasis was to hand over prime responsibility for the defeat of the Provisionals to the locally recruited security forces, the RUC and the Ulster Defence Regiment (UDR), the part-time soldiers whom many Catholics saw as the B-Specials in army uniform.[1]

In order to accomplish this, both the police and the part-time army were to be given more men and equipment. The British army, which up to this point had been the prime security force, was relegated to the role in which it had been originally introduced in 1969 – to aid the civil power. The political advantage in this change in emphasis was that the army could gradually fade into the background as the RUC and UDR took over responsibility for security. Further, if the strategy worked, the army could gradually be withdrawn to barracks with a view finally to withdrawing from Northern Ireland altogether. It was also a policy with political dividends because, if it worked, it would be applauded by a British public which was growing increasingly restless at losing British soldiers in a conflict they didn't care about or understand. This new policy was known as 'Primacy of the Police' or 'Ulsterization'. The authorities preferred the former term, as the latter had unpleasant overtones of 'Vietnamization'.

1. UDR was the *quid pro quo* after the Hunt Report recommended the abolition of the B-Specials in 1969.

Although this change in policy happened in 1976, the ground had been well prepared in advance, most significantly by Kenneth Newman, the man who became Chief Constable on 1 May 1976, having spent the previous three years as Deputy to the former Chief Constable, James Flanagan. The British government had appointed both policemen on the same day, 11 September 1973, with an eye to both the short-term and the long-term future. James Flanagan, the first Catholic ever to command the RUC, represented a short-term political advantage for the British government which was, at the time, anxious to bring Catholics and Protestants together in a power-sharing executive. The government reasoned that Catholics would be more likely to give their allegiance to the new political institutions and the police if the new Chief Constable was a Catholic. If Sir James, as he later became, was the policeman's policeman, Kenneth Newman was the politicians' long-term investment.

Kenneth Newman first came to the attention of civil servants and politicians in the Home Office in 1968 when he was a young Chief Superintendent in the Metropolitan Police, charged with organizing police tactics to contain the huge anti-Vietnam demonstration outside the American Embassy in Grosvenor Square in 1968. With a degree in law, a grasp of the new police technology and an understanding of management techniques, Kenneth Newman was exactly the kind of enlightened policeman the British government wanted to transform the RUC from a hick country force – which is how it was regarded by its cousins on the mainland – to the most modern and sophisticated police force in the United Kingdom. The government realized that the transformation could not be achieved overnight and that the heir apparent would need time to play himself in. The RUC was not the Metropolitan Police but a force that had faced a barrage of criticism and continuous physical assault since 1968. At heart, it remained deeply suspicious of foreigners from across the water, whether they were Chief Constables or Detective

Sergeants. Even as late as 1976, Special Branch officers from London found it difficult to get along with their colleagues in the RUC, whom they felt to be a 'different breed'. Kenneth Newman was, however, not a man to be daunted. He was, as everyone agreed, a professional to his finger tips. Kenneth Newman was the instrument the British chose to implement the new policy.

But the architect of this policy was the Permanent Under-Secretary, Frank Cooper, the Northern Ireland Office's senior civil servant. Cooper was a career diplomat in his early fifties, with a reputation as an 'arse kicker'. Those who worked with him hated him or loved him. His unorthodox methods often sent the eyebrows of his civil service colleagues shooting upwards, especially those in the Northern Ireland civil service, who had long been suspicious of the civil servants who came over from London in the wake of Direct Rule and took the reins from them. Cooper, educated at Manchester Grammar School and Oxford, was no stranger to the politics of terrorism, having negotiated with Archbishop Makarios in Cyprus. It was Cooper who, with the approval of the Secretary of State, Merlyn Rees, orchestrated the talks with the Provisionals at the NIO's country retreat at Laneside on the shores of Belfast Lough. Cooper and Rees were close, as they had once served as flight lieutenants together in the RAF (the myth that Cooper had been Rees's RAF superior is appealing but untrue). Rees and Cooper lived over the shop at Stormont Castle, a Walt Disney gothic stone building which now houses the British administration. Once the palatial home of Lord Craigavon, the first Prime Minister of Northern Ireland, it stands just below the even more extravagant Parliament buildings at Stormont, over which he once presided. Cooper and Rees lived in a specially converted flat which the civil service had generously equipped with a double bedroom for when Mrs Rees came over. The two flats were separated by a mess room, where the two men would often burn the midnight oil and kill the odd tumbler of whisky while discussing the broad

canvas of Irish history. If they sought guidance or information on any particular more immediate problem, Rees
was not above ringing his junior Ministers, civil servants or
even the Chief Constable himself at two o'clock in the
morning and telling them to get out of bed and come over.
It may not have made Rees popular, but at least everybody
knew what was going on. If not exactly suspicious of the
RUC, the Secretary of State liked to keep an eye on it.
Most days, one of his civil servants was round at RUC
HQ at Knock, not, it was insisted, to 'spy' on the police,
just to make sure that there were no problems.

Rees was determined to see that nothing untoward
happened while he was in charge of Northern Ireland: he
not only found the practices of which Britain was accused
at Strasbourg abhorrent, but realized that they would cause
the government still further grave embarrassment if
repeated. He demanded an assurance from Frank Cooper,
the Chief Constable James Flanagan, and the GOC Frank
King that there were no unauthorized interrogation techniques being used that he didn't know about. He told them
bluntly that he didn't want any 'messing around'. He
apparently made it clear he wasn't referring to 'the odd
kick in the balls', which could happen in even the most
genteel home counties police force, but the systematic use
of unacceptable methods.[1] All three gave him the assurance
he sought. He knew the political damage that such methods
would cause in the Catholic community whose support he
was trying to win. He knew the task was already uphill.
When the new GOC, David House, took over from Frank
King, Rees laid on a reception. He made a point of inviting
a Catholic school teacher from the border area who was
particularly virulent in his criticisms of the RUC. Lest the
new GOC should have any illusions, the school teacher

1. But from court decisions in 1977 it appears that such methods may
have already been used on a small scale when Merlyn Rees was still
Secretary of State. Terry Magill had his statement which he made at
Castlereagh on May 1976 rejected on the grounds of 'inhuman and
degrading treatment'.

left him in no doubt as to the strong feelings which the RUC excited in his area. Not, according to one Minister, that it would have made much difference. He remarked that talking to the GOC about civil liberties was 'like talking to a bloody wall'.

The third member of the Rees axis at Stormont was a civil servant called John Bourn, who had a Ph.D. from the London School of Economics gained in the days before LSE became a training ground for left-wing activists. Bourn was Frank Cooper's Deputy Under-Secretary, the number two civil servant at Stormont. As such he was in charge of Division Nine, the civil service unit which was responsible for the police. Traditionally Division Nine kept a low profile, given the sensitivities that political relationships with the police tended to arouse. Although some of its functions were administrative, Division Nine also had an important political role. Its business was to know what the police were up to and keep the politicians fully informed and warned of problems that might lie ahead. Three of its five functions listed in an internal document are of a political nature.

(a) Advice and briefing of Ministers of both a particular and general nature.

(b) Parliamentary work, including both primary and subordinate legislation, briefs for debates and submissions of draft answers to Parliamentary questions.

(c) Advice to the Chief Constable ... and the Police Authority on legislation and other matters which have relevance to the police service in Northern Ireland.

(Significantly, Division Nine was charged with the implementation of the recommendations of the Bennett Report.) It was based in Belfast, but liaised with Division Three in London, which had direct access to Westminster. This administrative chain meant that the government was kept fully in touch with all police matters – not least the allegations of ill-treatment.

In Merlyn Rees's day, Division Nine was based in Dundonald House, an oblong concrete office block which housed the government departments which administered Northern Ireland under Direct Rule. Dundonald House sits half a mile down the hill from Stormont Castle. Division Nine relayed its signals up the hill to the politicians in the Castle. In late 1976, it was recommended that Division Nine should be moved up the hill to be nearer the politicians. Civil servants would only have to walk down the corridor and knock on a door to alert the Secretary of State to any problems in the wind.

John Bourn was given the task of producing the document which would set out in detail the new policy the government was to follow once internment was ended. This is where the philosophy of 'primacy of the police' or 'Ulsterization' was born. The Committee that Bourn headed was Frank Cooper's brainchild. Amongst its members were a senior RUC officer, Jack Hermon, who went on to become Deputy Chief Constable and then Chief Constable; senior officers from Army HQ at Lisburn; civil servants from the Northern Ireland Office; and a representative from the internal security service, MI5. Bourn, who had come to Northern Ireland from the Ministry of Defence, was already familiar with the security problems of the province. He had worked for Denis Healey in 1969 when he had had to send the troops in to Derry and Belfast. The Report the Committee produced was then considered by a Ministerial Committee and went on to become a Cabinet document. The deliberations of the Bourn Committee were secret and so were its findings. The Report, which was never published and had a restricted circulation, became known publicly as 'The Way Ahead'.

When the new policy document was mentioned to the House of Commons on 2 July 1976, the security situation was in Merlyn Rees's words 'as grave as the Province has faced since the Troubles started'. Already that year six soldiers, seven UDR, fifteen RUC and 148 civilians had been killed. Informing the House that the Bourn Committee had finished its work, the Secretary of State explained the philosophy that lay behind it.

I would have liked to publish its results. But by their nature, it would not be in the public interest to disclose the details . . . The Committee has been concerned with long-term issues. It has taken a cool hard look at what the long-term situation demands.

The only way forward is the way in which law and order has always been established in this country – by the police working to the law and securing its effective administration . . .

At the heart of the Committee's conclusions is therefore the idea of securing police acceptance and effectiveness. By securing police effectiveness is meant the integration and acceptance of the police in the community to enable them to administer law and order effectively. It does not mean a return to the past. This is a particularly difficult and challenging task because of the legacy of Irish history. There is a traditional sensitivity and antipathy to the police. This stems from the history of the island over the last seven centuries, and particularly from the enactments of the eighteenth century. We have to recognize that the police are not acceptable in all areas of Northern Ireland today. The police will consequently have to overcome the legacy of the past as well as of the experience of the last seven years.

To increase the effectiveness of the police the Committee's main conclusions are as follows:

(a) An increase in the size of the force.
(b) The continuing introduction of special investigation teams.
(c) Improved arrangements for collecting and collating criminal intelligence.
(d) Flexible use of resources to concentrate on serious crime and preventative policing.
(e) A special effort will be needed to make the RUC more representative.

This will depend to some extent on political factors and the opinion leaders in the minority community speaking up more frequently for the RUC.

The occasion for the statement was the renewal of the

Emergency Provisions Act. In conclusion Merlyn Rees said:

It is because of the continuing emergency that I seek the renewal of these emergency powers. As I have said, the killings are continuing. In some ways the situation is as bad as the situation in 1972. It would be irresponsible of me to give up the existing emergency provisions.

Although Merlyn Rees couldn't say it, it would also have been pointless. Without the emergency legislation, the 'Way Ahead' wouldn't have got very far. The two were interdependent.

One of the members of the Bourn Committee was William Baird, a career civil servant who had learned to adjust to the political and administrative changes which had tumbled out of the chaos of 1969. He knew his way around the cold stone corridors of Stormont Castle and was familiar with the niceties of the institutional relationships between the police, the politicians and the public. Although as a good civil servant he did as he was told – to have done otherwise with a Permanent Under-Secretary like Frank Cooper would have been to invite trouble – Baird maintained an independence of mind, believing that dirty linen should be washed, but preferably not in public.

William Baird was also full-time Secretary of the Police Authority, which he believed was the crucial link in the chain between the public, the police and the politicians. Baird had witnessed the upheavals of the first half of the decade, and recognized that only a police force that was publicly accountable could gain the acceptability which had eluded it for more than half a century.

The Police Authority had been established in 1970 as a result of the Hunt Committee's recommendation that a public body 'representative of the community as a whole' should be set up to which the Chief Constable could be accountable.[1] Previously the Chief Constable had been accountable only to the Unionist government of the day, which Hunt regarded as an unsatisfactory situation, as it made allegations of the political partiality of the RUC difficult to refute. The Police Authority's main function was 'to secure the maintenance of an adequate and efficient police force'[2] and in order to do so had theoretically the authority to hire and fire the Chief Constable. In addition, it was charged with the important responsibility of keeping itself 'informed' as to the manner in which complaints from members of the public against members of the police force were dealt with by the Chief Constable.[3]

As the policy changed at the beginning of 1976, the Police Authority seemed ready to flex its muscles for the first time and was actively encouraged to do so by the politicians, who believed it had a crucial role to play in winning public acceptability for the RUC. In a confidential memorandum to the Secretary of State in April 1976, the Authority not only wished to have its existing powers confirmed but asked for more. Its message was blunt: it said that the police should be made even more accountable and that members of the Authority should attend the weekly security meetings held at Stormont Castle.

Merlyn Rees willingly confirmed the Police Authority's existing powers. He said:

> We see a continuing role for an independent Police Authority with significant powers

but he was not prepared to open the doors of the security meetings to its members.

But the fact remained that, despite appearances, the Police Authority could never be truly independent, as its members were appointed by the Secretary of State, not publicly elected, and its money came from central govern-

1. Hunt Report, pp. 84–8.
2. Police Act (NI) 1970 – I(2).
3. ibid., 12(I).

ment, not the ratepayers. It was not, therefore, surprising that most of its members were not inclined to bite the hand that fed it. The names of its seventeen members read like a Who's Who of Northern Ireland. Many members had more initials at the end of their names than they had at the front. There were six JPs, and a good number of OBEs, CBEs and MBEs. The Police Authority was an integral part of the Establishment.

The chairman was Alderman Myles Humphreys, JP, MIRTE (Member of the Institute of Road Transport Engineers), Lord Mayor of Belfast and Director of Quick Service Stations Ltd. Vice-chairman was Ivor Canavan, a Catholic business executive from Derry and a member of the Alliance Party. The Secretary of State had his own representative on the Authority, Tom Cromey, a former Irish rugby international and sports commentator, whose job was to keep an eye on the money the Police Authority spent and report back to Division Nine, which was responsible for allocating resources to the Police Authority.

The Authority had a vast £120 million budget to 'secure the maintenance of an adequate and efficient police force'. That money was used not only to pay policemen's wages but to equip and maintain the force. The RUC's needs were many and varied. Each request was reviewed and authorized by one of the Authority's many sub-committees. These are the items reviewed at one sub-committee meeting.

Special photographic equipment for the Special Patrol Group's Bronze Section covert surveillance work   £1,836.60
Camouflage suits, combat cap and camouflage boots for the RUC's counter-sniper unit   £2,850.00
Stand-by generators for use in future emergency   £439,000.00
Bullet-resistant glass for certain RUC stations   £76,000.00
Modification of toilets in Strabane RUC station from male to female use   £1,100.00

Tom Cromey's other job was to sniff the political wind and keep Stormont Castle and Division Nine fully informed of the mood of the Police Authority, especially where controversial matters were concerned. Tom Cromey was not only the head of Division Nine but the Secretary of State's eyes and ears on the Police Authority.

The attitude of two members of the Authority were a good political indicator. One was Donal Murphy, a Belfast solicitor with a passion for rowing, who was the representative of the legal profession on the Police Authority. Murphy was a good-humoured cynic by nature who often spoke out at Authority meetings when others would have preferred to remain silent. As a Catholic himself, Murphy believed that the Authority would do little to encourage Catholic support if it kept its head down when the going got rough.

The other was Jack Hassard, General Secretary of the Northern Ireland Postal Workers' Union, who was the Authority's trades union representative. Hassard was a Protestant with all the right credentials. He had been a Sergeant in the B-Specials and seen action against the IRA in the Border Campaign of 1956; he was a war hero, twice mentioned in dispatches; he had fought in North Africa and then in Italy, where he had wiped out a German machine-gun post single-handed. He had fought Communist guerillas in Malaya, when the only thing that had shaken him was the sight of his native trackers eating one of their Communist victims. Hassard's support for law and order was unquestionable.

When Merlyn Rees canvassed Hassard's name for appointment to the Police Authority, not everyone was enthusiastic. Hassard had been known to rock a few boats, and with a man like that on board most members of the Authority were liable to be sea-sick. Rees asked for any *good* reason why he should not be appointed. None was forthcoming. Hassard's political credentials too were excellent and somewhat rare in Northern Ireland. For years he had topped the poll in the local elections in his native Dungannon. Standing as an Independent, he had harvested the votes of both Catholics and Protestants in the town. If the people of Dungannon wanted anything fixing, Hassard was the man they went to. He lived in a council house on a mixed estate and worked in the post office in the market square. The post office stood next to the police station and Hassard knew all the policemen in it. They all knew him too and called him 'Jack'. If there was a new face in or around the station and Hassard wanted to know who he was and where he came from, the local police would tell him if they knew. There was little that Jack Hassard didn't know.

In the sectarian politics of Northern Ireland, Jack Hassard reminded Merlyn Rees of the kind of local politician he met across the water, but rarely in Northern Ireland. The Secretary of State thought that Hassard was just the man the Police Authority needed. At the end of the letter which confirmed his appointment, Merlyn Rees wrote: 'I'm sure you will find much satisfaction in your membership of the Authority.'

Merlyn Rees was keen to see the Authority work. At a private lunch at Police Authority Headquarters in River House, a grey modern office block with grimy windows in the centre of Belfast, one of Merlyn Rees's junior Ministers, Roland Moyle, gave the members of the Authority a pep talk. He explained the government's new policy and told his hosts that the Police Authority was 'the key factor' in securing police acceptance and effectiveness. 'If we fail in that,' he said, 'we fail all together.' He informed the members that the new Chief Constable who had just been appointed had agreed to keep them 'fully briefed' and hoped that this would mark the beginning of 'close links' between the Police Authority and the Chief Constable.

On the second Thursday of every month the six members of the Police Authority's Complaints Committee (four Protestants and two Catholics) met at RUC HQ to examine the Complaints Register. The Authority, buttressed by Merlyn Rees's assurances, believed that its Publicity & Complaints Committee, to give it its full title, exercised one of its most important statutory functions, that of 'keeping itself informed' as to the manner in which the Chief Constable handled complaints which members of the public made against his men.[1] The Committee had originally been mooted in July 1976, perhaps with more of an eye to publicity than complaints. In a July internal memorandum, the Authority said:

It is suggested that the Police Authority . . . may now be sufficiently established to warrant a more active publicity role and that this could best be achieved by the formation of a Publicity & Complaints Committee . . .
. . . It could for example arrange a panel of members who would, on appropriate occasions, act as spokesmen for the Authority for TV, Radio and Press purposes; take steps to promote the image of the Authority and publicize their work . . . The general aim would be to promote a larger and more dynamic role for the Authority.

One of the reasons for the greater emphasis on publicity – which grew less as the complaints increased – was that at the time of these deliberations in 1976, legislation was pending which would, in 1977, establish a Police Complaints Board for Northern Ireland. The Authority assumed that the new Board would inherit many of the responsibilities which it had formerly exercised. What the Authority did not know at the time was that, as far as allegations of ill-treatment were concerned, the new Police Complaints Board was virtually irrelevant, as it could concern itself only with matters of a disciplinary nature. As allegations of assault involved criminal proceedings, they automatically fell outside the new Board's terms of reference. Therefore the Police Authority's Complaints Committee remained the public's only point of contact with the police, as concern over the allegations grew.

The Complaints Committee's meetings were held monthly at RUC Headquarters at Knock, where its members met the Chief Constable's second-in-command,

1. Under Section 12(i) of Police Act (NI) 1970.

Senior Deputy Chief Constable (SDCC) Harry Baillie, who was responsible for complaints, and senior officers from the RUC's Complaints & Discipline Branch. The most important part of these meetings was the inspection of the records. A large loose-leaf binder with a grey plastic cover was produced. It bore the inscription 'Chief Constable's Complaints Register'. The Register indicated only the bare essentials: the registration of the complaint, its number and the stage which the investigation had reached. But the Committee was never allowed to read the detailed reports of the Investigating Officers contained in the confidential files that the Complaints & Discipline Branch compiled in each case. Occasionally, the files were produced, but not for inspection. Access to the files became a matter of bitter dispute. The Complaints Committee argued that without seeing the files it could not fulfil its statutory obligation under the 1970 Police Act to 'keep itself informed' as to how complaints were handled, while the RUC insisted that the contents of the files were confidential. The deadlock caused much acrimony and was never broken. Occasionally the Committee was treated to selected readings by the RUC, but no more. As Donal Murphy once remarked, the files could contain the complete works of Shakespeare for all the Complaints Committee knew. The crucial files that contained full details of the RUC's investigation, including all medical reports and statements taken from detectives and supervisory officers, were locked away in the Headquarters of the RUC's Complaints & Discipline Branch a few hundred yards down the road from RUC HQ at Ormiston House.

Ormiston House is a nineteenth-century gothic monument to a Harland & Wolff shipyard millionaire which his less prosperous descendants sold off to a prep school. The prep school had then sold it to the RUC. At first it became the Headquarters of the RUC's Fraud Squad and then, when complaints became more numerous than frauds, the Fraud Squad moved out and the Complaints & Discipline

Branch[1] moved in. Some policemen joked that there wasn't that much difference between the two!

The large country house of brown Dumfries stone stands in grounds which act as a sanctuary for wild life and a putting green for policemen. Above the lintel of the main entrance is a gargoyle with its hands over its eyes – or is it its ears? – with the motto 'Truth will prevail'. At the back of the house is a more obscure but no less appropriate message, 'He who tholes[2] will overcome'.

When a complaint of assault is made, it is registered at Ormiston House. An Investigating Officer – one of eighteen of Inspector rank and above – is assigned to investigate the complaint. He interviews the complainant and the detectives whom the police log shows interviewed him at the relevant times. He also interviews the uniformed police officers who were on duty at the time and those who were in charge of the prisoner. He requests medical reports from the medical officers resident at the Police Office[3] and, where they exist, from the individual's General Practitioner. He also asks for reports from the Scenes of Crime officers. (If a serious complaint is made, the interview room is immediately locked. The senior uniformed police officer keeps the key until the Scenes of Crime team arrive. They photograph the cell and conduct forensic tests on any hairs, fibres, etc. which they may find.) No police officer has ever admitted he has ill-treated a suspect. Occasionally he may admit that he was attacked by the prisoner and that the prisoner was injured in the process.

When a police officer makes such a statement, he enjoys the same rights as every other citizen; he can, if he wishes, remain silent. The atmosphere in which he makes a statement is very different from the atmosphere in which the complainant has often been induced to make his. The police officer exercises the rights which the complainant

1. Complaints & Discipline Branch was established by Kenneth Newman when he overhauled the RUC's complaints procedures.

2. An old Scottish word meaning, to labour with patience.

3. The official RUC term for Interrogation Centre.

has often been denied. On the basis of this evidence the Investigating Officer writes his report. Even some of the RUC's most bitter critics admit that the investigations are thorough and extensive, but there's a limit to the progress even the most persistent Investigating Officer can make, faced with a blanket denial that anything untoward happened. In the end he is invariably faced with conflicting allegations: the suspect, who says he was assaulted, and the detective, who denies it. Hence the importance of medical reports, especially those by doctors who examined the prisoner in custody.

Senior officers at Ormiston House bristle at the suggestion of an RUC 'wall of silence', as the expression carries unpleasant and embarrassing memories for the Force. It stems from an incident in April 1969 when forty-two-year-old Samuel Devenny was allegedly beaten up by a group of RUC policemen in his Bogside home during the Derry riots of that spring. He later died in hospital, it was thought as a result of the injuries he received. An inquiry was ordered but its findings were inconclusive. The then Chief Constable, an Englishman, Sir Arthur Young, who had been appalled at the attitudes of the Force he was appointed to command, said that the unsatisfactory result of the investigation was due to 'a conspiracy of silence' among members of the RUC.[1] it was an infamous case that few Catholics were wont to forget, believing that the RUC was either incapable or unwilling to root out its 'bad apples'. What annoys officers of the Complaints & Discipline Branch when the Devenny case is mentioned today is that Commander Kenneth Drury, the Metropolitan Police Officer appointed by Sir Arthur Young to head the Devenny investigation, was later gaoled following the Porn Squad corruption trial. A senior officer in Complaints & Discipline scathingly dismissed remarks about the 'wall of silence'. 'Look at that cowboy in gaol in London,' he said. 'It's the Met that knows all about "walls of silence". They've had more handouts than the Salvation Army.'

1. 4 November 1970.

I was given a tour of Ormiston House. I was shown the store room, stacked with files of complaint investigations. I was not allowed to see any. I was taken to 'Knock Petty Sessions', the room where disciplinary hearings are heard in the presence of the Chief Constable. I was shown large offices with police officers and clerks poring over paper work and files with life-size colour posters of Starsky and Hutch looking down on their work from above. I passed the office of the Investigating Officers. (They are known in the RUC as the 'Kneecappers'.) Half a dozen men were sitting at desks. I popped my head round the door – I wasn't taken inside – and asked if they had ever come across a 'wall of silence'. There was a five-second silence and a nervous shuffling of paper before one of them said 'No'.

An investigation can take months. When it is finished, the Senior Deputy Chief Constable (Harry Baillie) is notified of the result and he in turn informs the Chief Constable. The files are then sent to the Office of the Director of Public Prosecutions in the Royal Courts of Justice in Belfast's city centre. The Director has to decide whether the evidence contained in the file is sufficient to merit the prosecution of a police officer.

Since 1972, Charles Barry Shaw, one-time officer in the anti-tank regiment of the Royal Artillery, has been the Director of Public Prosecutions for Northern Ireland. He has one of the most difficult and controversial jobs in the province. Barry Shaw has a standing equivalent to that of a High Court judge and works directly to the Attorney-General in London, the highest law officer in the United Kingdom.

Before the DPP's office was set up, the RUC decided whether or not the evidence they had collected was strong enough to merit a prosecution. Because of the close connections between the RUC and the Unionist government at Stormont, there remained a degree of unease about the impartiality of some prosecutions, and it was not deemed a good thing anyway that the police should be so closely connected with the courts.[1] A working party under Mr Justice McDermott was established in 1970 and concluded that policemen should be concerned with police work and should not, in addition, be required to prosecute an accused against whom they considered a prima facie case existed. The Report said:

> Anything which tends to suggest to the public mind the suspicion of an alliance between the court and the police cannot but be prejudicial.[2]

It therefore recommended the establishment of an independent Department of Public Prosecutions under the control of a Director who would be responsible for deciding whether or not a prosecution should be brought and the handling of all prosecutions in all courts. The Director was to be appointed by the Secretary of State.

As far as this book is concerned, the Director has two main functions. First, he has to assess the police evidence on the basis of which they have charged the suspect. As in about 75 per cent of cases involving terrorist suspects the only evidence the police have is a statement obtained under interrogation, the Director has to decide whether those statements will withstand the scrutiny of the court and not be excluded by Section 6 of the Emergency Provisions Act. Secondly, where a suspect alleges ill-treatment at the hands of police officers, the Director has to decide on the basis of the Complaints & Discipline file whether the evidence is strong enough to merit the prosecution of a particular police officer. This is often a most difficult decision, as the Director has to consider not only whether an individual

1. Hunt Report, paras. 84 and 142.
2. Citation of para. 381 of Royal Commission on the Police, 1962.

police officer is clearly identified but whether that officer is *likely* to be convicted if he does decide to prosecute.[1]

Each individual case has to be assessed on its merits. The Director has to weigh the credibility in court of the word of a suspected terrorist against that of a respected police officer who is trying to protect the community against terrorism. He knows that invariably the complainant is a bad witness, prone to exaggeration and lies, however true the substance of his allegations may be: that the police officer is trained and practised at giving evidence in the witness box and unlikely to be intimidated or confused by cross-examination.

The Director also has to be convinced 'beyond reasonable doubt' – the standard of proof required – that the medical evidence is conclusive: in other words, that the injuries were not self-inflicted or already on the suspect's body when brought into police custody. This often involves fine medical judgements, such as for example determining the age of a bruise by its colour or deciding whether or not a perforated eardrum can be self-inflicted. The Director has to weigh other considerations too: how the court is likely to react to a conflict of medical opinion; how doctors will stand up to cross-examination; how credible the RUC's explanation of an injury is likely to be; whether doctors are likely to admit the 'possibility' of self-infliction however convinced they may be of the unlikelihood of it. The Director and his staff of criminal lawyers who assess each case have no resident medical expert, although they

1. The DPP for England and Wales, Sir Thomas Hetherington, faced similar problems which received wide publicity. On 27 January 1980, the Commons Home Affairs Committee announced that it was to hold an inquiry into death in police custody following the DPP's announcement that there was insufficient evidence to bring charges against the Merseyside police officers involved in the case of Jimmy Kelly, a Liverpool labourer who died in police custody following his arrest in June 1979. The case received great public attention and resulted in the Home Office's disclosure that, since 1970, 245 people had died in police hands. The Commons Committee, however, was empowered to examine only procedures, not individual cases.

may summon the police and the doctors to clarify certain points. In the end it is a matter of their judgement. The Director is always able to refer the file back to the Chief Constable for further information.

It is most important to remember that the DPP's function is not to decide whether a suspect has been assaulted, but whether an individual policeman can be successfully prosecuted for the assault. This was seldom clearly understood by the public, who assumed that when the Chief Constable announced that the Director had decided not to prosecute a police officer, the suspect had *not* been ill-treated. It was a confusion that appears to have caused the Director much concern. On one occasion, albeit late in the day, in November 1978, he clearly reminded Harry Baillie, the Senior Deputy Chief Constable:

> It is not, for example, my function to determine whether or not an individual was assaulted. My function is to determine whether or not the evidence is sufficient upon which to direct the initiation of criminal proceedings in respect of such alleged assault.

The Director may have many reasons for deciding not to prosecute a suspected terrorist or a policeman, but he insists that his reasons remain confidential. If he decides not to prosecute a suspected terrorist, it may be because he believes that the statement on which the prosecution is based is unlikely to withstand the scrutiny of Section 6. There may be other reasons too. If he decides not to prosecute a police officer, there may be many more reasons: problems of identification, conflicting medical evidence of injuries, alternative explanations of their origin, or the strength of the police officer as a witness and the weakness of the complainant. But in neither case does the Director's decision not to prosecute necessarily mean that the suspect did not carry out the crime.

In effect, the way in which the complaints system, said to be the most rigorous in the United Kingdom, was operated meant that the Director of Public Prosecutions was expected to perform a function that was not his to perform. Theoretically the police could discipline an officer whom the DPP had declined to prosecute, but the Catch-22 was that he could not be disciplined for an offence material to the criminal charge which the Director had already considered. A police officer could not be placed in 'double jeopardy'.

All this has to be borne in mind when the official statistics are examined. They represent only part of the picture. In the period 1 July 1976 to 1 October 1979, 3,312 persons appeared at the Belfast City Commission charged with terrorist offences. Twenty-eight statements were ruled inadmissible in court, and in fifteen cases the Director declined to prosecute on the basis that he was not satisfied by the prosecution proofs in relation to Section 6. (It is significant that in both instances most of these cases appear to concern statements obtained in 1977 and the first four months of 1978.) For the same period the DPP directed prosecutions for assault against fourteen police officers in six cases. All fourteen were acquitted.

At the end of the day the Complaints Committee, in its attempts to find out how complaints were being dealt with, faced two problems which proved insuperable. First was the Chief Constable's insistence that once an investigation of a complaint had begun – which was invariably immediately – the matter was *sub judice*, and therefore could not be discussed. The Police Authority believed the Chief Constable's position to be of doubtful legal validity, and at one point they considered seeking legal advice to challenge it. An internal memorandum summed up the Police Authority's frustrations.

Lack of access to police files has hindered the Police Authority in their investigation of allegations against the RUC. However the other factor inhibiting investigation has been the detailed and rigorous application of the *sub judice* rule by the Chief Constable.

The Authority was also frustrated by its inability to discover the grounds on which the DPP reached his decisions, as the Director jealously guarded his independence and seldom gave even the Chief Constable any detailed explanation. The Authority was not privy to these communications and when the DPP's decision was delayed for some time, as frequently happened, the Authority found it difficult to discover the reason why. The memorandum concluded:

The Authority would suggest that individual cases can be assessed quickly as to whether in the broad sense the prisoner was unfairly treated while in custody. It is not necessary to determine whether he was so treated by A or B or C etc. If the assessment is that what has happened should not have happened then there is a need to discuss with doctors and the Authority safeguards, including, if necessary, those which go to the fundamentals of the interrogation process. The doctor has his professional standards to satisfy – the Authority have a statutory duty to discharge.

By the early summer of 1976, the RUC's senior management had been completely reshuffled. A new triumvirate had been installed at the top to implement 'The Way Ahead'. There were rumours that James Flanagan was not keen to vacate his seat, but the Police Authority, presumably on instructions from above, declined to extend the two and a half year period for which he had been appointed. During the three years he had served as James Flanagan's Deputy, Kenneth Newman had laid down the new structures which were the framework of 'The Way Ahead'. The government was not prepared to change its timetable, so James Flanagan, now with his knighthood, stepped aside for the new English Chief Constable.

Harry Baillie moved into the number two position as Senior Deputy Chief Constable (SDCC). Baillie was the opposite of the new Chief, a Northern Ireland Protestant who had risen through the ranks of the RUC since his young days as a Detective Constable in Cookstown. He was a giant of a man, bluff, slowly spoken, with blue eyes and considerable charm. The new Chief Constable was small, crisp and efficient. Harry Baillie was responsible for the 'Kneecappers', the RUC's Complaints & Discipline Branch.

The new number three was Jack Hermon, another home-produced policeman, who had also served his apprentice-ship in Cookstown. He became Deputy Chief Constable (DCC) with special responsibility for Operations, which included the running of the new Interrogation Centres which were planned. Jack Hermon had spent the past two years reorganizing the RUC's training schemes, while Kenneth Newman was reorganizing the Force. He also had responsibility for operations along the border, which he knew well, especially the areas around County Fermanagh, where he had been the local Boy Scout District Commissioner.

Hermon was a weathered six-footer who had been brought up in the old school, but had rapidly embraced the methods of the new. It was Hermon not Newman who had sat on the Bourn Committee. By the time Kenneth Newman became Chief Constable, his reorganization of the RUC was complete. He left the existing administrative framework intact. The province remained divided into three operational regions, North, South and Belfast, which were then subdivided into sixteen Divisions. Kenneth Newman saw that these boundaries, although administratively convenient, actively hindered the prevention and detection of terrorist crime. To the IRA each Regional and Divisional boundary represented an invisible border across which they could escape. An IRA Active Service Unit (ASU) based in one Divisional area could carry out an operation in another and escape to a third. Each Divisional Headquarters would have a file on the individuals concerned, but would seldom match them up. The IRA had little respect for administrative convenience. Faced with a mobile and elusive enemy, the old system of collecting and using intelligence was plainly inadequate. It was like a dinosaur chasing a ferret.

Kenneth Newman instituted three major changes. First,

he centralized intelligence. At the RUC's headquarters at Knock, three miles from the centre of Belfast, he established a Criminal Intelligence Section. Feeding information into it were three new Criminal Intelligence Units based in the province's three Regions and feeding information into them were similar units in the Divisions. Every scrap of intelligence, every forensic and ballistic detail was fed into the system. Each unit had access to each piece of information. When a suspect was charged at a police station, a special intelligence form, called an FP4, was automatically filled in, which gave details of the prisoner's alias, nicknames, haunts, accent, scars, tattoos and 'modus operandi' (the word on the FP4). Each completed form was forwarded to the Criminal Intelligence Section at Headquarters. In addition, the RUC had access to the army's computer at Thiepval Barracks, Lisburn, whose 'P' section, the 'people' bank, contained details of over half the population of Northern Ireland.

The new Criminal Intelligence Unit also had wider access to computerized intelligence data banks. The RUC's Special Branch could use the Metropolitan Police's Special Branch computer, believed to be at New Scotland Yard, with its records of 1·3 million people. Such liaisons were made possible by the establishment of the National Joint Unit (NJU), set up specifically to deal with 'the Irish problem' in the wake of the Birmingham bombs and the introduction of the Prevention of Terrorism Act.[1] The RUC had never had its own computer, and all intelligence was recorded and collated by hand. When I asked a senior officer why there was no computer, he said that guerilla wars were not won by machines and the Vietcong didn't have computers. Kenneth Newman developed one of the most sophisticated intelligence networks of any police force in Western Europe.

His second change was the reorganization of the CID. In addition to the existing Divisional CID, he introduced

1. McKay, Peak and Margolis, 'Terminal Surveillance', *Time Out*, No. 469, 13 April 1979.

four Regional Crime Squads to combat serious terrorist
crime. The concept of the Crime Squad had been born on
the mainland in response to the growing problem of serious
crime, and had already been adopted in principle in
Northern Ireland when James Flanagan set up the 'A'
Squad to deal with the waves of sectarian murders carried
out between 1972 and 1974. The 'A' Squad's most famous
success was the detection and conviction of the UVF's
East Antrim gang.[1] Kenneth Newman reorganized and
strengthened the 'A' Squad and changed its name to the
Headquarters Crime Squad. It was supported by three new
Regional Crime Squads, each based on one of the three
operational areas, North, South and Belfast. North
Regional Crime Squad was based in Derry, South in
Armagh and Belfast at Castlereagh. The Squads were
recruited from existing members of the CID, each one
hand-picked for his particular qualities: inactivity was not
one of them, a senior officer remarked. Most of them were
young detectives, most of them were keen and ambitious,
and they had often had little experience.

Each Regional Crime Squad consisted of about twenty
detectives, three or four of them from the Special Branch.
The usual composition of a Squad was one Detective
Inspector, three Detective Sergeants and fifteen Detective
Constables, plus a Woman Police Constable (WPC) to do
the paper work. The Squad was then subdivided for
operational purposes into four units of five detectives:
invariably one member of each unit was a Special Branch
officer. But these structures and permutations were not
rigid, as the essence of the Regional Crime Squad was its
flexibility. As a rule each Squad concentrated its attention
on the Region in which it was based, with Headquarters
Crime Squad often acting as a 'fire brigade' operation,
moving in and helping out where and when necessary. The
function of the Regional Crime Squad was to smash the
Provisional IRA, in particular the ASUs (Active Service

1. See Appendix 1.

Units) which its own structure so closely resembled. The Chief Constable said its role was

to target the most active members of terrorist organizations. The squads are not limited by divisional boundaries and can, therefore, adopt a more comprehensive and concentrated approach to the problem of terrorism.[1]

These four Regional Crime Squads, totalling little more than eighty detectives, were the new Chief Constable's shock troops. They carried out most of the interrogations. Kenneth Newman made it clear that they didn't organize tea parties. Although the crimes that each Squad investigated were usually restricted to its own particular area, most of the interrogations were carried out at Castlereagh. The Crime Squads were answerable to Chief Superintendent William Mooney, the Head of the CID. He was answerable to DCC Hermon, who controlled Operations, and he was answerable to the Chief Constable.

The Chief Constable's third and most important change was never announced as such. He made Castlereagh a full-time, centralized, specialist Interrogation Centre, Palace Barracks five years on, the synthesis of his reorganization of Intelligence and the CID. The Criminal Intelligence Unit collated the information, passed it on to the Regional Crime Squads, who interrogated terrorist suspects detained at Castlereagh under the emergency legislation for two to seven days. Here, held incommunicado, without access to solicitors or relatives, suspects made the confessions and signed the statements which were the only evidence offered by the prosecution in the majority of cases that came before the new Diplock courts. Castlereagh was to be the cutting edge of the government's new policy.

1. Chief Constable's Report, 1976.

3. Getting Results

'The cumulative effect of these measures will, I trust,
become increasingly noticeable in the year ahead.'

Kenneth Newman, 1976 Chief Constable's Report

Kenneth Newman became Chief Constable on 1 May 1976
during a period of violence which was, as Merlyn Rees had
told the House of Commons, worse than anything since
1972. He had been in office barely a fortnight when he
faced carnage on a dreadful scale. This was the toll of one
weekend, 15 May 1976.

On the Saturday three policemen were killed and one
seriously injured in a landmine explosion at Belcoo, near
the border with the Republic in County Fermanagh. One
policeman was shot dead and two others injured in an
attack on their car in Warrenpoint, County Down. Two
men were killed and thirteen injured in a pub explosion
near Unity Flats in Belfast. Three men were killed and
two women seriously injured in another pub explosion at
Charlemont, County Armagh. Two men and one woman
were seriously injured in a sub-machine-gun attack in
the same town. On the Sunday, two men were shot dead
outside a social club in Belfast's Ardoyne district and a
reserve policeman was murdered near his home at Ben-
burb, County Tyrone. On the Monday three more
civilians were killed. Kenneth Newman did not need
reminding that the security forces faced a crisis of
confidence.

Following the weekend of violence, there were wholesale
arrests. The Secretary of State, Merlyn Rees, signed seven-
day detention orders on eighteen of the men who had been

lifted. Most of them were interrogated at Castlereagh. One of them was Terry Magill.

Magill was arrested by the police and army at his mother's council house in Belfast's Turf Lodge district at 4 am. (The knock on the door usually came in the early morning, when most people were in bed and unlikely to cause a commotion when one of their neighbours was being arrested, especially in an area as hostile to the security forces as Turf Lodge.)

Magill was medically examined and fingerprinted. He told me that the first three days were easy: it was all 'just talk'. He was questioned about various incidents, including two murders and the bombing of two hotels. He was asked to sign statements. He said he knew nothing and refused. He alleged the 'rough stuff' started on the fourth day, when he continued to say he knew nothing. He claimed his hair was pulled and he was slapped around the face. Then, he alleged, he was burned with a cigarette on the wrist, between the fingers, on his arms, on his back and on his privates. He agreed to sign four statements, two admitting to murder and two involving the bombing of hotels, one of them the Russell Court. He said the pain was too much, so he signed. I asked him why he didn't hold out for another three days to avoid spending the rest of his life in gaol. He said that the pressure was too great and he couldn't stand the pain any more. I asked him if he registered a complaint while he was at Castlereagh. He said he didn't but waited until he was out of the place. He saw a doctor only when he was being charged at Townhall Street police station. The doctor noted the burn marks on Terry Magill's body.

I suggested it would not have been too difficult to have inflicted the burns on himself. He pointed out that prisoners did not have access to cigarettes: all their belongings were taken off them when they entered Castlereagh. Occasionally an interrogator might offer a cigarette, but he would not stand there and let the suspect burn himself with it. There was no police note of Magill having self-inflicted burns which there should have been had that been the cause.

Terry Magill's case came to court a year later. On 8 June 1977 His Honour Judge McGrath acquitted him. He said that the prosecution had not proved beyond reasonable doubt that inhuman and degrading treatment had not been used and that the statements were voluntary. No one was more surprised than Magill. He told me that beating the charge was like admitting that the R U C had burned him with cigarettes. It was more than Magill had expected from British justice.

The following month there was no let-up in the violence. On 2 June, Detective Constable McAdam, believed to be one of the Special Branch officers who interrogated Terry Magill, was shot dead on the Falls Road outside the Royal Victoria Hospital, where he was picking up a relative. Within hours of the shooting, Matthew Bradley, a twenty-four-year-old unemployed tiler from Ballymurphy, was arrested and taken to Springfield Road R U C station barely two hundred yards from the hospital where Constable McAdam was shot. In court, Bradley alleged that on entering the interrogation room he was attacked by seven detectives: he said they kicked him, punched him and pulled his hair. He was examined by a Police Surgeon, Dr Robert Irwin, who found multiple bruising all over his body and a 'collar' of bruising around his neck. Dr Irwin concluded that Bradley had received a number of blows to the body and that most of the injuries would have been difficult to self-inflict. The detectives alleged that Bradley had gone beserk and attacked them. He was charged not with the murder of Constable McAdam but with assaulting his interrogators.

At his trial in November 1977, His Honour Judge Brown dismissed Bradley's version of events as 'manifest lies', despite the doctor's opinion that the collar of bruising could only have been caused by systematic blows from another person. The judge preferred other medical evidence that Bradley had attacked the police officers, and duly sentenced the alleged assailant. Bradley appealed. In August 1978, three appeal court judges, headed by the Lord Chief Justice, Sir Robert Lowry, quashed Bradley's conviction. Bradley was released after spending fifteen months in gaol, six of them on remand.

The continuing violence of the early summer barely registered on the mainland. The British media had long grown weary of devoting more than a few column inches to the depressing catalogue of killings and bombings. Only a new spectacular would make the front pages.

On 21 July 1976, the Provisional IRA assassinated Christopher Ewart-Biggs, the newly appointed British Ambassador to Dublin. A remote-control bomb was detonated in a culvert under the road which the Ambassador took to the Embassy every morning. The Jaguar was blown off the road and ended up in a crater ten feet deep. A young civil servant from Stormont Castle, Judith Cook, was also killed. Her colleague, Brian Cubbon, narrowly escaped. To the Provisionals, had they known he was in the car, Cubbon was a target almost as important as the Ambassador. Educated at Bury Grammar School and Trinity College Cambridge, he had just succeeded his fellow Lancastrian Frank Cooper as Permanent Under-Secretary at the Northern Ireland Office. Cooper had gone on to higher things, now with a knighthood, at the Ministry of Defence. Brian Cubbon had the task of implementing the policies which Sir Frank Cooper and his colleagues had formulated in the Bourn Report.

The Ambassador was no ordinary target. The Provisionals believed him to be a British spy-master, an important link in the sophisticated intelligence network the British had now built up on both sides of the border. Ewart-Biggs was a career Foreign Office diplomat who had served in many post-war trouble spots, including Cyprus and the Middle East. He was believed to have been attached to Century House,[1] an anonymous office block on the South

1. Chapman Pincher, *Inside Story*, Sidgwick & Jackson.

Bank of the Thames that houses Britain's Secret Intelligence Service (SIS). The press played down the connections. The fact that the Provisionals had assassinated a British Ambassador was more than enough to fill the front pages, especially one as elegant as the monocled Christopher Ewart-Biggs.

Five days after the assassination, the new Chief Constable, Kenneth Newman, issued an important new Headquarters directive on terrorist suspects. It was coded S B 16/13 and marked 'Secret'. Dated 26 July 1976, it cancelled the previous directive which had been issued three days before Kenneth Newman became Chief Constable. This new directive was issued to all Divisional Commanders to give them new guidance and direction.

The new instructions made it clear that from then on responsibility for the command and control of the interrogation system lay with the Chief Constable himself and that all members of the Force involved in and concerned with interrogations were responsible to him for compliance in both the spirit and the letter of the directive.

The importance of the directive in the light of what subsequently happened lay in the distinction it made between an 'interview' – the result of which criminal charges were to be preferred – and an 'interrogation' conducted for the purpose of obtaining intelligence. The directive stipulated that the Judges Rules, the suspect's main safeguard from abuse during his detention in police custody (see Appendix 1), applied to an 'interview': it clearly implied, however, that the Judges Rules did *not* apply to an 'interrogation'.

The system the directive laid down institutionalized the difference between 'interview' and 'interrogation'. CID and Special Branch officers were ordered to decide whether a suspect should be interviewed or interrogated when he entered police custody.

Although the directive specifically forbade the use of the Five Techniques and stressed that prisoners were to be treated humanely and not threatened, insulted or subjected to torture, inhuman or degrading treatment, the fact that the Judges Rules seemed not to apply to 'interrogation' appeared to give detectives an unaccustomed freedom. Add to this the greater latitude which Section 6 of the Emergency Provisions Act had already given the RUC in their questioning of terrorist suspects – Section 6 was the cornerstone of the Act – and the climate was now created in which subsequent abuses might grow, however well meaning the authors of both Act and directive may have been in their intentions at the time.

There was unease in some quarters of the RUC at the direction the Force seemed to be taking under the new Chief Constable. This unease was never publicly expressed and was spoken of only in the most private of conversations. My description of the two events that follow is deliberately and necessarily vague in order to protect the identities of the police officers who provided me with the information, at considerable risk to their own careers. To give names, dates and locations would be to place my informants in jeopardy. The absence of detail is a reflection of my caution, not lack of clarity on the part of those who gave me the inside information. The two events described happened a few months after Kenneth Newman became Chief Constable and indicate how the men on the ground – the detectives of the Regional Crime Squads – saw their new role in 'The Way Ahead'.

The first event happened in the early summer of 1976, when the Chief Constable called a meeting of the new Regional Crime Squads at the Castlereagh Headquarters of the Belfast Regional Crime Squad. There were around 100 men present, most of them CID and Special Branch, from the most senior levels down to Detective Constable. It was the first time that most of the audience had met the new Chief Constable. He outlined the philosophy of 'Primacy of the Police', and explained the role of the new Regional Crime Squads with charts showing their structures and relationships with the other sections of the Force, like the Criminal Intelligence Unit, that were to provide the back-up facilities. The audience seems to have been impressed by what appears to have been a good management presentation. The Chief Constable reminded them of the vicious enemy they were facing: the only way to defeat the IRA was the rigorous application of the law to put them behind bars. He said he wanted results within the law and suggested that those who got them would enhance their chances of promotion.

But important questions still remained. As will be shown, the precise interpretation of Section 6, the section of the law that governs the admissibility of statements, remained unclear. It was impossible to gauge the effect of the Chief Constable's words on young, enthusiastic and often inexperienced detectives charged with the job of obtaining confessions that would help to defeat the IRA.

In the weeks that followed there appear to have been more meetings of senior officers of the Crime Squads at which the same points were emphasized when tactics and strategy were discussed. Again the Chief Constable stressed the need to obtain results within the law.

The results that the Chief Constable and the British government wanted did not become immediately apparent, but both parties had always known that it would take time for the new policy to bear fruit. Every month the RUC compiled mountains of statistics which they looked to for signs of an improvement in the security situation. So far they had seen little to encourage them. The RUC also compiled statistics of complaints of Assault During Interview (ADI) which, viewed overall, tended to rise and fall in response to the level of violence or a particular push by the security forces as a result of political pressure. In July 1976 there were only seven complaints of assault during interview – the second lowest level recorded for any month in the whole of the period 1976–9. The Directive SB 16/13 was issued at the end of July 1976. In August complaints of assault during interview shot up to twenty-one.

Traditionally August was always a difficult month,

when the climax of the Protestant marching season coincided with the anniversary of internment. But in August 1976 the tensions were heightened by demonstrations mounted by the paramilitaries of both sides, in protest against the government's abolition of Special Category status. At one point there were over a hundred shooting incidents on three consecutive days. On 20 August, the Chief Constable made a statement to offer the public some reassurance:

Terrorism continues to bring death and destruction to Northern Ireland . . . I will not be satisfied until the shooting and the whole squalid catalogue of criminality is brought to a finish . . . Our purpose is to put behind bars those criminals who up to now have perhaps regarded themselves as being beyond the reach of the law . . . Even in the past fifteen days, at a time when disorder and violence have been portrayed widely, the steady less-publicized work of the police has produced some significant results. Sixty-two people have been arrested and charged with serious terrorist type offences and a large number of others are still being questioned . . . The intention is that the law should be enforced even more effectively for the good of all the people of Northern Ireland and I earnestly ask for all the help and support the people can give us.

One of the twenty-one complaints of Assault During Interview registered in August 1976 was made by Michael McNaught, a sixteen-year-old Catholic from a middle-class home in the predominantly Protestant Waterside area of Derry. He was arrested at 6.30 am on Monday, 23 August, and taken to Strand Road RUC station in Derry, which was the Headquarters of the North Regional Crime Squad. He was interrogated about the murder of WPC Linda Bagley, who had been shot at point-blank range by the Provisional IRA earlier in the year. McNaught had already been arrested and questioned at the time of the murder and been released without charge.

Four others were charged with Michael McNaught for the murder of WPC Bagley. None of them were charged

with pulling the trigger. Michael McNaught was charged
with acting look-out, or 'scouting', on the basis of a verbal
admission made during interrogation. McNaught had not
signed any statements. The case came to court nearly a
year later and it is worth examining it in some detail, as the
judge's verdict shows just how much latitude Section 6
gave the RUC's detectives, and the case reveals how
crucial it was to the success of the government's new policy.

In May 1977 the five accused, four men and a woman,
appeared before Lord Justice McGonigal at Belfast City
Commission, charged with a series of offences which ranged
from murder to membership of a proscribed organization.
A former Second World War commando and a founder
member of the SAS, Lord Justice McGonigal had no
sympathy for those who sought to subvert the state. The
main evidence before him was verbal and written statements made in police custody. Four of the five accused
challenged their statements on the grounds that they
contravened Section 6 of the Emergency Provisions Act.
The defence argued that they had been obtained by the
use of torture, inhuman and degrading treatment. The
defence also maintained that the statements submitted by
the Crown had not been *made* by the accused but had been
put to them as facts and questions and then been written
down as if they represented their own words.

On 19 May 1977, after a lengthy trial, Lord Justice
McGonigal delivered a celebrated and, to many, notorious
judgement. He began by stating that Parliament had taken
the wording and standards of Section 6 from Article 3 of
the European Convention on Human Rights, which stated
that 'No one shall be subjected to torture or inhuman or
degrading treatment or punishment'. He said that as
Parliament had drawn Section 6 from the European
Convention, he looked to the European Commission to
define the terms 'torture, inhuman and degrading treatment'. The European Commission of Human Rights had
recently defined the terms in the torture case that had been

brought against the Greek Colonels. In the Greek case, the Commission defined 'inhuman treatment' as

At least such treatment as deliberately causes severe suffering, mental or physical.

'Torture' was

inhuman treatment which has a purpose, such as the obtaining of information or confession, or the infliction of punishment, and it is generally an aggravated form of inhuman treatment.

'Degrading treatment' was

treatment or punishment of an individual which grossly humiliates him before others or drives him to act against his will.[1]

Lord Justice McGonigal also quoted what he believed to be an important paragraph in the Greek case which covered treatment which did not fall into any of the above three categories:

Finally the Commission distinguished between acts prohibited by Article Three and what it called 'a certain roughness of treatment'.

The Commission considered that such roughness was tolerated by most detainees and even taken for granted. It

may take the form of slaps or blows of the hand on the head or face. This underlines the fact that the point up to which prisoners and the public may accept physical violence as being neither cruel nor excessive varies between different societies and even between different sections of them.[2]

The judge said that treatment had therefore to be of a somewhat extreme nature to fall into the categories of torture, inhuman and degrading treatment as specified in Section 6 of the Emergency Provisions Act.

Inhuman treatment is, for example, treatment causing *severe*

1. ECHR Yearbook 12, p. 186.
2. ibid., p. 501.

suffering. Torture is an *aggravated* form of inhuman treatment and degrading conduct is conduct which *grossly* humiliates. The use of these terms is again underlined by the report's reference to 'a certain roughness of conduct' which does not fall within any of the categories ... It appears to accept a degree of physical violence which could never be tolerated by the courts under the common law test and, if the words in Section 6 are to be construed in the same sense as the words used in Article Three, it leaves it open to an interviewer to use a moderate degree of physical ill-treatment for the purpose of inducing a person to make a statement. It appears to me that this is the way the words must be construed and that that is the effect of the Section.

It was a remarkable statement that clearly said that interrogators could ill-treat suspects within the framework of Section 6. Nothing could illustrate more plainly the dangerous latitude that Section 6 gave the RUC's interrogators and the crucial importance of Section 6 to the successful operation of Castlereagh and the Diplock courts.

Nevertheless, the judge added that the courts would not permit physical ill-treatment of a lesser degree which, on the strict interpretation of Section 6, would not necessarily make the statements inadmissible. He said it

would be repugnant to all the principles of justice to allow such conduct to be used as a means towards an end, however desirable that end may be made to appear.

The judge then told the court that he had additional powers of 'judicial discretion' which, properly used, acted as an extra statutory control over the way in which statements were induced and obtained. He stressed, however, that these powers were *not* to be used to 'defeat the will of Parliament' as expressed in Section 6. In other words, if a degree of ill-treatment falling short of that required by Section 6 (which had to be *gross*) was used to induce a statement, the judge did not automatically have to use his 'discretion' to exclude it. The judge said that he had not only to consider the conduct itself but the effect it was likely to have on the suspect against whom it was used, in particular whether it was likely to drive him to 'act against his will or conscience'.

So even the exercise of 'judicial discretion' had qualifications and did not automatically restrict an interrogator's activities.

The judge then considered Michael McNaught's case. In court, Lord Justice McGonigal said that McNaught had given an account of what, if he was right, must have been an almost continuous course of ill-treatment stretching over all the interviews he had had. McNaught said that in the first interview he was struck thirty times hard enough to hurt, mostly to the stomach; that he had also had his hair pulled, and his stomach was sore the next day. In the second interview McNaught had said he had been hit again in the stomach and that by the end of the interview he had received dozens of blows. In the third interview he said he had been punched in the stomach, the kidneys and the back more than fifty times and slapped around the face with an open hand. He said that his mouth had been burnt with a lighted cigarette, that he had been punched in the face and his nose made to bleed. He had also said that he had been made to strip and was struck in the testicles and around the kidneys. Lord Justice McGonigal remarked that this treatment was such that it was difficult to understand how anyone who had received it would not obviously be in pain and under severe stress and fear.

He also said that McNaught had made a written complaint about his treatment on the day after his interviews, but that there were considerable discrepancies between the allegations he had made in the complaint and the allegations which he had made while giving evidence in court. He had also been examined by Dr Mitchell on behalf of the Crown and by Dr Stone, his own doctor. Both doctors had found signs of injury to the nose. Dr Stone had found that the nose was bleeding, and Dr Mitchell had found that both it and the lip were swollen. But neither doctor had found any other sign of injury, no bruising, no tenderness, and nothing to indicate that the terrific assault which McNaught had described had taken place. Nor did he appear to Dr Stone, his own doctor, either distressed, nervous or agitated. Lord Justice McGonigal noted:

> Neither doctor found any other injury, no bruisings, no tenderness and nothing to indicate that the terrific assault described by the accused had taken place. He did not appear to his own doctor distressed, nervous or agitated.

But although he believed that McNaught had not only exaggerated but lied in the course of giving evidence, the judge felt that he could not discount the allegations entirely:

> The evidence as a whole leaves me in a state of doubt. The onus is on the Crown and the fact McNaught's evidence cannot be relied on as proof of his allegations is not, therefore, conclusive.
>
> It is clear that he did sustain an injury to his nose which left it swollen and caused it to bleed. There is no suggestion on the Crown evidence of how or when that injury was received and it appears to me from its nature and from the relevant times,[1] that it must have been received during the period covering the interviews. That injury could have been caused by one blow and in itself would not in my opinion bring the case within Section 6.

Lord Justice McGonigal was not convinced that, had it been the only blow, it would have induced or influenced the making of the statement. He concluded:

> It has been denied by the Crown witnesses that *any* blow was struck. That is clearly wrong and that being so it may be that other denials of some degree of ill-treatment are also wrong and that McNaught may have been punched to the stomach or other places in a way that did not leave any bruises or lasting tenderness but which at the time hurt and frightened.
>
> Accepting as I do that there was an injury to the nose, I could not be satisfied in the way that I have to be that there was no

1. i.e. the interview schedules the police produced in court.

other ill-treatment which operated on McNaught's mind to induce him to make a statement. It does not appear to me from the medical evidence that such treatment, if received, amounts to torture or inhuman or degrading treatment in the sense in which I have held these words were used, but it does appear to me that it is treatment that, if received, could have affected McNaught's mind and induced him to make a statement and it is therefore treatment that requires me in the exercise of my judicial discretion to exclude it. I therefore hold that the statement made by McNaught is not admissible in evidence.

Michael McNaught was released. His four co-defendants were sentenced. But the importance of the case extended beyond the fact that McNaught was acquitted. One of Northern Ireland's most senior judges had clearly stated that Section 6 permitted a degree of ill-treatment to induce statements. It seemed to many, disturbed by the latitude that Section 6 already gave interrogators once the common law test was abolished, that the courts were now licensing a degree of ill-treatment as long as it was not 'gross'. Among some sections of the legal profession, the McGonigal judgement became known as the 'Torturers' Charter'. Privately, his senior colleagues criticized Lord Justice McGonigal's interpretation of Section 6 in the belief that he had rashly confused European and English Law. But the damage had been done.

With this case very much in mind, the Bennett Report concluded:

The uncertainty, despite the standards upheld and applied by the courts, about what is permissible and what is not short of the use of physical violence or ill-treatment, may tempt police officers to see how far they can go and what they can get away with.[1]

In September 1976, Merlyn Rees vacated Stormont

1. Bennett Report (Report of the Committee of Inquiry into Police Interrogation Procedures in Northern Ireland), March 1979, para. 84, p. 31.

Castle for the Home Office and left Northern Ireland to a
Secretary of State who was temperamentally more at home
with the tough security policy the government had now
decided to pursue. Roy Mason was Yorkshire born and
bred, and was proud of it. He was hard-working and
ambitious. Like many of his fellow Yorkshiremen, he was
blunt, straightforward and stubborn. People may have felt
ambivalent about Merlyn Rees, but Roy Mason attracted
few mixed feelings. He was a black-and-white person who
saw issues in black-and-white terms. His road to the top
had been hard. At the age of fourteen he had started work
down a Yorkshire coalmine and never forgotten the experience. He found his way into politics through his union
work for the NUM and a TUC scholarship to the London
School of Economics. Firmly on the right wing of the
Labour Party, his trades union connections, and the fact
that he had once been a real worker, stood him in good
stead with his leader James Callaghan, who needed all the
trades union support he could get to survive the difficult
industrial climate of the mid-seventies.

Callaghan sent Mason to Northern Ireland because he
wanted a clear, unequivocal line to be taken, the priority
being the defeat of terrorism, not further attempts to
shuffle the well-thumbed political cards. Mason was the
man for the job. It was an easy move for him to make,
from one set of generals to another, from Minister of
Defence to Secretary of State for Northern Ireland. Roy
Mason felt at home with the military: one of his colleagues
said that he greeted a man with a uniform like a long-lost
brother.

Nor was Northern Ireland the graveyard of political
careers that it was popularly supposed to be. It had
certainly not hindered the political advancement of William
Whitelaw and Merlyn Rees. To most observers, whoever
held the Northern Ireland post was on a hiding to nothing.
But in fact, it even had distinct advantages for the
ambitious politician as it offered its incumbent constant
exposure to the media. (Before Roy Mason took over, his

civil servants at the Ministry of Defence informed their opposite numbers at the NIO that they would be sending over Roy Mason's books of press cuttings which they said should be kept up to date to keep the Minister happy.) To the media, the new tough pipe-smoking Minister who marched round the province in a safari suit epitomized the government's determination to defeat terrorism. It was exactly what Jim Callaghan wanted, not least to reassure the Ulster Unionist MPs at Westminster whose support he needed to maintain his slender majority in the House of Commons. The changes were now complete. Northern Ireland had a new GOC, a new Chief Constable, a new Permanent Under-Secretary, and a new Secretary of State to lead the team. The new policy had new men.

Roy Mason's style and approach to the Irish problem were very different from those of his predecessor. Rees was a conciliator, a listener, a man of compromise, which some saw as indecision. Mason knew what he wanted, gave orders and expected them to be obeyed. Some called it arrogance. Rees devoured volumes of Irish history and understood the nuances of Irish politics. Mason had no time for history; security concerned the present not the past. Results were what mattered. The new Secretary of State was a natural partner for the new Chief Constable.

Ministers noticed the change when Roy Mason took over. There were no more regular round-table discussions at the end of the day when ideas were floated and anxieties aired. There were no late-night sessions over a dram in the Secretary of State's flat. Contacts with the Provisionals were broken off and Laneside ceased to serve tea to the paramilitaries. There were no more flying visits to Castlereagh such as Merlyn Rees had occasionally made, to keep an eye on things. Roy Mason believed that the RUC should be left to get on with the job without any interference from the politicians.

For the new Secretary of State, the highlight of the week was the Monday morning security meeting held in the ministerial conference room at Stormont Castle. At one

end is a huge bay window that overlooks the Castle's green
lawns and the greenhouses and stables in the distance. At
the other end is the door leading off to the SOS's office.
The Northern Ireland Cabinet met here before Stormont
was abolished in 1972, and the British took over: it had
seen many changes in Prime Ministers and policies since
the eruption of the Civil Rights movement called into
question the assumptions on which the Northern Irish state
had been built. In the centre of the room is a polished
thirty-foot table where the Secretary of State, the GOC
and the Chief Constable sat at the weekly security meetings, flanked by civil servants, police and army officers.
Above the fireplace is a huge faded oil painting, an
Arcadian idyll with shepherds and peasants reclining at
sunset. During the meetings, civil servants were said to
gaze longingly at it.

According to Ministers who attended the Monday morning meetings, the mood tended to be 'gung ho': 'We're
beating them, the bastards are on the run, we're scaring
the life out of them,' were the kind of sentiments frequently
expressed. A Minister told me he sometimes felt like
pinning medals on everybody. The Chief Constable would
recite the number of arrests made and charges brought
that week as evidence of progress in the battle against
terrorism.

The RUC kept a scoreboard as the results started to
come in. At the end of 1976 the Chief Constable announced
that the new Regional Crime Squads had successfully
eliminated complete terrorist units in various parts of the
province.[1] Charges against the Provisional IRA were more
than double those in 1975, an increase of 121 per cent; 708
suspects were charged, more than double those in 1975.
Charges for murder and attempted murder increased by 7
per cent, use and possession of explosives by 115 per cent,
miscellaneous charges – hijacking, arson and membership
of illegal organizations – by 187 per cent. But complaints
of assault during interview also more than doubled. They

1. 1976 Annual Report.

increased by 113 per cent. In 1975 there had been 180 such complaints: in 1976 there were 384. But to the Monday morning security meetings, they were not the main priority.

Not that any politicians or policemen who attended the security meetings needed any reminder of the possible pitfalls in a security police obsessed with results. Roy Mason took over from Merlyn Rees in September 1976, the month the European Commission published its Report and found the British government guilty of 'torture, inhuman and degrading treatment'.

Part Two

Part One

4. The Rafferty File

'The Regional Crime Squads were successful in eliminating complete terrorist units in various parts of the province.'

Kenneth Newman, 1976 Chief Constable's Report

By the autumn of 1976 the new Regional Crime Squads were beginning to bite. One of the Provisional I R A units they eliminated was a cell in East Tyrone. The case of James Rafferty arose out of its detection and destruction.

James Rafferty was interrogated at Omagh R U C station for three days in November 1976, in connection with the activities of that Provisional I R A Active Service Unit. He was released without charge and spent the following four days in hospital recovering from his injuries. The Rafferty case is not only one of the earliest and most serious of the allegations of the period, but one which remains, at the time of writing (1980), unresolved. The case is a constant thread that runs through the period covered by this book. The conditions under which Rafferty was arrested, the allegations he made, the evidence of the doctors who examined him, the way in which his complaint was handled, the reaction of the D P P, and the frustrations of the Police Authority are common to many other cases. James Rafferty's complaint was just one of the forty-one complaints of Assault During Interview registered in November 1976.

Within one week in the autumn of 1976, the Provisional I R A struck three times in one small country area of East Tyrone. On 28 October a postman who was a member of the U D R was shot dead while delivering letters in the Cappagh district. On 2 November, an R U C reservist was wounded in Fintona; and on 4 November another R U C reservist was injured in a booby-trap explosion.

On Tuesday, 9 November 1976, three men from County Tyrone were arrested under Section 10 of the Emergency Provisions Act. They were Patrick O'Neill, Michael Boyle and Peter Kane. They were taken to Omagh RUC station where they were interrogated by the local CID and Regional Crime Squad detectives. A team of twenty-three detectives was involved in the subsequent interrogations. As a result of information obtained from these initial interrogations, four more men were arrested and brought to Omagh on Thursday, 11 November. They were James Rafferty, Edward Hurson, Peter Nugent and Kevin O'Brien.

These latest incidents apart, the Crime Squad had been investigating a series of incidents in the Cappagh district of County Tyrone which stretched back four years to 1972. They included the bombing of a sewage works, the murder of a policeman in 1973, a booby trap in 1974, an attack on a convoy in 1975, and the ambush of a UDR patrol in 1976. It was the kind of exercise for which the Regional Crime Squads had been designed: to pinpoint an area and investigate past and present crimes committed in it; to detain and question suspects and, where possible, to obtain statements which would clear the books going back over a number of years.

James Rafferty and Peter Nugent were interrogated and released without charge. As a result of three days of intensive interrogation the other five were charged on twenty-nine counts with offences ranging from conspiracy to murder and causing explosions, to belonging to a proscribed organization. The only evidence against them were verbal admissions and written statements made during interrogation at Omagh. No forensic evidence was produced, although explosives were alleged to have been the unit's speciality.

The case came to court on 28 November 1977 before His Honour Judge Rowland. Initially all five refused to recog-

nize the court,[1] which was tantamount to an admission of
I R A membership. However, they changed their minds and
pleaded not guilty. Two of the accused, Boyle and Hurson,
challenged the admissibility of their statements on the
grounds that they had been induced by torture, inhuman
and degrading treatment.

Passing judgement and sentence in court, His Honour
Judge Rowland reviewed all the evidence he had heard. In
court, Boyle had said that he had been slapped around the
head, kicked in the back a number of times and punched
in the stomach with a closed fist. He said that as a result he
was mixed up and confused: all he wanted to do was to
escape from the hands of his interrogators, so he agreed to
their suggestion that he had joined the I R A and handled
explosives and guns. At Omagh, Boyle did *not* complain.
It was only when taken to be charged before a Special
Court at Cookstown that he told a doctor what had
happened to him. Dr Johnson asked him, 'Do you want to
tell me anything about yourself since you have been
detained?' Boyle replied that he had been 'hit several times
on the head by a plain-clothes policeman at Omagh police
station'. Dr Johnson examined Boyle but found no signs of
injury. After he had been charged at the Special Court,
Boyle was examined by his own doctor, Dr Kathleen
McNeece. She said he looked pale and confused but found
no medical evidence to support the allegations he made. In
court Judge Rowland said:

I regard the medical evidence as important because it is one
criterion which can properly be adopted to resolve a conflict of
allegations . . . The ill-treatment alleged by Boyle was of such a
nature and degree that one would undoubtedly have expected
visible signs of injury . . . I am satisfied beyond a reasonable
doubt that the accused was not maltreated . . . I have come to the
conclusion I am not faced in this case with a wholesale conspiracy

1. The I R A do not recognize the legitimacy of the British presence in
the North of Ireland and therefore do not recognize the legality of their
courts.

by police officers and gaolers who looked after the accused to tell
a farrago of lies in court.

The judge admitted Boyle's statement.

He then considered Hurson's allegations made in court,
admitting that the evidence 'clearly establishes a prima
facie case of Section 6 treatment'. Hurson alleged he had
been punched in the stomach with fists, kicked in the
testicles, hit around the head, bent over a table and had his
head banged against the wall. He told the court that while
he was being subjected to this treatment, he heard James
Rafferty 'shouting and screaming'. He said he thought that
Rafferty was being beaten up and that he would get the
same treatment if he didn't cooperate, so he agreed to
make verbal admissions and sign a statement. Like Boyle,
Hurson made *no* complaint at Omagh, but waited until he
reached Cookstown RUC station to be charged before the
Special Court. Again, Hurson complained to a doctor, Dr
Henry. When Detective Inspector Farr at Omagh heard
that Hurson had complained at Cookstown, he arranged
for Hurson to be interviewed again. Two detectives then
obtained the same series of admissions in Cookstown that
Hurson had made in Omagh. Hurson never made any
allegations about his treatment in Cookstown; but did say
in court that the two detectives told him that if he did not
confess he would be sent back to Omagh for more. The
judge said that he didn't believe Hurson.

Again, the police denied that Hurson had been ill-
treated in any way. Again, the judge turned to the doctors'
reports 'to seek the means of resolving the evidential
conflict'. Following his interrogation, Hurson was examined by six doctors over the following week.

Judge Rowland first reviewed the evidence of Dr Henry,
who had examined Hurson at Cookstown Police Station,
where he had been brought to be charged. He said that
Hurson had told Dr Henry that he had had his head
hammered by hands and fists; he had been punched in the
privates and stomach; and that his hair and ears had been

pulled. Hurson told the doctor that he had been well treated in Cookstown. The judge then summarized Dr Henry's report. There were signs of tenderness and slight swelling at the back of the head; tenderness of the right side of the neck; tenderness over the spine; tenderness and swelling over the cord which leads from the testicles to the abdomen; and tenderness of the neck. The doctor said, however, that he found no marks, discolouration or bruising anywhere on Hurson's body. His blood pressure was a normal 140/180. Had Hurson been as severely beaten as he alleged, Dr Henry said that he would have expected to find marks.

Later the same afternoon, he was examined by Dr Johnson. He did not note the complaints that Hurson had made about his alleged ill-treatment at Omagh. His examination showed: tenderness at the back of the head, upper neck and lower back; the left spermatic cord was thickened and tender from the testicle up towards the abdomen; the left buttock was tender. He found no evidence of bruising.

Judge Rowland also said that Hurson had been examined by his own doctor, Dr Kathleen McNeece, at 5 pm on 13 November. She had recorded that he was pale but not confused and able to recount clearly what had happened at Omagh. She found nothing abnormal about the testicles and no marks or bruising on the stomach, although it was tender when she pressed it; the region around the left kidney was tender; there was tenderness over the back; there was redness of the roots of his hair at the back of his head, and his ears appeared very red. She found no swelling or discolouration anywhere. Nevertheless, she felt that Hurson's complaints were quite genuine.

Judge Rowland said that Dr Dean had examined Hurson at 12.20 am on Sunday, 14 November, and had found tenderness on the head, scalp, neck and lower back but no signs of bruising or swelling carrying on. At 11 am on 15 November, Judge Rowland said that Dr Watson, the prison doctor at Crumlin Road, examined Hurson and had found no scars or marks of any significance.

Finally, on Wednesday, 19 November, a week after his interrogation, Judge Rowland said that Hurson was examined by Dr Hendron, a Belfast GP. Dr Hendron found tenderness over both testicles and the stomach; soreness on the right side of his head; his ears were also inflamed. Dr Hendron said that he was convinced that Hurson was telling the truth at this examination.

Assessing the medical evidence Judge Rowland said:

> My conclusion about the medical evidence is that there was virtually no objective signs of recent injury to the accused. Having observed the accused in the witness box and in court over a number of days and having heard the way he answered questions, I am in no doubt that the tenderness he complained of was purely subjective and that apart from one fairly insignificant swelling at the back of the head, there was nothing consistent with the severe treatment he described . . . The swelling at the back of the head was so insignificant that it was difficult to see how it could have been caused by hand slapping *and even if it were, that is not the kind of maltreatment embraced by Section 6* [my italics]. His evidence is not capable of reasonable credence and I reject it.

James Rafferty, whom Hurson alleged he had heard 'shouting and screaming' at Omagh, was also called to give evidence. Judge Rowland said that he 'was not impressed' by it and it was of 'no assistance to Hurson's case'.

The trial lasted sixteen days. All five accused were found guilty and sentenced for terms ranging from fifteen to twenty years. The judge had no doubt he was locking up an Active Service Unit of the Provisional IRA. He told them on passing sentence:

> It is quite clear from the evidence contained in your statements that all five of you were operating as a group of terrorists whose sole purpose was to spread terror throughout the community and cause as much damage and destruction as you could both to life and to property . . . You were taking two risks when you associated with this organization, one was the risk of detection sooner or later and the other was the risk of severe punishment

if you were caught. Both these risks have now come home to roost and you now know what you can expect.

But this wasn't the end of the story. Hurson appealed on the grounds that Judge Rowland had not paid sufficient attention to the medical evidence. The Court of Criminal Appeal did not accept the plea, but did order a retrial. Hurson's retrial took place at Belfast City Commission in September 1979, before Mr Justice Murray in Court Number 1.

The judge entered the high-ceilinged courtroom from a door to the right of the Royal Coat of Arms on the wall above his red-leather chair. As the judge's tipstaff[1] announced, 'This Court now stands open, God Save the Queen', the court muttered a barely audible reply. The acoustics in Court Number 1 are dreadful: it's often difficult to hear justice being done. The hard wooden benches that rise in tiers from the back of the court for members of the public are empty except for the odd relative who wanders in. The press benches are equally deserted: in Belfast newspapers tend to report sentences not trials. Murder cases are ten a penny. The judicial machinery grinds on largely unnoticed and unreported, as dozens of convicted terrorists are consigned to the Maze prison. The Hurson retrial was a rare interruption in the process. But the case was not unnoticed or unwatched by the police, the judiciary and the DPP. All were aware of its importance, not least the RUC. They knew that, with Rafferty's complaint still unresolved, among the issues at stake should Hurson be acquitted were the methods used by the Crime Squads and CID in cracking terrorist cells such as that in East Tyrone. If Hurson's statements were rejected by the judge, and Rafferty's complaint upheld, a question mark might be placed over the way in which the statements of the rest of the ASU had been obtained.

The most populated benches were those occupied by seventeen RUC detectives to the right of the dock. They

1. The judge's amanuensis.

sat expressionless, occasionally leaning forward to whisper something and occasionally smiling when Hurson's girl-friends were mentioned. Most of them were in their twenties and thirties, fashionably dressed by High Street tailors, many sporting moustaches. Hurson stood in the dock surrounded by prison officers with their peaked caps pulled down well over their eyes. Hurson looked young, pale and neatly dressed in a black cord jacket and open-necked striped shirt. He was softly spoken, his thick Irish country accent even more difficult to understand given the acoustical problems in the courtroom. Mr Justice Murray listens to evidence leaning forward like a doctor at a patient's bedside. Crown counsel was John Creaney, a thick-set barrister and a heavyweight in court. Hurson's defence counsel was John Curran, a thin, earnest QC with glasses, who takes time to build up a head of steam. The two are frequent adversaries in statement fights. As Curran admitted, his client Hurson was 'not a person of very great intelligence'. He had never heard of Armistice Day, the date on which he was arrested. Hurson was not impressive in the witness box.

Cross-examined about his interrogations, he kept repeating, 'I just can't remember.' Giving evidence, Dr Henry, who was the first doctor to examine him when he arrived at Cookstown, said that he had 'seen worse injuries in a game of rugby'. Curran pointed out that injuries consistent with a game of rugby should not happen in police custody. Dr Johnson said that the medical evidence which he observed was 'consistent with roughing up', but did not constitute 'serious assault'. He did not believe that it would cause a suspect to speak rather than remain silent.

The Crown then suggested that such signs as were observed might have been the result of Hurson's attempt to inflict injuries on himself. Curran pointed out that it was improper for the Crown to suggest self-infliction as an explanation when the question of self-infliction had not once been addressed by Crown counsel to any of the five

doctors who took the witness stand. Creaney said Hurson
had made no complaint at Omagh. Curran said he had
been frightened to do so: he had complained within ten
minutes of arriving at Cookstown police station. He
reminded the judge that the Crown must establish that
there was no reasonable possibility of injury and said that
the way the Crown presented its case was that no one had
even heard of ill-treatment and nothing at all had happened
to Hurson at Omagh.

He suggested that if the doctors were asked to put
their hands on the Bible and swear that nothing had
happened to Hurson, they would not do it. The Crown,
he concluded, had failed to remove the doubt from the
mind of the court. Curran also argued that the statements
he made in Cookstown should be declared inadmissible
as they were made while he was still under the influence
of what had happened to him in Omagh. He made the
point that Inspector Farr of Omagh told the detectives
in Cookstown to take further statements from Hurson
only after he was informed that Hurson had made a
complaint, and only after Hurson had been sitting in
Cookstown police station *for two hours*.

After a four-day trial, Mr Justice Murray rejected the
statements that Hurson had made at Omagh, on the
grounds that the Crown had not totally dispelled the doubt
from his mind that Hurson had been ill-treated in police
custody at Omagh. However, he did accept the statements
that Hurson had subsequently made while in custody at
Cookstown RUC station.

Hurson was handcuffed and taken away to serve the rest
of his sentence in the H Blocks at the Maze prison.
Hurson's defence appealed again to have the Cookstown
statements also rejected. At the time of writing, the appeal
is still pending.

Although Mr Justice Murray upheld Judge Rowland's
conviction of Hurson, the fact that he rejected the statements that Hurson had made in Omagh cast some doubt
on the RUC's insistence that none of the suspects arrested

in the swoop in East Tyrone had been ill-treated while in
custody at Omagh. The verdict, although of little consola-
tion to Hurson, at least added weight to the allegations
that James Rafferty had made about what happened to
him at Omagh in November 1976.

Twenty-four-year-old James Rafferty lived and worked
part-time on his mother's twenty-six-acre farm at Augh-
nagar, a few miles to the north-west of Dungannon, in the
shadow of the Cappagh mountain. Rafferty was a strong,
healthy red-head with a Zapata moustache and a ruddy
complexion that suggested a life spent outdoors. He had
not been interned and never been in trouble with the
police.

Just before dawn on Thursday, 11 November 1976, the
police and army arrived at the Rafferty farmhouse. The
family were asleep. The house was searched and James
Rafferty arrested under Section 10 of the Emergency
Provisions Act. He was taken to Omagh RUC station,
where he was photographed, finger-printed and medically
examined. His mother had warned the uniformed police
who had arrested him that her son suffered from epilepsy.
The doctor asked him about an injury to his finger. Rafferty
explained that he had caught it in a sand-grading machine
in 1969.

He was then taken to an interview room. This is
Rafferty's account to me of what he alleged happened. The
two detectives asked him about his farm, the kind of crops
he planted and about his family. They sat at one side of a
table and Rafferty at the other. They seemed 'very nice':
he never thought that there would be 'rough stuff' to come.
Two other detectives entered the room: one showed him
a rifle, 'like the old ·303s the UDR used', and said it
belonged to him. Rafferty denied it. One of the detectives
then hit him in the stomach with his fist. The detective
again said that it was Rafferty's gun, and again Rafferty
denied it.

Rafferty did know about guns, as he was a member of a

clay pigeon shooting club. The gun he was being shown was not used for shooting clay pigeons. A detective then accused him of being a member of the IRA. Rafferty said he wasn't. The detective then admitted that the gun wasn't his, but had been found on Rafferty's farm and was in Rafferty's care. Rafferty denied it. He was then banged on the side of the head.

Rafferty alleged that the ill-treatment got worse in the subsequent interviews. He was accused of being the OC of the Provisionals' Cappagh unit. He said he wasn't. He was accused of being a murderer. He denied it. He was made to stand against the wall and beaten and prodded in the stomach. One detective jumped up and down, pulling his hair furiously. A gun fell out of his pocket as he did so. He said he was going to 'kill the bastard'. The room had no windows. The only light was from a naked bulb hanging from the ceiling. One detective pulled his moustache as if he was trying to lift him by it. Rafferty yelled out and screamed. A detective tried to lift him up under the ears. Rafferty screamed and yelled again.

He was given a break at one stage: a 'nice young detective' came in and said that if Rafferty admitted to either the Cappagh quarry explosion or the bombing of a petrol station he'd be out in five years' time. If he didn't confess to them, the detective said he was going to be in for thirty years. Rafferty said he wasn't involved in any of them. 'Come on, James,' Rafferty alleged the detective said, 'take one of those wee jobs.' Rafferty still refused.

He was put against the wall again and beaten around the stomach. He lost all sense of time. He remembered looking at a detective's watch and seeing that it was 11.45: he assumed it to be nearly midnight. He was confused and exhausted. He was made to strip to his underpants and told to perform exercises, step-ups on a chair, while counting out loud. If he lost count, he was made to start again. He was made to run on the spot. He was exhausted. He alleged that he had already been kicked around the room and hit with a closed fist.

Rafferty said he saw no point in asking for a doctor, as he thought it would do no good. It never occurred to him to ask for a solicitor. The interviews lasted for nearly three days. On the last day, a uniformed policeman saw him in his cell and asked him if he wanted to see a doctor. Rafferty said no. The policeman came back later and asked him again. This time Rafferty said yes.

He was examined by Dr O'Neill on behalf of his own GP, who wasn't available, and the doctor who was acting for the police. Dr O'Neill noted that Rafferty was tender around the forehead and scalp, and had four or five bruises one to two inches in diameter in the area of the stomach. He also had abrasions and bruising on the lower back. Both doctors agreed that Rafferty should receive urgent hospital treatment. Rafferty was told there were no charges being made against him and he was being released. The uniformed inspector at Omagh asked Rafferty if he wanted to make a complaint. He said he did. When he went outside, escorted by uniformed RUC officers, he met his mother and sister. He says that they were shocked when they saw his condition and turned on the uniformed policemen. They said they thought the police 'couldn't do this any more'. Rafferty said the uniformed men were not responsible for his condition.

Shortly after midnight on Sunday morning, Rafferty was taken to Tyrone County Hospital in Omagh in a police car. His own doctor, Dr Katherine McNeece, was able to visit him that day. Rafferty told her what had happened. She noted a small linear laceration of approximately one to one and a half inches long over the base of the spine and some bruising over his stomach. She says she did not do a full examination, as he had already been given a thorough examination by the consultant on admission.

The consultant, Mr McMurray, a Fellow of the Royal College of Surgeons, recorded Rafferty's complaints: he said he had been kicked and punched in the abdomen, been pulled by the hair and knocked unconscious. On examination he noted that Rafferty was suffering from a degree of amnesia and had difficulty in maintaining his balance. There were 'multiple dark black bruises on his upper abdomen', and a bruise and abrasion at the base of the spine above the bottom. On close examination of the scalp Mr McMurray observed reddening areas around the hair roots. Rafferty's skull was X-rayed. There were no fractures. By the following Wednesday, the consultant decided that Rafferty was fit to go home.

Mr McMurray examined Rafferty again three months later. He complained of headaches and dizzy spells; he experienced feelings of depression and insecurity and had violent dreams of being threatened and shot. Mr McMurray's opinion was that Rafferty was 'a genuine person'. He noted that Rafferty's physical injuries had resolved satisfactorily and the symptoms of which he now complained were 'due to a mild degree of concussion' Rafferty had experienced. He felt the symptoms may be in part due to 'the physical side of his ordeal' and 'the mental stress which this incident has caused'.

Rafferty's mother complained to Councillor Jack Hassard of Dungannon, who was a member of the Police Authority's Complaints Committee. Hassard acted swiftly. The day he was due to visit Rafferty in hospital, he wrote to William Baird, the Secretary of the Police Authority, and suggested that the Authority set up a Tribunal of Inquiry 'into this alleged torture' as the Authority was empowered to do under the 1970 Police Act.[1] The Tribunal could only be established where a complaint related to 'a matter affecting or appearing to affect the public interest'. William Baird acted with equal speed and informed Harry Baillie, the Senior Deputy Chief Constable in charge of Complaints & Discipline, of Jack Hassard's concern. Baird told Baillie that he understood that James Rafferty 'has been sufficiently severely beaten to necessitate his being admitted to Omagh Hospital'. He also passed on Hassard's request that Mr Baillie should have inquiries made so that

1. 1970 Police Act (NI), Section 13(2).

the RUC would have some answers ready for the meeting of the Complaints Committee the following week.

A few days later Hassard wrote to Baird again. He said he had been given the 'run around' by the RUC in Omagh. He had rung them to find out which hospital Rafferty was in. They said that Rafferty wasn't in Tyrone County Hospital in Omagh, but the South Tyrone Hospital in Dungannon. Hassard checked and told the RUC they were wrong. The officer he spoke to at Omagh said that he had been given the information by the CID. 'Let me say,' wrote Hassard, 'that Mr Rafferty was taken from Omagh RUC station by police car, so one would think that the driver would have known whether he was in Omagh or Dungannon.' Hassard was right. SDCC Baillie later admitted that the CID had 'misinformed uniformed staff regarding the hospital to which Mr Rafferty had been admitted'.[1]

The RUC acted swiftly too. An Investigating Officer was detailed to investigate Rafferty's complaint the day he was discharged from hospital. Hassard then wrote directly to SDCC Baillie, giving the names of police officers reported to have been involved in the alleged brutalities at Omagh. He wrote:

These names may help investigators because as is expected there will be a wall of silence and not many volunteers to admit the alleged torture which has acted as a great recruiting campaign for the Provos. I am sure that if they (the Provos) had their way they would knight Messrs [he mentions the detectives' names]: instead they will probably return to the killing of decent uni-formed officers. This is why I feel so concerned.

Hassard also said that he was very impressed with the Investigating Officer and felt sure that he would 'carry out his duty'.

By the middle of January 1977, the RUC's investigation was complete.

There was an air of disquiet surrounding the first meeting

1. At Complaints Committee meeting, 1 March 1977.

of the Complaints Committee of 1977. On Friday afternoon, 7 January, a depleted Committee – Hassard and
another member were absent – met SDCC Baillie at RUC
Headquarters. The meetings were confidential, so few
besides those who sat around the conference table knew of
the concern that was expressed that day. The need for
secrecy was even greater, given the atmosphere in which
the meeting was held. The previous day, news had been
leaked of some after-dinner indiscretions attributed to the
new Secretary of State, Roy Mason, who had, up to this
stage, been playing himself in gently.

Although the security situation showed little signs of
improvement, at least Roy Mason had the burgeoning
Peace Movement to divert attention from the pressing
security and political problems he faced. The occasion of
the alleged indiscretions had been a dinner the previous
November, hosted by the Chairman of the BBC, Sir
Michael Swann, held at the Culloden Hotel in Belfast to
celebrate the opening of the BBC's new studios in Belfast.
Among the guests were Roy Mason, the Deputy GOC and
other notables of the province.

Mr Mason is reported to have attacked the BBC for its
support of terrorism by reporting the activities and statements made by the leaders of paramilitary organizations.
The unexpected tirade took the host and some of his guests
aback. The Secretary of State allegedly repeated his view
that statements made by the IRA and other terrorist
organizations should not be reported: and the BBC should
not be used by the IRA as a weapon in their propaganda
war. This exchange became known as 'the second battle of
Culloden'.

Ivor Canavan, the Catholic business executive from
Derry who chaired the Authority's Complaints Committee,
can scarcely have been unaware of the storm caused by the
Secretary of State's reported remarks. He knew that the
subject to be discussed at the meeting – the ill-treatment
of suspects in police custody – constituted a political
minefield. If word were to leak out that the Complaints

Committee were worried, it would have undoubtedly given the media and the IRA a field day. Roy Mason would not have been pleased.

Ivor Canavan proceeded with caution. He noted the clear increase in complaints, especially those alleging assaults, and said that his impression from contacts with 'reasonable people of substance' indicated that there was a feeling of unease in regard to allegations of police irregularity while interrogating prisoners. SDCC Baillie told the Committee that twice as many Provisional IRA members were charged in 1976 as in 1975, and said that in a lot of cases their only defence was to allege coercion in the eliciting of statements. His colleague, Chief Superintendent Cordner, mentioned the new regulations that had been introduced to enable investigating officers in the Complaints & Discipline Branch to identify the detectives who had interviewed the complainant at the time of the alleged assault. He said that every policeman knew that his job was at risk if he acted outside the regulations. Mr Baillie then referred to the allegation about misconduct at Omagh RUC station and said that 'prosecutions were pending'.

The Chairman said that this was what should happen where appropriate, but reminded SDCC Baillie and Mr Cordner that there were those who alleged that, although there may not be enough evidence to *prove* a case in court, there was plenty of substance in many complaints of ill-treatment. He told them he felt it essential that everything should be done to ensure that this 'degree of suspicion' would diminish, as the 'aura of suspicion' survived a 'not guilty' verdict. SDCC Baillie said the police view was that it was foolish and counter-productive to resort to physical tactics in the questioning of prisoners, as such methods were an admission of defeat. Chief Superintendent Cordner informed the Committee that the Rafferty case was now *sub judice* and was going to the DPP 'soon'. In other words, discussion of the Rafferty case was now officially closed.

On 20 January 1977, the RUC informed Jack Hassard that its investigation of the Rafferty case was complete: the file had now been sent to the DPP and he would be 'advised of the DPP's direction' in due course. As the Investigating Officer had apparently recommended the prosecution of certain policemen who had interrogated Rafferty at Omagh, there was no reason to believe that there would be any undue delay in the DPP's decision. But Hassard wasn't satisfied. He was worried that once the RUC had invoked the so-called *sub judice* rule, the Rafferty case would be swept under the carpet. Hassard wanted everything brought out into the open. As he was on first-name terms with many of the police in his area, he knew that they too were uneasy at what was happening during some interrogations. They had expressed concern to Jack Hassard that they were having to pay for the actions of 'outsiders'.

The Police Authority had greeted Hassard's proposal for a Tribunal of Inquiry into the Rafferty case with little enthusiasm. They felt that such matters should be resolved internally without publicity, lest they should not only incur the wrath of the Chief Constable and Secretary of State, but also fuel the IRA's propaganda campaign. They bought time by persuading Hassard to suspend his motion calling for the Tribunal, on the grounds that the Complaints Committee would lay aside time to discuss the Rafferty case with SDCC Baillie. Hassard reluctantly agreed to bide his time and wait for the DPP's decision.

On 3 March 1977, the Police Authority sent a confidential minute to Chief Superintendent Cordner, whose department held all the files, notifying him that the Complaints Committee wished to devote 'some time' to the Rafferty case at their next meeting, and suggested that he bring the Rafferty file with him. The Authority acknowledged that 'there might be some difficulty in meeting this request'. There was.

Hassard was furious and repeated his demand for a Tribunal: he said that that was the only way in which complainant and the police could be fairly treated. The Authority then wrote to SDCC Baillie and informed him that the Complaints Committee were going to hold a Special Meeting on 22 March 1977 to discuss Jack Hassard's demand for a Tribunal.

It would therefore be appreciated if you and your team could be in a position to answer any detailed questions which may be put and, to this end, you will no doubt arrange to be in possession of the file in the case.

The meeting was inconclusive: no file was produced, although it appears that some medical reports were made available to the Committee. Hassard remarked that 'multiple dark bruises on the stomach' weren't caused by Rafferty's epilepsy. What particularly angered him was that he was put out of the room while Rafferty's case was being discussed. The police argued that, because Hassard was one of those who had made an official complaint in Rafferty's case, he was an interested person and therefore should not be party to a discussion of his case. Hassard protested. The Committee excluded him by a unanimous vote. He told them it was 'a damned disgrace' and stood in the corridor 'like a stuffed dummy' for twenty minutes. He wasn't told what transpired in his absence. He had no allies on the Complaints Committee. All he was informed was that the Rafferty file 'was still with the DDP'.

Hassard was undaunted. Three days after he had been 'put out', he wrote to Barry Shaw, the DPP. He asked him if he had received all the medical reports as he was concerned, as a Justice of the Peace, that the Director should reach his decision only when he was in possession 'of all the facts in this most serious case'. Hassard worked for the Post Office. He sent all his important letters by registered mail. His letter to Barry Shaw was registered on 28 March 1977. He received no reply or acknowledgement that it had been received.

By the summer of 1977, neither Hassard nor the Complaints Committee had received any further word on the

DPP's decision in the Rafferty case. On 22 July Hassard sent the DPP another registered letter. The Post Office had already acknowledged that his previous letter had been received by the DPP's office, three days after it had been posted in Dungannon.

Three weeks later, Hassard received a reply to his reminder. The Director said that he regretted there had been 'some error with regard to our correspondence' and assured Hassard that he had received his original letter and sent a reply a week later. For whatever reason, Hassard never received the letter. All it had said was that the Director would consider all the facts.

By autumn 1977, there was still no word from the DPP. The Complaints Committee thought the delay now intolerable, and wrote to Kenneth Newman, asking him what was going on. The Chief Constable told them that his discussions with the Director were confidential and that he could not enter into correspondence on the matter. The Committee then decided to ask him if the DPP had referred the file back to the RUC and, if so, how many times and when. The Committee then asked the Secretary, William Baird, to speak to SDCC Baillie to see if 'any headway' could be made in getting information as to what had happened to the Rafferty file.

Still no satisfactory answers were given. It was not until the meeting of an increasingly frustrated Complaints Committee on 22 October 1977 that the mystery was solved. But its solution posed even more serious questions. It 'came to light' that the DPP had returned the Rafferty file to the RUC on 13 May for further information; it had been with the police for the past six months; SDCC Baillie gave the Committee no 'satisfactory answer' why the police had not informed them of the fact.

On 7 November the Complaints Committee wrote to SDCC Baillie, demanding an official explanation of why they had been kept in the dark. On 24 November SDCC Baillie replied and admitted that there had been 'a break-down in communication'.

In December 1977, a year after he had made the original suggestion, Hassard tabled a motion demanding once again that a Tribunal be set up to investigate Rafferty's complaint. Again discussion of the motion was postponed.

In January William Baird had a meeting with the DPP. The Director informed him that he could give no estimate of the date when he would announce his decision; he did say that he now had all the information he desired and had assigned one of his staff full-time to the Rafferty case.

At the February meeting of the Authority, Hassard said they had been given the 'brush off' by the DPP, and repeated his demand for a Tribunal. Ivor Canavan then explained the reason for the Director's continued delay. He said that the Director was awaiting the outcome of the retrial of Edward Hurson, the suspect who had been interrogated at the time of Rafferty's arrest, and who had allegedly heard Rafferty's screams and shouts in Omagh police station. Nevertheless, Ivor Canavan conceded that the police had still not offered an 'adequate' explanation as to why the Authority had not been informed. Discussion of Hassard's motion was deferred once again.

In March 1978, the Complaints Committee outlined its views on a Tribunal in a draft paper.

The choice of a case for tribunal investigation must be made very carefully. First it should ideally avoid conflict of a direct nature with the DPP. Secondly it would need to centre carefully around the 'manner' in which the police have carried out their investigation. At least part of the criteria would seem to be met in the Rafferty case.

The delay is prima facie reprehensible and additionally there has not been (to put it no higher) complete openness on the part of the Complaints & Discipline Branch . . . the time is suitable now to seek a Tribunal.

The Chief Constable was also asked to produce a report on the RUC's investigation of Rafferty's complaint, a prerogative the Police Authority also claimed it had under the Police Act.¹ The Chief Constable refused on the grounds that 'it was not necessary to the Authority in order to discharge their functions'. The Authority felt it was going round in circles: it decided to inform Roy Mason that if the DPP did not make an early decision the Authority was going to set up a Tribunal.

The final showdown between Jack Hassard and the Chief Constable came at the meeting of the Police Authority in June 1978. Hassard raised the subject of Rafferty. The members of the Authority sighed, chewed their pencils and looked at the ceiling, as Hassard said they always did when he mentioned the subject. The Chief Constable said that 'one complainant in whose complaint Mr Hassard was interested', that is, Rafferty, was a man 'suspected of having committed a number of serious offences'. Hassard then produced a firearms certificate which the RUC had issued to Rafferty only three months previously and passed it round for inspection. The certificate was numbered A239856 and dated 20 March 1978. It gave James Rafferty, who was a member of a clay pigeon shooting club, the right to possess a double-barrelled 12-bore shot gun de luxe number 86148. The certificate was stamped RUC Headquarters and signed for by a Chief Inspector 'for Chief Constable, Royal Ulster Constabulary'. If Rafferty was a man 'suspected of serious offences', asked Jack Hassard, why had the RUC given him a gun licence?

Hassard's patience was exhausted, as almost two years after his original demand the Police Authority still had not taken the decisive step of setting up a Tribunal. Hassard accused the Police Authority of being about as independent as a sausage without a skin. At long last, in October 1978, the Authority announced its decision to set up a Tribunal to inquire into James Rafferty's complaint.

The Tribunal was finally appointed in the spring of 1979.

1. Police Act (NI) 1970, Section 15(2): 'The Chief Constable shall whenever so required by the Minister or the Police Authority, submit to him or them reports in writing on such matters as may be specified in the requirement', i.e. to maintain an adequate and efficient police force.

Its Chairman was Peter Gibson, QC, brother of rugby international Mike Gibson. By the summer of 1980 the Tribunal still had not started its inquiries. Nearly four years after James Rafferty was discharged from Omagh Hospital, his complaint remained unresolved.

5. Laying Down the Rules

'I have personally set about creating a system which, as far as humanly possible, is designed to prevent any potential police abuse of persons in custody.'

Kenneth Newman, 24 June 1977

When Ivor Canavan, the Chairman of the Complaints Committee, told Kenneth Newman's deputy of 'the feeling of unease' in January 1977, he was told by the RUC that the new regulations, which involved medical examinations before, during and after questioning and a record of all the movements of the prisoner and his custodians, were designed not only to prevent ill-treatment but to identify any police officer suspected of it. On paper the safeguards were extensive.

When a suspect was detained, he was offered a medical examination before his interrogation began. If he arrived during normal working hours, it was offered by a full-time Medical Officer employed by the DHSS and seconded to the Police Authority to carry out examinations of persons in custody. If he arrived at night or early morning he would be seen by a doctor employed on a part-time basis. These doctors were usually drawn from local hospitals and general practice and came in when required. Both sets of doctors were usually referred to as 'Police Doctors', although technically neither group was employed or paid by the RUC.

These initial medical examinations were crucial. They were meant to establish not only whether a suspect was fit for interrogation – the last thing the police wanted on their hands was a prisoner with a heart attack – but whether he was already injured when he entered police custody.

Whatever the causes of such injuries – whether they were
the result of a fight during arrest or a pub brawl – it was
important to establish that they had not been received
in *police* custody. The police feared that a suspect
might deliberately injure himself beforehand, in order to
allege that he had been beaten up during interrogation,
in the hope that any statements he made would be
declared inadmissible. These initial examinations, like
all the regulations, were designed to protect the
police from false allegations as well as the suspect from
ill-treatment.

The examination was voluntary. Many suspects declined
it, often for no sinister motive. They said they had no
complaint, felt perfectly healthy and therefore saw no point
in having a medical examination. In court a prosecuting
counsel might attempt to make much of a suspect's refusal.
(In a case in 1979,[1] His Honour Judge Brown interrupted
Crown counsel who was imputing a sinister motive to the
defendant's refusal of a medical examination. Counsel
called the accused 'a very cunning gentleman and a very
cunning liar'. The judge said that if he had been arrested
and had no complaint to make other than that of being
arrested at 6 am, and did not suffer from asthma or
diabetes, he saw no reason why he should be examined
either, as there would be nothing to find.) At Castlereagh
more than fifty per cent of suspects declined this initial
examination. Some doctors were more persistent than
others in explaining the advantage of an initial examination
to suspects.

The doctor would take his own notes of the examination
and then enter the basic details on the Prisoner Arrest
Form. This form, 38/17A, is for both police and prisoner,
and later for the courts, the most important piece of
documentation where allegations of ill-treatment are concerned. It details the prisoner's history from the point of
his arrest to either his release or removal to prison on
remand. The form itself is twelve pages long. Various other

1. *R.* v. *J. J. McGrath and T. McGrath*, 9 July 1979.

forms are attached to it. The first form indicates the section of the emergency legislation under which the prisoner has been detained. This is either form EP, which signifies a three-day detention order under the Emergency Provisions Act, or form PT, which indicates a seven-day detention under the Prevention of Terrorism Act. (Once a person is arrested, the police cannot change the section under which he has been held. For example, if he has been arrested under Section 10, the police can't change it to Section 12 because they decide they want to question him for another four days.)

The Prisoner Arrest Form goes everywhere with the prisoner. At every stage of his journey he is signed for on receipt like a registered parcel. The Prisoner Arrest Form is designed to identify every police officer who comes into contact with the prisoner during his stay in police custody. It lists the names and ranks of every uniformed officer in charge of the prisoner and the times at which he came on and went off duty; the name, rank and number of every detective who interviewed him, the times at which the interviews started and finished, and the name of the person in charge; the records of every meal the prisoner was offered and the amount of it he consumed; all requests the prisoner made (for example, to see a doctor); and details of any complaint he made.

At the end of the form are three 'Prisoner Complaint Certificates'. The prisoner is given three lines on which to give details of his complaint. He then signs it. His signature is witnessed and then countersigned by the officer in charge. Often the prisoner makes his complaint to the doctor, not a police officer. Many suspects appeared genuinely frightened that, if they complained to the police, word would get back to their interrogators, who, they said, would call them back for more.

A more detailed record of the prisoner's medical examination is made on the Prisoner Medical Form (38/17B) which is then attached to the Prisoner Arrest Form (38/17A). This is signed by the Medical Officer and notes, among other things, whether there are allegations of ill-treatment and whether the medical evidence is consistent with them. There is also space for 'general observations', including 'note of Refusal'. These records are only completed and held by those doctors who examine suspects on behalf of the police. Although they are available to officers from Complaints & Discipline Branch who investigate allegations of ill-treatment, they are disclosed to the complainant only if and when his case comes to court. These Police Doctors' reports are vital confirmation of any findings a prisoner's GP may make.

The Prisoner Medical Form also covers a prisoner's initial, intermediate and final examination. The final examination is the most important, as this is the stage at which injuries are generally noted. Sometimes the doctor will mark them on an outline drawing which is then attached to the Prisoner Medical Form. Again this final examination is not obligatory. Many suspects decline, although they may later complain and on examination be shown to have injuries.

At Castlereagh only slightly more than 50 per cent of prisoners consented to the final examination. Again it appears that many were afraid to do so, and waited until they reached Townhall Street police station, where they were taken to be charged, before they made a complaint and consented to medical examination. It appears that some just wanted to get out of Castlereagh as fast as possible; others were worried that if they complained and agreed to medical examination on the spot, they would be subjected to more of the treatment they alleged they had already received; suspects often alleged that detectives threatened them with further beatings if they made a complaint.

Dr Alexander, who became Castlereagh's Senior Medical Officer at the end of 1977, admitted that Castlereagh had a bad name and prisoners seemed inclined to wait until they went elsewhere before consenting to a medical examination.[1] Dr Russell, one of Dr Alexander's seven part-

1. Meeting of the Hermon Committee, 20 April 1978.

time assistants, admitted[1] that sometimes prisoners had been so fearful after examination that they had asked for their medical records to be destroyed.

A prisoner was also allowed to see his own General Practitioner on request, but until the middle of 1977 he had to make a personal request to see him and had to specify him by name. Before then a GP was not given access to a prisoner at the request of family or friends. But the suspect was denied the most important safeguard of all: access to a solicitor.

Even the most detailed records do not necessarily establish the truth. In many cases a complainant's only satisfaction is a settlement in a civil action for damages in the courts. Here the standard of proof required is 'the balance of probabilities', which is less than 'proof beyond reasonable doubt', the criterion of the criminal courts. Over half a million pounds of public money was paid in compensation to persons who made complaints following internment. Because the time scale between registration of complaint, notification of civil action and eventual settlement is often up to three years and more, few claims arising out of incidents in the period covered by this book have been settled. By the end of 1979, according to the Police Authority, only three claims had been settled. They involved incidents in September and December 1976 and February 1977. The total amount paid was £1,250. None of the three settlements involved Castlereagh. Two, however, involved Omagh police station, where James Rafferty had been interrogated. One of them involved Peter Farrell.

On 10 December 1976, a month after Rafferty's interrogation, a UDR man and his wife were injured in a landmine explosion near Ballygawley, a few miles south of Cappagh.

1. Special meeting of Complaints Committee with three groups of doctors, 19 May 1978.

Eleven days later, at 6.20 am, Peter Farrell, a twenty-three-year-old clerical worker, was arrested at his home in Ballygawley under Section 10 of the EPA. Farrell was well known locally. He was a keen amateur footballer and banjo-picker in a popular folk singing group, which used to play engagements two or three times a week on both sides of the border.

Farrell was taken to Omagh police station on 21 December 1976. He was examined and found to be fit. He was taken to the police station's 'strongroom'. He made no allegations of ill-treatment during his interrogation. In statements which he later made to his solicitor and the RUC's Complaints & Discipline Branch, he said that detectives questioned him about explosives. They then produced ammunition which they said they had found in his house and told him he could get two or three years for possession. Farrell said the bullets were those which he had had on the strap of his banjo for decoration; they were not live bullets and had often been examined by the security forces as he crossed the border with his folk singing group. He alleged that the detectives kept insisting that it was live ammunition and said that if he didn't confess to keeping live ammunition in his house they would bring the whole family of five in for questioning. The detectives told him that membership of the IRA was a lesser offence and it would be better for him to admit to that than have his family brought in. Farrell said he was not a member of the IRA and would not admit to membership. He said the detectives kept pushing words down his throat. A uniformed policeman came into the room and Farrell asked him if he could see his solicitor as he had been told by the detectives that he would be out that night. The policeman said he wasn't sure whether he could see one or not and left the room to check. Farrell said 'there seemed to be a loud roar of laughter'.

Farrell was taken out of the strongroom, a few feet along the well-lit corridor to the flight of stairs which led to the cells beneath. Farrell told the RUC Investigating Officer that at the top of the stairs – there were nine steps with a concrete landing at the bottom – he was pushed in the back by a policeman. He remembered nothing more until he woke up in hospital the next day with five stitches in the back of his head.

An ambulance took him from Omagh police station to Tyrone County Hospital. Farrell was not charged with any offence. James Rafferty had made the same trip the previous month. Farrell was examined at 1.30 am by the consultant surgeon. By this time the hospital's casualty department had already put five stitches in the back of his head. The surgeon noted the injury and an apparent tenderness in the right lower back. No other abnormalities were noticed. Farrell complained of headaches and pain at the bottom of his back. The consultant also noted that he was suffering from amnesia and couldn't remember how the injury had occurred.

Farrell spent Christmas in hospital under observation and was released on 4 January 1977. He went straight to see his local GP, as he still complained of pains in his chest, back and shoulders. He said he had headaches, was depressed and was nervous of being rearrested by the security forces. He was placed under a consultant psychiatrist. The psychiatrist, who observed Farrell over a period of months, was concerned by his mental condition. He was unable to return to work for six months. He had become an intense worrier and stopped playing in the folk group. He sometimes trembled without reason and suffered from palpitations. He had lost a stone in weight. He suffered from nightmares in which he relived the incident and would wake up screaming and shouting. He still suffered from headaches, dizziness and a pain in the back. The psychiatrist analysed his condition as 'an anxiety state of severe intensity', which he said was a direct consequence of the incident in Omagh police station. He said Farrell had undergone 'tremendous psychological suffering' for a person normally healthy and able to withstand stress. Had he seen the patient earlier, he said he would have considered admission to a psychiatric hospital.

The consultant psychiatrist believed that the 'irritating factor' in Farrell's case was that the fact that he had been questioned might make some people suspect that he had been involved.

On 16 March 1977, Farrell instructed his solicitor to register a complaint with the RUC. It was received by the Complaints & Discipline Branch two days later. The same Investigating Officer as had investigated Rafferty's complaint was detailed to investigate Farrell's. In Farrell's civil action for damages against the Chief Constable in September 1979, the police records were inspected, in particular the Prisoner Arrest Form.[1] The form showed that Farrell's condition was 'all regular' until the last entry: under 'Remarks' it was noted: 'prisoner fell down stairs and was removed to hospital'.

The court heard that when the accounts book in the Sergeant's office at Omagh was inspected, it noted that at 9.55 pm the prisoner was injured as he was being brought downstairs to his cell for the night. It recorded that he fell from the top of the stairs to the landing and was knocked unconscious. But the court also learned that the duty officer of the day's report was rather more specific. It noted that the prisoner was injured *when he fainted* as he was being taken down the stairs at the station. It said that as a result he cut his head and was taken to hospital for attention. It said that he received five stitches after falling from the top step down nine stairs onto concrete.

As part of the prosecution evidence in the civil action a consulting engineer was commissioned to do a survey of the location where the incident took place. In his report the engineer concluded:

It can be pointed out that it is not likely that a person would fall in the normal way on these stairs for the following reasons:

1. Technically its equivalent at the time: the full PAF was formalized later.

1. The stairs commence a distance of 3ft 2ins. from the edge of the corridor so that a person turning the corner does not immediately come upon the stairs.
2. The stairs are of good construction dimensionally and are fitted with a hand rail.

The civil action was heard in the High Court before Mr Justice Hutton on 11 September 1979. Peter Farrell was awarded £600 damages.

Speaking in the House of Commons on 23 February 1977, Roy Mason said:

A democracy functions by the will of the people and the rule of law. It cannot behave like a totalitarian state nor is it right that it should. Its security forces exist to defend the rights of its citizens and not to limit them.

While the Secretary of State was enunciating these principles, nineteen-year-old Paul Duffy was being interrogated at Omagh. His occupation was described as 'joiner'. His home was in Stewartstown, a small town that lies between Cookstown and Coalisland in the corner of East Tyrone that borders Lough Neagh. It is an area of strong Republican traditions and close family ties. Duffy was arrested at his home at 5.30 am on Monday morning, 21 February 1977. He was taken to Cookstown police station a few miles away, given a medical examination and found to be in good health. Duffy's only infirmity at the time was in his right leg: his knee cap had been removed following a road accident. That afternoon he was flown by helicopter to Omagh RUC station for interrogation. Other youths from the area had been arrested about the same time and were also helicoptered to Omagh.

Duffy was interrogated by teams of detectives from Omagh, Dungannon, Armagh and the Regional Crime Squad. They questioned him in particular about an ambush the previous April in which a policeman was killed at Dernagh crossroads, a mile or so outside Coalisland. Three other policemen were injured in the attack. The dead constable was married and had two children, aged eight and one.

Duffy said his first interview on Monday afternoon 'wasn't too bad', although he alleged that he was slapped and kicked around. He said that he asked to see a solicitor and was told never to ask that question again: slaps to the head and punches to the stomach followed. The detectives discovered his bad knee. He said they continued to punch him on the back and stomach and slap him around the face. Duffy made similar allegations about the treatment he received at the hands of the next two detectives: most of the punches were in the back and stomach; he said they seemed to concentrate on his knee and made him squat against the wall a lot. He said that the next two detectives were 'nice' to him. Monday's interviews ended at 12.32 am on Tuesday morning.

The police called a doctor, who examined Duffy at 1.30 am on Tuesday morning. Duffy complained of ill-treatment. Dr Connolly found tenderness around the back of the skull, both sides of the face, the shoulder and stomach. (If Duffy's allegations were true, it was too soon for bruises to show.) Duffy alleged the ill-treatment continued on Tuesday. A detective came into the room and said he had better tell all he knew before he came back to deal with him the next morning. He said that he had 'got all the other boys broke' and was going to spend all the next day with him.

On Wednesday morning Duffy was interviewed by Detective Constable Latimer of the Regional Crime Squad and Detective Sergeant Boyd of Armagh CID. The interview lasted from 10.15 am to 12.30 pm. Duffy alleged that DC Latimer was the detective who had threatened him the night before and that the two of them were 'by far the worst'. He alleged they started knocking and kicking his injured knee and making him squat to put pressure on it; they made him strip and do press-ups; they made him run on the spot with his underpants over his head. At one stage Duffy alleged that he was given three quick punches on the chin and a crown was knocked off one of his teeth. They said that if he didn't talk they'd smother him. Duffy alleged they put his jacket over his head. One of the detectives then caught his eye and made it bleed. Duffy said that one suggested to the other that he'd been trying to escape. They kept insisting that he was responsible for the murder at Dernagh crossroads and continued hitting him in the stomach, asking him if he knew it would leave no marks.[1] Duffy denied any involvement.

When Duffy was returned to his cell at lunchtime, he was visited by Detective Inspector Farr, who was one of the police officers in charge of the interrogations. D I Farr's notes of the conversation read:

Saw small abrasion on right eyelid. Asked him what had happened. Said he got it on door getting out. Hard to talk to. Refused to talk to me. Declined to comment further about interviews. Asked if he had complaint to make. Said not. No apparent sign of ill-treatment. Only visible mark abrasion on eye. At 12.25 pm informed by D C Latimer that when he and D S Boyd were interviewing Duffy, he had tried to escape by the door.

The uniformed duty inspector, Inspector Weir, visited Duffy after Inspector Farr had notified him about the eye injury. He wrote in the station's Occurrence Book:

I spoke to Duffy in cell. Appeared physically fit. Had no complaints. There is a graze above right eye. Asked him about it. Replied tried to get out.

Duffy complained about the pain in his knee and a doctor was called. Dr McClements noted the abrasion and wrote 'this chap complained of maltreatment by the R U C'. He referred Duffy to the casualty department of Tyrone County Hospital. But before Duffy was escorted there he made a statement of complaint to Inspector Weir, the uniformed duty inspector who had visited him three hours

1. Bruising only tends to occur where flesh meets bone: the stomach is a fleshy area unlikely to bruise, except along the costal margin where the stomach meets the rib cage.

earlier. This time Duffy did make a complaint but refused to sign the complaint form. He said it was because he didn't know whether he was going to be subjected to further ill-treatment.

At the hospital Duffy was seen by the casualty doctor. His knee was bandaged and the bruise and abrasion over his eye were cleaned and dressed.

When he was brought back to Omagh police station, Duffy said he was interviewed by 'two quite reasonable men'. He was shown a hand-written statement by another prisoner that implicated him in the murder at Dernagh crossroads: the prisoner stated that Duffy had taken his car to use in the ambush. Duffy denied it. The detectives said that the others would get lesser sentences for cooperating with the police and advised him to do the same; they told him that they now had 'all the facts' and were going to charge him. The interview finished just before midnight on Wednesday. Duffy was then given a final medical examination by the doctor who had examined him two days earlier. Dr Connolly recorded the abrasion over the eye and noted that a crown was missing from the upper front tooth. He also noted that Duffy's elbow, chest, hip, jaw and back of neck were tender.

Duffy was released at 12.57 am on Thursday morning. No charges were made.

That evening, on his return to Stewartstown, he was examined by his own doctor, Dr Dowdall: he noticed marked bruising above and below the right knee, bruising over the front of the skull and severe tenderness at the back; there was also bruising over the jaw which 'could have been caused by a punch or punches with a closed fist'. He also observed that the crown on the tooth was missing. Duffy was given sedatives and referred to a dentist.

Duffy's complaint was taken up by the Complaints & Discipline Branch. The Chief Inspector who had been assigned to investigate the cases of James Rafferty and Peter Farrell was detailed to Duffy's complaint. The papers were sent to the DPP. No prosecution was directed.

His solicitor, who was his uncle, Paddy Duffy, advised
on a civil action. Paul Duffy sued the Chief Constable for
damages but was unable to take part in the proceedings.
On 26 February 1978, exactly a year after his interrogation
at Omagh, Paul Duffy was shot dead a few miles from his
home, in a British army 'stake-out' of a farmhouse at
Ardboe. The soldiers who shot him were believed to be
members of the SAS. The army said they shot Duffy while
he was visiting an IRA 'dump'. Paul Duffy was given a
military funeral by the Provisional IRA. They said he had
been killed while on 'active service'. The man who was
with Paul Duffy at the time of the 'stake-out', Martin
McGuckin, was wounded. He was arrested and charged,
but the charges against him were apparently later withdrawn.

The Chief Constable contested Duffy's civil action. The
case came to court in July 1979, and lasted five days.
Despite opposition from the Chief Constable's defence
counsel, Mr Justice Murray agreed that Paul Duffy's two
statements of complaint – one to Inspector Weir, the other
to the Complaints & Discipline Investigating Officer –
should be admitted as evidence, as Duffy was unable to
give evidence himself. The defence argued strongly against
the proposal, on the grounds that this would identify and
expose certain detectives. The judge said that they would
have the opportunity to defend themselves.

All the police officers denied Duffy's allegations.[1] Under
cross-examination DC Latimer and DS Boyd, who interviewed Duffy on Wednesday morning, denied they
assaulted him. DS Boyd said he did not strike Duffy on
the mouth and denied looking for any part of his tooth. He
alleged that during the interview on Wednesday morning
Duffy tried to escape through a window and that he and
DC Latimer had tried to prevent him by closing the
window on him and thereby causing some injury to the
face. He said he was unable to explain how Duffy received

1. The following is based on a newspaper report in the *Tyrone Democrat*,
2 August 1979.

his other injuries and could not understand why he had been sent to hospital. D I Farr, who admitted that he was one of the people in charge of the investigations being conducted at Omagh police station, was also unable to explain how Duffy had received his injuries and did not know why it was necessary to have him sent to Tyrone County Hospital.

During re-examination, counsel for the police started to recall Duffy's alleged escape attempt. The judge intervened and said it was too late after five days to start making a case which had never been put to any of the witnesses during cross-examination: he said that no suggestion had ever been made by the defence that Duffy had received his injuries while trying to escape or that the injuries were self-inflicted. The judge adjourned the court until the afternoon. A deal was done outside the courtroom. When the court resumed, it was announced that the case had been settled. Paul Duffy received £550 for his injuries. Posthumously.

6. 'An Assault of Marked Severity'

> 'Just what was going on in the police station on those days in January? Information obtained by the technique involved is, by its nature, unreliable and consequently the confession of guilt in relation to certain offences lacks validity.'
>
> Report of consultant psychiatrist on Robert Barclay,
> 21 June 1977

Of the four Regional Crime Squads set up by the Chief Constable, Headquarters Crime Squad, successor of his predecessor's 'A' Squad, was regarded as the elite. In the competition for results in 1977, Headquarters Crime Squad came out on top. It undertook more operations, interviewed more suspects and charged more persons than any of its three rivals – Belfast, North and South Regional Crime Squads. In 1977 it conducted 252 operations, interviewed 1,106 suspects and charged 359 persons. The essence of each squad was its mobility and expertise in, amongst other things, interrogation. All the Crime Squad's skills were placed at the disposal of the Divisional CID. The Chief Constable stood firmly behind the work of all his detectives, whether Crime Squad or Divisional CID. He said that their methods of operation were 'painstakingly examined in court' and throughout they maintained an 'objective and professional approach' to the investigation of 'many vicious crimes committed by some very callous individuals'.[1]

Headquarters Crime Squad was the most mobile of all and took an 'overall' view of serious crime across the province, whereas the other three squads tended to concentrate on crime in the particular area in which they were based. 'HQ' was the 'topping-up' squad. In January 1977 detectives from HQ Crime Squad were interrogating at Omagh RUC station. Two statements they obtained from

1. Annual Report, 1978.

twenty-nine-year-old Robert Barclay were among their first successes in 1977.

At 1.30 am on Sunday, 2 January, Robert Barclay was coming home from the pub – closing time tends to be flexible in rural parts of the North, especially in the border areas where Robert Barclay lived. Barclay was about 5 ft 10 ins., with dark hair and eyebrows, sallow complexion and sharp features. As the parish priest who had known him for twenty years observed, 'he was of quiet disposition and a good worker'. The only failing he noticed with pastoral disapproval was that 'he took some strong drink, sometimes more than was good for him'. He did say that he never knew or heard of Barclay being a member of any illegal organization. Barclay had been in steady employment for four years as a mechanical-digger driver. His employers thought highly of him. They said he was an honest, willing and dependable worker.

Barclay lived and worked at the other end of County Tyrone from James Rafferty, Peter Farrell and Paul Duffy. His home was near Castlederg, the last outpost before Tyrone becomes Donegal and Northern Ireland, Eire. The border was only a couple of miles away. It's a sparsely populated area, crossed with fields, hedgerows and narrow country lanes, a natural hunting ground for the Provisional I R A, with the sanctuary of the Republic literally only a few minutes away. Police and army who patrolled the frontier district were easily exposed to ambush and booby traps.

There doesn't appear to have been any particular incident that triggered the arrest of Robert Barclay: in those parts any youth wandering about at 1.30 am is liable to be lifted if he comes across the security forces. Barclay was taken to Castlederg R U C station, where he was formally arrested under Section 10 as a suspected terrorist. He was then transferred to Omagh police station, fifteen miles away, where he alleged he was ill-treated by his investigators.

I cite the case of Robert Barclay in some detail because

it illustrates the difficulties a court of law faces in assessing whether allegations made by a suspected terrorist are fact or fiction. Medical evidence is crucial in this assessment and in Robert Barclay's case there was a clear conflict. How such a conflict is resolved is a matter for the judge in the Diplock court. The case also illustrates the other important stage in the judicial process whereby the RUC investigates the complaint and then submits its report to the DPP. The DPP reaches his decision whether to prosecute a particular police officer or officers on the evidence placed before him. In the case of Robert Barclay, the DPP decided against prosecuting any police officers, a decision clearly vindicated by events when the subsequent private prosecution brought by Robert Barclay against two of the interrogators failed. Both detectives were acquitted of the charge against them. The case also deserves detailed examination because a transcript of the original trial exists as the case went to appeal – invariably the only circumstances in which transcripts of trials are produced. There was also a detailed record of the proceedings of the private prosecution brought by Robert Barclay against Detective Constables French and Newell. I quote extensively from both, not only to illustrate the complexities of the case, and in particular the conflict over the medical evidence, but also to give some flavour of a Diplock trial.

Robert Barclay's case came to court on 30 November 1977, nearly a year after his arrest. The trial, heard before His Honour Judge Rowland, lasted three days and centred round the admissibility of the statements which Robert Barclay had made to the police following his interrogation at Omagh RUC station.

As is customary in such cases, all the doctors involved in the examination of the accused, gave evidence and were subjected to cross-examination in court.

The court heard Dr Craig say that he had examined Barclay between 4.20 and 4.35 on the morning of his arrest, Sunday, 2 January, after his arrival at Omagh RUC station from Castlederg. He said that Barclay made no complaints and that he found no signs of injury. Giving evidence in court Robert Barclay said he was interviewed on Sunday morning and asked about his family and general matters. He made no complaint. He said he didn't make any complaint either concerning the second interview he had on Sunday afternoon. On Monday, 3 January, Barclay said he was interviewed again in the morning, but was not subjected to any ill-treatment, nor did he have any complaint of ill-treatment to make with regard to his interview on Monday afternoon. It was only during his interview on Monday evening that Barclay said he was ill-treated. As his Counsel, John Curran, QC, told the court, the kernel of the allegations which Barclay made concerning his interview on Monday evening concerned punches to the stomach, punches to the face and punches to the ear and eye. In his submission Mr Curran said that on the basis of the medical evidence there was 'crystal-clear evidence' that his client had sustained injuries while in police custody in Omagh 'consistent with a fairly severe beating'.[1]

Barclay made no further allegations of ill-treatment. The court was told that he'd signed statements on Tuesday afternoon. In the first, taken at 3.52 pm, he admitted acting as look-out while weapons or explosives were being brought across the border. In the second, taken at 3.55 pm, he admitted to picking up four masked IRA men with guns at the border. On the basis of these two statements Barclay was charged with possessing firearms and with communicating information which was likely to be of use to terrorists.

Omagh courthouse is a splendid monument to British justice in the eighteenth century, when the royal writ ran throughout all of Ireland's thirty-two counties. It stands at the top of the hill of Omagh's High Street like some neglected Athenian temple built of brown sandstone

1. The details of the allegations Barclay made are outlined in the proceedings of the private prosecution he brought against Detective Constables French and Newell.

instead of white marble. On four pillars of the colonnade are four words daubed in white paint, still discernible despite the efforts of the caretaker to remove them. They spell out the Provisionals' slogan: 'We shall rise again'. Although a listed building, its upkeep has not been a priority in view of the more pressing problems that Omagh has faced. The big clock above the colonnade has had three new faces since 1969 – each one shattered by bombs in the High Street. It suits the pigeons well, which now use the clock as a nesting place.

Inside the courthouse is the magistrates' room where Special Courts are held. Omagh Courthouse was the setting for a strange encounter involving Robert Barclay, his solicitor Patrick Fahy and a police officer who at Barclay's trial was not named.

Giving evidence in court, Patrick Fahy said that he had seen his client briefly in the courthouse while he was still under police escort. He said that the lighting on the landing where he met Barclay was not particularly good. He said he then saw him in the magistrates' room where he was being charged, but at neither stage did he see any injuries on Barclay or hear him make any complaint.

Mr Fahy told the court that as he left Omagh Courthouse and crossed the street to return to his office, he passed a uniformed police constable standing on the footpath opposite the point where his colleagues were leading Barclay into the police transit van outside the courthouse's side entrance. Fahy said the constable stopped him and asked him if he had seen Barclay's face. He suggested he take a look at his eye. Fahy crossed the road to the police van and, to start the conversation, asked Barclay if there was any message he wished to be conveyed to his relatives. When Barclay came to the door of the van, Fahy asked him what had happened to his eye. Barclay said nothing, but brushed his fringe back from his right eye. Fahy saw a lump across his eyebrow.

The court then heard that Robert Barclay was taken from Omagh to Belfast to be remanded in custody at the

Crumlin Road prison, but that before he left he was examined by Dr O'Neill, a local GP who was on police rota duty that day. Giving evidence in court, Dr O'Neill said that he conducted a brief examination on Barclay at around 1 o'clock on Wednesday, 5 January 1977, in an office at Omagh Police Station. He said he found no signs of injury and noted that Barclay made no complaints. He said he saw no evidence that Barclay had a black eye. The court was then told that when Barclay arrived at Crumlin Road prison he was first examined by Dr J. D. Watson, the Senior Medical Officer at the prison. In court Dr Watson said that he examined Barclay at approximately 4.45 pm and asked him whether he had any allegations of assault. Dr Watson said his records noted that he made allegations that he had been assaulted by the RUC in Omagh Station on 3 January 1977 and complained that he had been punched on the face and around the head and stomach. Dr Watson was asked the results of his examination. He said he had noted that Barclay had a black eye and that the left side of his nose was bruised, although it did not appear to be fractured. He said that his right ear was swollen and blackened around the outside and that there were two small cuts on the jaw but he found no evidence of fracture. He also said that he noted an extensive bruise measuring 9 cm×8 cm on the abdominal wall to the left of the umbilicus. Dr Watson also produced the standard sketch form of the human body on which he had noted the signs of injury.

The court also heard from Dr Lee, a casualty officer at Dundonald Hospital in Belfast, who had examined Robert Barclay at around 6.45 pm on Wednesday afternoon, on the instructions of his solicitor. In his evidence Dr Lee said that Barclay had complained that he had been hit around the face, chest and abdomen. He said that Barclay told him he had been assaulted on the evening of the 3 January. Dr Lee then repeated what he had found when he had examined the prisoner. He described him as being 'quite alert and coherent', although there were 'external signs of trauma'. He said that there was a large periorbital haematoma[1] around the right eye which was swollen and tender, as well as a small area of bruising and swelling beneath his left eye. He also noted that the right ear lobe was extensively bruised, swollen and quite tender. There was also further mild swelling and tenderness around the bottom of the skull at the back of his head. Further there were two small abrasions on his left lower jaw. He said that on Barclay's chest he had found marked tenderness over the fourth to sixth ribs but there were no external signs of injury. On the abdomen he'd noted a circumscribed area of bruising about 3 ins. × 4 ins. Dr Lee said that he had found it 'markedly tender'. He said that Barclay exhibited a slight rebound when he touched it which indicated 'a clinical sign of injury to deeper tissues'.

This was the general framework of the *voir dire* – the statement fight, the process whereby the court decided whether Barclay's statements were admissible as evidence. The following verbatim extracts from the court transcripts are quoted to give some indication of the difficulties the court faced in reaching its verdict, in particular over reconciling the clear disparity in the medical evidence between the observations of Dr O'Neill and those of Dr Watson and Dr Lee.

First Paddy Fahy, Barclay's solicitor, was cross-examined about his 'tip-off' from the police constable. It was, at least as far as the defence was concerned, a rare breach in the 'wall of silence': they were concerned to proceed with caution, lest revelation of his identity led to reprisals against him by his colleagues for 'breaking ranks'.

DEFENCE QC: What was the effect of that conversation?

P. FAHY: Well, as a consequence of what I was told by that officer, I went to the van to which I could see Mr Barclay had been brought. It was parked a distance across the street from the

1. Severe bruising round the eye.

courthouse – a distance of some twenty yards. My purpose in going to the van at that stage was to have a look at Mr Barclay's face in view of what I had been informed by the police officer. As I went towards the police van – Mr Barclay was inside the van or entering the van at that point in time – I shouted across to him, 'Is there any message which you want me to give to any of your people?' And my reason for doing this was that I wanted to have a reason for going to the police van.

PROS. QC: I don't think we need to have the witness's internal reasoning processes, if Your Honour pleases.

JUDGE: No, we will just stick to the facts.

FAHY: I went across to him and said to him, 'Let me see your eye.'

DEF. QC: Can you tell His Honour, were there police within earshot of this conversation?

FAHY: Yes there was.

DEF. QC: How many?

FAHY: I can't be sure. I would have thought four, possibly five, but that is only a rough estimation. I can't be sure.

DEF. QC: What happened then?

FAHY: When I asked him that question he lifted his hair which was falling down over his right eye. He lifted his hair back from the right eye slightly, and I was able to see at that time what appeared to me to be a lump over his right eye.

I had very little time but I said to him, 'What happened to your eye?' and he did not answer me at that time. He simply shook his head. He was then moved from me or I moved away from him. At any rate I left the scene of the police van at that stage, Your Honour.

DEF. QC: Now can you tell His Honour at this stage anything about the colour of that lump you saw at that time?

FAHY: No. I cannot say anything about the colour of the lump. The light was poor. There were no other lights available than perhaps the internal lighting of the van but I could not comment on the colouring of that lump. Certainly there was nothing that struck me about the colouring of it.

Paddy Fahy was then cross-examined by prosecuting counsel.

PROS. QC: Do you know who that police officer was?

FAHY: Yes I do.

PROS. QC: Who was it?

FAHY: I am not willing to name the police officer, Your Honour.

JUDGE: Why not? Is it not relevant?

FAHY: Your Honour, I do not think it is relevant and I am not going to. I feel that it would be wrong of me to name the police officer who in those circumstances passed on a certain amount of information to me. I think it would be wrong to place him in any position of danger or jeopardy so far as his name is concerned. If you wish, I can do it to you privately; that is, if Your Honour wishes. I would not want to get him into any trouble.

JUDGE: I do not believe in trying this case privately. I am trying it publicly; either the information is relevant or it is not. It would be hearsay evidence, the content of the conversation would be hearsay.

DEF. QC: In fact Your Honour will appreciate that I did not ask the witness what he was told.

JUDGE: That is absolutely right.

PROS. QC: I am just asking for his name.

FAHY: As I say, Your Honour, I know the man's name. I can give it but I think it would be wrong of me to place his job in jeopardy, which I believe that I would be doing by giving his name in open court. That is my only reason.

JUDGE: I will leave it at that then.

PROS. QC: I do not want to press it any further, while not accepting the reasons.

FAHY: I think, Your Honour, I could say that as far as the reasons are concerned, I cannot see how this name is relevant, but I am willing to give it to Your Honour in private and it can be checked and verified.

JUDGE: I accept that you can give it, Mr Fahy, but the point so far as I am concerned is that I will not try these cases with notes being passed up to the judge. I will try them on the basis that justice must be seen to be done. It does not put the matter any further that you can put his name on a piece of paper and pass it up. I accept your word as an officer of the court. I accept that writing it on a piece of paper does not make the trial right. I would prefer to leave it in the circumstances and I think we have decided to leave it where it is.

Then the doctors were called for cross-examination. First Dr Lee, who examined Barclay at Crumlin Road gaol at 6.45 pm on Wednesday evening. He was questioned about the time scale of Barclay's injuries.

DEF. QC: Now can you assist His Honour in relation to this: in terms of the time scale within which these injuries might have been sustained, he apparently alleged to you that he had been assaulted on 3 January; from what you saw, can you say or can you make any comment about that?

DR LEE: Well the difficulty arises in dating bruises, as I'm sure Your Honour knows. It depends on a number of things, but I feel that generally the injuries and the bruising were in keeping with the time scale of the alleged assault. The bruises on the ear lobe and on the eye were well organized and were already resolving.

JUDGE: Does that mean well established, as it were, well organized?

DR LEE: Yes.

JUDGE: Does that mean that they were beginning to disappear?

DR LEE: Well the bruise was beginning to dissolve and you could see this by the colouring.

DEF. QC: Can I ask you this: in your judgement is there any possibility that these bruises and marks that you found could have been created between 1 o'clock on the day in which you saw him and 6 o'clock when you saw him?

DR LEE: In my opinion there could have been no possibility that they could have been created on that day.

JUDGE: That is between 1 pm on the 5th?

DR LEE: Yes.

JUDGE: And 6.45 pm on the 5th, is that right?

DR LEE: Yes.

JUDGE: Now what do you say to that?

DR LEE: In immediate bruising you get signs of acute inflammation. You get more redness than bruising and in fact the type of bruising he had would not normally appear in most tissues until around at least 24 hours following the injury.

DEF. QC: Now can we take it a stage further? I mentioned 1 o'clock because it was suggested no complaint was made to a doctor and he found no injury on him. Have you any comment to make about this?

DR LEE: No.

DEF. QC: Now can I ask you this? Is there any likelihood in your view that the injuries that you saw and the marks that you saw could have been created at all on the 5th; never mind 1 o'clock on the 5th; could they have been created that day at all?

DR LEE: No, I do not think that there is any possibility that they could have been created on that day at all.

Dr Lee was then cross-examined by prosecuting counsel.

PROS. QC: Is it your opinion doctor that this bruising could not have occurred on the 5th?

DR LEE: Yes, that is correct.

PROS. QC: And is that based on the colour of the bruising or what?

DR LEE: Well, not simply the colours but the nature of the swelling.

PROS. QC: Could it have been caused on the 4th?

DR LEE: It is possible.

PROS. QC: And you have no comment to make on the fact that an examination by another doctor at 1 o'clock or so on the 5th would appear not to have found the sort of bruising that you found?

DR LEE: No, I have no comment.

DEF. QC: I want to ask you: how long did your examination take in fact overall?

DR LEE: I am not sure. I am just recollecting. I think it would have been in the region of half an hour to 35 minutes.

JUDGE: But really when you saw him he had a black eye?

DR LEE: Yes.

JUDGE: That is really what it comes to?

DR LEE: The swollen area. And these were the most striking things.

JUDGE: Now with regard to the swelling, was the eye swollen?

DR LEE: Above the eye was swollen. The periorbital haematoma[1] where the bruising comes down and breaks down to give you a complete ring, this in itself would take about 24 hours to achieve. There was no swelling beneath the eye so that the trauma had occurred above the eye and the bleeding had tracked down to give a complete ring around the eyes. I should say the eye.

JUDGE: What is the first thing that happens when trauma is applied?

DR LEE: There is a fluid swelling. It starts off within minutes of the injury and this continues and then later what we term the bruising takes over when the blood is leaked out and starts to be dissolved and is carried away.

JUDGE: And then the discolouration continues or comes?

DR LEE: Yes.

JUDGE: Does the swelling usually subside?

DR LEE: It usually subsides.

JUDGE: After how long?

DR LEE: It varies in different tissues.

JUDGE: You cannot generalize?

DR LEE: No.

JUDGE: May I take it that what you saw there at 7 should have been there at 1 o'clock?

DR LEE: Yes.

JUDGE: And it was striking, wasn't it?

DR LEE: It was, yes.

JUDGE: Is there any medical explanation for this?

DR LEE: Well, as to what occurred in an earlier part of the evidence, when I saw Mr Barclay his hair was quite long and well down and dishevelled and it certainly could have hidden the ear. I cannot recollect just now how it might have hidden anything else. It might well be possible that it could hide the eye.

1. Severe swelling round the eye.

JUDGE: I also gather you to say that his hair was down but that did not stop you from seeing the black eye.

DR LEE: No, it did not.

JUDGE: And may I take it that if his hair was down at 1 o'clock it would not have stopped the other doctor from seeing the black eye?

DR LEE: No.

JUDGE: You can see what I am up against here?

DR LEE: Yes.

JUDGE: And you have no medical comment to make on this?

DR LEE: No, Your Honour.

Dr Watson was then called. He was the Senior Medical Officer at Crumlin Road gaol and had examined Barclay at 4.45 pm on the Wednesday.

DEF. QC: Doctor, in terms of the allegation of being assaulted in the way he described on 3 January, were your findings consistent with such an assault?

DR WATSON: They would be consistent.

DEF. QC: And for example, I gather you were in court when Dr Lee was in court giving his evidence. Would you agree that from the nature and colouring of the various bruises on the eye and ear, these general features, it would be quite clear these injuries did not occur on the 5th?

DR WATSON: That would be my opinion. That they did not occur.

DEF. QC: And probably not on the 4th, but more likely on the 3rd?

DR WATSON: About 48 hours prior to my seeing him would be my estimation.

DEF. QC: In a general way, would it require considerable force applied to this person to leave marks like that in 48 hours? Would it be consistent with fairly substantial punching?

DR WATSON: Yes, you cannot generalize. People vary. But on the whole, a reasonable amount, certainly some force, was used.

DEF. QC: To put it in the vernacular, would it be quite obvious that he had some form of beating?

DR WATSON: There was some form of direct violence applied to him.

Dr O'Neill, the Omagh GP who had examined Barclay at 1 pm on Wednesday at Omagh RUC station, then took the stand. He was asked where he had seen Barclay.

DR O'NEILL: It was just an office. It was not a medical room. It was just an office there. There is no proper medical room in Omagh Barracks for examination. This is just one of the rooms. It is sort of improvised really.

PROS. QC: And did you ask him if he had any complaints?

DR O'NEILL: Yes, I asked the accused if he had any complaints of ill-treatment since his arrest and if he had had enough food and sleep. He said that he had no complaint and that he did not allege any assault or ill-treatment during his stay in custody.

PROS. QC: Did you examine him?

DR O'NEILL: Yes, I examined him after that.

PROS. QC: And this was at the request of the RUC?

DR O'NEILL: It was at the request of the RUC, yes.

PROS. QC: How did you examine him?

DR O'NEILL: Well, it is probably just more by way of observations really and I am nearly certain all I did do was to get him to lift up his shirt just to have a look at his abdomen. He had no complaint really and I was not expecting to find or see anything and neither I did. I did not observe anything at that particular time, except I think I noted on one of my other forms that he had an appendicitis scar on his abdomen.

PROS. QC: Did you see anything else?

DR O'NEILL: Not according to my evidence here or to my report. I saw no evidence of physical maltreatment and I did not observe any injuries or any bruises on his body.

PROS. QC: Thank you.

DEF. QC: Doctor, you first saw this man some time around 1 o'clock, is that right? I think that is what you have marked there.

DR O'NEILL: Yes, that would be correct.

DEF. QC: And the records appear to show that he was returned to his cell at a quarter past one, so that, could I put it to you this way, you had a fairly short examination of him in fact?

DR O'NEILL: Yes, that would be correct, yes.

DEF. QC: Now could I ask you this: is there a difference between the situation in which you as a doctor are asked to examine a person who is making complaints about ill-treatment and the situation when you are examining someone with no complaints?

DR O'NEILL: Well I think that naturally there would be. If a person is making complaints of an injury being inflicted in a particular spot, you will be very careful to scrutinize it very thoroughly. If a person does not make a complaint and says that there has been no maltreatment, it is unlikely that you will be very thorough in your investigation of him.

DEF. QC: And for example, may I put it to you this way: that in lifting up a person's shirt a thing like an appendicitis scar would be very obvious: anyone could see it on a cursory glance?

DR O'NEILL: Yes, this was obvious.

DEF. QC: And would it be fair to say to you that you were not aware of any particular allegations which might leave bruising or marks and therefore you were not looking for them?

DR O'NEILL: Yes, that is probably correct. Well, if there were no allegations of injury or bruises, well you would not expect to be searching for them very thoroughly really.

JUDGE: I am faced with a great difficulty here. At 1 o'clock you saw no black eye, is that not right?

DR O'NEILL: Yes, well I did not observe it.

JUDGE: And at 5 o'clock another doctor sees a black eye; is that fair?

DEF. QC: The witness says he did not observe it.

JUDGE: I am just trying to get at the facts now.

DEF. QC: But again, to be absolutely fair to you, I think you have already admitted that there may have been things that you just didn't see. What we are referring to is bruising which Dr Watson and Dr Lee both found, consistent with a beating on 3 January. That is really 48 hours earlier almost. That is what they found at 4.45 and 6.45 respectively. If there had been such an assault at that time, may we take it that in the ordinary way you would have expected to see some signs of that when you examined him, if you had been alerted to the matter?

DR O'NEILL: Yes, I would have expected to see some signs if I was alerted.

JUDGE: Can I ask this: what was the light like in the room when you were looking at him?

DR O'NEILL: Well, the lights in these rooms are not good really as far as that. There is quite a high wall in front of the building and this is blocking the light coming into the room where we were, so that during the day the light in this is not very good, and even with the light on – it is just an ordinary bulb really – there is no fluorescent type lighting in these rooms, so far as I can recall, but I know the facilities for examining patients – medical facilities – are poor in Omagh and there is no couch even or a room where you could put a patient lying down. You just have to examine them as they are standing.

JUDGE: I mean as far as I can make out, you continued to examine him under some difficulty, but the real key to your examination was that there was no complaint and therefore it was not a very thorough examination?

DR O'NEILL: Well, that would be correct.

Barclay's defence counsel, John Curran, then made his final submission:

Your Honour has met a wall of silence, there is not the least indication that any person in Omagh RUC station inflicted any injury upon the accused; and one has the other matter: that first of all there is not the least suggestion put to the accused that the injuries were self-inflicted as it is sometimes a suggestion made in these cases. That is the first point. Secondly, there is no suggestion of any other accidental or other ways the injuries might have occurred. For example, in some cases it is heard of people falling down police station steps and injuries were caused accidentally. There is no suggestion of any type, in this case, and ultimately one has to face up to the situation that someone, or more, or a number of witnesses called on behalf of the Crown who have denied that this man sustained injury, on the balance of probabilities are being untruthful about this matter.

The prosecuting counsel, Patrick Markey, then made his final submission:

The first matter is, was there any ill-treatment by the police and in particular, and indeed in the way the case has been presented, it can only be ill-treatment at the hands of Detective Constables French and Newell so far as the allegations made by the accused are concerned; and the first thing is that they completely deny any allegations of assault or ill-treatment. The situation is that they repelled any suggestion of ill-treatment and certainly deny the sort of ill-treatment which the accused through his own mouth describes was meted out by either of these officers.

He must have been a very hardy man to have withstood that for a period of 4½ hours without making any sort of admission of any kind.

So far as the medical evidence is concerned, the medical evidence is difficult in this sense, that the findings of the different doctors at different times are extremely hard to reconcile on any sensible basis.

Of course, there are all sorts of various time scales that have been advanced before Your Honour about when bruises appear and when discolouration appears and the different stages of it, and it is rather hard in a sense to reconcile the medical evidence about that because none of the doctors appear to be able to agree with any great precision about these matters.

So far as these matters are concerned, I then leave it and submit that the Crown evidence, through the mouths of the police officers on this aspect, is credible evidence and unshaken.

The Crown then covered itself, just in case.

While it is the Crown case, on the evidence, that no ill-treatment occurred, certainly if any ill-treatment did occur, solace and control came, in my respectful submission, by the time the statements were made.

On 2 December 1977, Judge Rowland delivered his verdict. He said that it was impossible that Dr O'Neill would have failed to see injuries if they had been there. He was satisfied beyond reasonable doubt that Barclay had suffered no physical or mental abuse. He therefore admitted the two statements and sentenced him to seven years. Robert Barclay, prisoner number CI358/77, returned to the Maze prison to serve his sentence.

The defence launched an appeal at once. The three Appeal Court judges, Sir Robert Lowry, the Lord Chief Justice, Lord Justice Gibson and Mr Justice O'Donnell delivered their verdict on 13 April 1978. These are the notes of the judgement taken in court at the time.

The conviction was unsafe and unsatisfactory in the light of all the evidence: the learned trial judge's inferences from the facts and in particular the medical evidence were unreasonable: the findings of fact in the *voir dire* were unsustainable in the light of all the medical evidence: there was clear evidence that the accused had sustained serious injuries whilst in custody at Omagh RUC station: from all the medical evidence, the learned trial judge ought to have found that on the probabilities such injuries were sustained at the time and place alleged by the accused, namely the evening of 3 January 1977 at Omagh RUC station; there was no proper basis for preferring the results of an 'observation' by Dr O'Neill at Omagh RUC station at 1 pm on 5 January 1977 to whom no complaint had been made, to the findings of Drs Watson and Lee at 4.45 and 6.45 on the same day at Crumlin Road prison when they had –

(a) received detailed complaints of ill-treatment from the accused.
(b) examined him with reference to such complaints.
(c) agreed upon their findings almost exactly, although they examined him separately.
(d) discounted the possibility of their findings being consistent with injuries inflicted on 5 January 1977.

The judgement continued:

The learned trial judge's findings of fact were against the evidence: the inexplicable inconsistencies in the Crown medical evidence on the vital issue of injuries and their causation ought to have been resolved in the light of all the evidence; the learned trial judge ought to have excluded the verbal and written admissions and there being no other evidence against the accused, ought to have acquitted him.

Robert Barclay was released, after serving a total of sixteen months in prison.

Robert Barclay's acquittal was not the end of the story. While he was remanded in custody between his arrest and trial, two things happened. First, he was examined by the same consultant psychiatrist as had examined Peter Farrell. The psychiatrist wrote that Barclay was a mature, normal, hardworking individual who might be expected to have had fairly good stress tolerance, but that five months after his interrogation the symptoms and signs of anxiety were still quite marked. He remarked that it could be at least another year before the anxiety symptoms wore off and that being detained in prison awaiting trial could well be a complicating factor. The consultant psychiatrist also passed a judgement:

> Quite a number of questions arise here. The first that comes to mind are the reliability of the information obtained in interrogation and the validity of the confession. Just what was going on in the police station on those days in early January? I have seen some other cases where rough handling has been alleged and by any standards Mr Barclay's account is impressive. Information obtained by the technique involved is by its nature unreliable and consequently the confession of guilt in relation to certain offences lack validity.

The second, and more important, event was the history of what happened to the complaint that Barclay registered following his interrogation. The complaint was processed by the RUC's Complaints & Discipline Branch on 27 January 1977. An investigation was conducted and the papers sent to the DPP. On 9 August 1977 the RUC informed Barclay's solicitor that the DPP had directed 'no prosecution' against any police officer. But Barclay's defence were not prepared to let the matter rest there and took the unprecedented step of taking out a private prosecution against DCs French and Newell. A summons was served on them in Belfast and they were charged in Omagh. The magistrate remanded them in custody and the two detectives were taken to Crumlin Road gaol. They were granted bail of £500 the same day.

The private prosecution was heard before Lord Justice Gibson at Belfast City Commission on 23 April 1979. Judge Gibson had been one of the three Judges of Appeal who had quashed Barclay's sentence almost exactly a year earlier. Again Paddy Fahy was cross-examined about the police constable who he said had tipped him off about Barclay's eye outside Omagh courthouse. Again Fahy declined to name him for the same reasons, although pushed to do so by counsel acting for French and Newell. Judge Gibson resolved the deadlock by ordering Fahy to name the policeman. Fahy did so. The constable, Ben Quinn, was not in court – he was believed to have gone sick.

Much of the private prosecution was a replay of the original trial, with the doctors giving the same evidence under cross-examination. Giving evidence in court, this time for the prosecution, Barclay detailed the assaults he said he had received at the hands of Detective Constables French and Newell during his interview on the Monday evening. He said that the interview started at 6.45 pm. At the beginning he told the court that three men came in and asked him if he knew who they were. They identified themselves as CID from Belfast. Barclay said that they did not tell him their names. They were the two accused, Detective Constables French and Newell, and Sergeant McKimm. After about thirty minutes Barclay said that Detective Sergeant McKimm left and that he was alone with the two remaining detectives until 11 pm. At 7 pm Barclay said he was given a cup of tea and told to drink it quickly because there were a few hard hours ahead. He said that Newell reached across the table and spilt the tea over his second sandwich and reached to catch him by his shirt. Barclay said he remained seated for ten to fifteen minutes and then was made to get up with his back to the wall, his feet apart and arms out in front of him for about fifteen to twenty minutes. He said that McKimm loosened his buttons, felt his muscles and said that he was tense, so he must be telling lies. This went on for about fifteen to twenty minutes, then McKimm left and he was told to sit down again. Fifteen minutes later he was told to get up. He said that French stood behind him and Newell in front. He said he was slapped around the face with French standing three to four feet behind him and Newell three to four feet in front. He said that both were slapping him with open hands and this went on for fifteen minutes. He said they called him a liar. He was told to sit down and then told to get up again. He said that French stood in front and Newell behind and both thumped him with their fists on his head, face and stomach. One of them said he wanted to give him a right going over. After the interview Barclay told the court he had swelling around his eye and he was sore around his ribs. He said that he had received about a dozen blows with the fist from both men. He said they told him they could easily take him to a country road and pretend that he was showing them an arms dump and that he had run away and they had been forced to shoot him. Barclay then said that about 10.15 to 10.30 pm he was told to sit down and questioned about bombs in Castlederg. He made no admissions and denied everything. When he returned to his cell he was sore all over and didn't know whether he was coming or going. He never saw either French or Newell again. Under cross-examination Barclay told the court that the following morning he had seen Detective Sergeant McKimm and another police officer on a number of occasions. Barclay said what he had already said in court at the original trial, that McKimm had passed remarks on the condition of his eye, asking what had happened to it. Barclay said he had told him he had got it from two men the night before. At that point he said McKimm took off his coat and watch, put the watch in his coat pocket, and threatened that if he had any complaint about the eye he would thump his head into the ventilator hole and give him a real going over.

Detective Constable Kenneth Stanley French was the first witness for the defence. Detective Constable French had a clear record. He said that neither he nor Detective Constable Newell had either punched, injured or threatened Barclay. He said that no tea had been spilt and that Barclay had eaten his sandwiches and drunk his tea. He told the court that he had taken all the notes and that neither Detective Constable Newell nor Detective Sergeant McKimm had made any notes at all. He denied that Barclay was made to stand and had been forced to hold his arms out: nor, he said, did Detective Sergeant McKimm pull up Barclay's shirt and feel his muscles. Detective Constable French said that at the end of the interview there were no signs of any injury. He told the court that he had taken fourteen and a half pages of notes on the interview and that Barclay had made no admission except that he had put a false disc and plates on his vehicle. He also said that Detective Sergeant McKimm had introduced everybody by name.

Detective Constable French told the court that they had reason to believe that Barclay was a member of the IRA and that they had cautioned him when they told him they believed he was involved in terrorism in the Castlederg area. He said that Barclay denied both allegations. They had asked him about his car and he admitted that he had changed the tax disc to avoid an MOT test, and agreed that this was not the act of an honest man. Detective Constable French said that they had put it to Barclay once more that he was an IRA member and he said that he definitely was not. They asked him if he had 'chummed' with any known members. Barclay said he didn't know any, and that if he were a member he would tell them. Detective Constable French said that they asked Barclay if he accepted that he kept company with members of the IRA, and in reply he said that he probably did, but didn't know that they were members. Again he denied membership. Detective Constable French said they then suggested that Barclay was deeply involved and again he denied it. They also put other matters to him, including information from the Gardai and that they had no doubt that he was a member, and a high-ranking one at that. Barclay replied that 'honestly' he was not. They said that even if he wasn't sworn in he was deeply involved and in the constant company of members. Finally they asked him if he would like to consider his position, and Barclay said he would. Detective Constable French said they told him that they would see him again the next morning. In fact, they said that they didn't interview him the next day or see Barclay again. Neither were at the Special Court in Omagh.

Under cross-examination Detective Constable French said that they never got Barclay to make any admission, that no injuries were observed on him, nor did he or Barclay ever got off their seats during the four hours of interview. In court Detective Constable French admitted that he might have raised his voice possibly when Barclay denied membership, and may perhaps have spoken in a louder tone, but not, he stressed, in order to frighten him, just to bring home that they had no doubt that Barclay was a member. Detective Constable French said that he could offer no help in explaining how Barclay had been injured. Further he said that he didn't know Constable Ben Quinn – the man whom Patrick Fahy had just named in court – but he understood that Constable Quinn was sick, and remarked that as someone had produced a sick-line list that morning.

Giving evidence in court, Detective Constable William Alastair Newell said that neither he nor anyone else had touched or threatened Barclay or his family. He said that he too had been seated all the time, as were Barclay and Detective Sergeant McKimm. He told the court that nothing untoward had happened. Then under cross-examination he said that the interview had been entirely friendly but couldn't remember whether he had raised his voice. He pointed out that in prison members of the IRA on remand were directed to make charges and told against whom they were to make them. He said that at times during the interviews he did tell Barclay that he was lying. He admitted however that it would be odd for Barclay to inflict injuries on himself and then not make any allegations to Dr O'Neill when he was being examined.

The fifth witness in court was Detective Sergeant William McKimm. He said that he had been present at the start of the interview, when all were introduced by name and rank. He said they had had tea and sandwiches but that he hadn't seen any tea spilt. He denied that Newell had reached out to grab Barclay and that Barclay had ever been forced to stand up with his arms out. He said that he hadn't unbuttoned Barclay's shirt to feel his muscles. He made it clear that while he was in the room there was no violence. As far as the interview on the morning of the following day was concerned, he said he did not see anything wrong with Barclay's eye or make any remark about it. Nor did his colleague say that Barclay would get 'a real going over' if he made a complaint.

Under cross-examination Detective Sergeant McKimm said that if the accused misbehaved it would be a reflection on him and he was answerable for their behaviour, even when they were not in his presence. He said that there was a hole in the room for ventilation.

The trial lasted two days. On 25 April 1979, Lord Justice Gibson acquitted Detective Constables French and Newell. In his judgement he said:

There was undoubtedly, as I thought, strong prima facie evidence in this case that the complainant, Mr Barclay, had been assaulted. He was undoubtedly undamaged when he entered Omagh police station and there is no doubt that when he reached Crumlin Road prison he was suffering from injuries which I am satisfied did not occur either in Crumlin Road prison or on the way from Omagh. He therefore undoubtedly had sustained injuries while he was in Omagh police station.

The question for my determination was whether the complainant had satisfied me beyond reasonable doubt that these injuries had been occasioned by the two accused and that they had been done in the nature of an assault by them. The only direct evidence of this was of course the evidence of Mr Barclay himself and therefore the first interest for me was to examine his evidence with some care to ascertain how far he was a reliable and honest witness.

Lord Justice Gibson concluded that Barclay was not an honest, reliable witness. He pointed out that Barclay had admitted that he had falsified the particulars of his car in order to deceive the authorities, which clearly pointed to the fact that he was a person who on occasion for his own purposes could and did resort to dishonesty. He also said that Barclay was clearly wrong when he said that both French and Newell had taken notes. There was no question or doubt about who had taken the notes, as they were clearly all in the one handwriting and that that handwriting belonged to Detective Constable French. The judge said he was satisfied that the notes were contemporary and were taken almost entirely during the interview. He also referred to 'a certain evasiveness' in Barclay's answers. He said that he was placing some importance on the notes in reaching his decision because he often found in cases such as this that he was astonished to find how bare were the notes of interviews which had lasted for a long time. He sometimes found that the notes were a mere page or two and they were supposed to be a full record of what took place over a matter of hours. However, in this case he said that the notes were very full and detailed and extended over no less than fourteen and a half pages of fairly close-written paper. The judge also said that he did not believe the allegations that Barclay had made concerning Detective Sergeant McKimm and his colleague. He said he was satisfied that there had never been a conversation about the eye.

Altogether I do not find Mr Barclay's evidence, apart from the allegations of actual physical violence against him, to be satisfactory or such as in itself carried any assurance that I could rely on. Now lacking that I turn to see what the other evidence was, how far it would bear out and corroborate his evidence, or how far it would contradict the evidence of the complainant, or whether it was merely neutral. That of course turns mainly on the medical evidence.

Altogether the conclusion I have reached is that there is no clear medical or other corroboration of the accused, Mr Fahy's evidence when you put it against the medical evidence just does not support it because after that period of time you would not expect swelling and no discolouration. Dr O'Neill, who saw nothing, and the other doctors can only say that these injuries were probably almost certainly more than 24 hours old, but then we are trying to put it into a period which is 48 hours before. So I have come to the conclusion that there is not any clear corroboration of the evidence of Mr Barclay and, for instance, that the injuries could equally well have happened as regards time at least, say, during the night of the 3rd/4th when he was alone in his cell.

They are the sort of injuries that could physically be inflicted by a man on himself, although it is right to say that Dr Watson said it would be unlikely. But there is not any reason why a man could not bang his ear, for instance, against a wall or damage his eye against some object in his cell. One does know, of course, of cases where people have bruised their bodies in such circumstances.

While the evidence is that it would be unlikely, having regard to the variety of injuries, that he caused it himself, certainly it was possible and the evidence does not clearly establish otherwise and so, having regard to the standard of proof which is required in a case like this to eliminate any doubt in the matter, I am left really at the end of the case in the situation where I just do not know how he was injured and that being so, as I have said, I have no alternative but to acquit.

Robert Barclay's civil action for damages has not yet come to trial.

I asked a senior police officer what had happened to Detective Constable's French and Newell of Headquarters Crime Squad. He told me that 'cognisance' had been taken 'for action as and when'.

Of course, the R U C insist that these allegations must be kept in perspective and placed in the context of the total number of people detained and charged during any particular period. From 1 July 1976 to 31 October 1977 – when the new Interrogation Centre at Gough Barracks opened – 118 terrorist suspects were interrogated at Omagh R U C Station. Thirty-eight were charged and eighty were released. Of the thirty-eight who were charged, thirty made complaints against the police regarding their interrogation. This is the broad perspective. More specifically, for the period November 1976 to February 1977, thirty-six terrorist suspects were interrogated at Omagh. Ten of them made complaints of Assault During Interview (A D I). In November 1976, fourteen suspects were detained and six complained. One of them was James Rafferty. In December 1976, when Peter Farrell was interrogated, three suspects were detained and one complained. In January 1977, nine were detained and one complained. He was Robert Barclay. In February 1977, ten were detained and two complained. One of them was Paul Duffy.

7. Castlereagh

> 'The accommodation and facilities are modern. These are supported by medical inspections, detailed documentary records of the prisoner's stay in police custody and supervision by uniformed officers who are responsible for the welfare of prisoners.'
>
> Castlereagh: RUC Fact Sheet

By early 1977, Castlereagh had been operating as a full-time Interrogation Centre for around nine months. There had been allegations made about Castlereagh, but so far few had paid them much attention on the grounds that allegations of police brutality were all part of the propaganda war which most people took in their stride. The allegations that emanated from other police stations in the province, particularly Omagh and Springfield Road in Belfast, may also have diverted attention from Castlereagh. Apart from a few odd bruises and abrasions noted in the autumn of 1976, doctors who examined prisoners coming from Castlereagh saw little to arouse any degree of concern. They did however note a slight change in the pattern of allegations and in the signs they observed in the closing months of 1976.

The first sign was prisoners complaining of having their wrists bent backwards and forwards. 'Dorsi-flexing', as it's called, is a particularly painful method of inflicting punishment and, unless carried to extremes, leaves no marks. Doctors began to notice slight swelling of the wrist in some cases. William Campbell was a typical case. He was arrested on 6 November 1976 and taken to Castlereagh. He made the familiar allegations of being slapped and punched, but also complained that he had had his wrist bent back and then had it banged against the wall. The doctor who examined him said there was no sign of any injuries or bruising but there was a slight swelling around the joint where the wrist meets the hand, which could, he admitted, have been self-inflicted. The second sign was bruising on the costal margin – the point where the stomach meets the rib cage – an area susceptible to bruising if punches strayed from the sensitive but visually unresponsive target of the stomach. Marks like this were found on Francis McDonnell on 9 December 1976, although at the time they were not thought to be what the doctors called 'significant', meaning injuries they deemed unlikely to have been self-inflicted.

All suspects detained at Castlereagh were offered a medical examination on entry and exit as they were at all police stations. At Castlereagh the system had grown up in a somewhat haphazard way. Originally, before Castlereagh became an Interrogation Centre in 1976, administered and staffed by the RUC, interrogations were carried out by the army and police in a few Nissen huts in the back yard of Castlereagh police station, better known in those days as Ladas Drive, the RUC's Divisional HQ in Belfast.

In those early days, medical examinations were the responsibility of doctors from the Royal Army Medical Corps. But the army doctors got bored: there were few suspects to examine and little to see when they did; there appeared to be no cases of ill-treatment; internment took care of most suspects and the standard of evidence required to lock up a prisoner in Long Kesh required little pressure on the part of the interrogators.

In the winter of 1974–5, the army doctors threatened revolt: this wasn't what they had joined the RAMC for. They delivered an ultimatum. The Home Office told the Northern Ireland Office that they had better find other doctors quickly as the army doctors were refusing to carry out further examinations. The Northern Ireland Office passed the problem to the Police Authority, who were told to find somebody else to do the unpopular job.

The Police Authority first turned to the Police Surgeons,[1] whom they already employed to do routine police work,

1. Their proper title is 'Forensic Medical Officer': they were popularly known as 'Police Surgeons'.

like examining drunken drivers. They spoke to Dr Robert Irwin, who was Secretary of the newly formed Forensic Medical Officers Association. Dr Irwin was a busy man. Besides running a general practice in a tough Republican area – he was a Protestant – his hands were already full with police work, having examined over 300 corpses, many of them victims of sectarian killings. Dr Irwin consulted his colleagues and they too were not keen on the new job they were being offered. The Police Authority explained their dilemma and begged the Association to reconsider its position, faced as they were with the prospect of having no doctors in a few days' time. Reluctantly the Police Surgeons agreed, but only on the understanding that they were helping out in a crisis and replacements were to be found as soon as possible. In effect, the Police Surgeons provided medical cover at Castlereagh for about three months and soon discovered why the army got bored. They saw no cases of ill-treatment and found themselves examining individuals who were perfectly healthy. They kept up the pressure on the Police Authority to find replacements.

The Police Authority were desperate. They discussed the problem with Dr Terence Baird, the Chief Medical Officer at the DHSS. Dr Baird was sympathetic to the Police Authority's problem, but many of his doctors worked in the prison medical service and could not be spared. In the end, he scouted around and plundered the Medical Referees Service, the group of doctors who decide, for example, whether sick leaves are genuine. He managed to persuade, perhaps by the offer of promotion, a veteran of the Second World War to take on the job. Dr Ernest Page had been a navy man too. He had been involved in midget submarine operations against the German navy. He was a big man of some fifteen stone: his friends used to joke that they must have stood him on the slipway and built the midget submarine round him. But Dr Page was only interested in working nine till five, which still left the Police Authority with the problem of filling the other sixteen hours of the day. Finally they persuaded some local

GPs and Registrars from the city's hospitals to do some 'moonlighting' and provide 'silent-hour' cover. They were to work a rota system and were called out only if necessary. There was no stampede to work at Castlereagh.

Part of Dr Robert Irwin's routine job as a Police Surgeon was to examine prisoners who were brought into police stations. One of the stations he covered was Townhall Street, the rear of which is a heavily guarded Victorian fortress down a back alley near the city centre. Townhall Street is the police station to which suspects are brought to be charged after their interrogation at Castlereagh. The journey from Castlereagh to Townhall Street takes about fifteen minutes. Once there, the prisoner is officially handed over and signed for on the Prisoner Arrest Form. He is asked if he has any complaints. Initially prisoners were not formally asked if they wanted a medical examination and were only examined on request. However, the situation changed in 1977 when the Police Surgeons at Townhall Street began to see a growing number of prisoners coming from Castlereagh with injuries. Senior police officers at Townhall Street became concerned that they might be blamed for the injuries and were anxious to put themselves and their men in the clear. They discussed the problem with Dr Irwin and their own superiors and, as a result, it was decided to offer a medical examination to every prisoner who arrived at Townhall Street from Castlereagh, whether he requested it or not.

When I visited Townhall Street the police were at great pains to point out that no prisoner had ever been injured at their police station. When I asked them about injured prisoners arriving from Castlereagh, they said that was something on which they could not comment. I asked them for their opinion. They said they did not have opinions. Dr Irwin said that he had only ever seen one prisoner with an injury received while in custody at Townhall Street, and that injury was self-inflicted.

The Police Surgeons worked on a rota system at Townhall Street. If a prisoner said he wanted to see a doctor, the officer would refer to the chart on the wall above the desk and ring whichever of the four doctors was on duty at the time. Within half an hour, Dr Irwin or one of his colleagues would arrive to see the suspect. The examinations were conducted in a small room just down the corridor from the main office. There was an old-fashioned wooden couch in the corner, a desk, a light and a chair. Here a prisoner would often make his first complaint of ill-treatment and, significantly, he would make it to a doctor not to a policeman.

In many cases prisoners told the doctors they had been frightened to complain at Castlereagh or had wanted to get out of the place as fast as they could. Prisoners told doctors that they had been warned by detectives at Castlereagh not to complain and threatened with 'more of the same' if they did. Even at Townhall Street, and later at Crumlin Road prison where they went on remand, some prisoners refused to complain, although doctors clearly observed marks on their bodies. If a suspect complained to a doctor, the doctor automatically informed the police.

It was here, in the medical room of Townhall Street police station, that Dr Irwin and his fellow Police Surgeons began to see injuries on prisoners coming from Castlereagh. The odd injuries they had seen towards the end of 1976 became more frequent in the early months of 1977. Seldom did the police offer any explanation for the injuries the doctors saw. If a prisoner accidentally injured himself, or deliberately injured himself in order to corroborate his allegations of ill-treatment, the police were obliged to record the incident and inform the doctor accordingly. Similarly, if a policeman injured himself, or alleged he was injured by a prisoner, it was his duty to make a report and inform the Medical Officer. At Townhall Street the Police Surgeons were seeing *unexplained* injuries on prisoners. Admittedly abrasions could be self-inflicted while the prisoner was in transit in the police van from Castlereagh to Townhall Street, but many of the bruises and other injuries the doctors observed were, in their view, impossible to inflict in this way. (A new 'injury-proof' transit van was introduced only in July 1978, when most of the injuries had ceased.) Further, because only about 50 per cent agreed to medical examinations before they left Castlereagh, it was often only at Townhall Street that the injuries were first observed and a complaint first made. I asked Dr Page, who remained at Castlereagh until the autumn of 1977, if he had seen many injuries. He said 'No comment'. As a detective remarked, the medical room was in the wrong part of the building anyway, at the end of the cell block, not the interrogation room corridor.

When the prisoner had been examined at Townhall Street, he was taken downstairs to the Dickensian cells in the bowels of the station. They have steel doors, no windows, concrete floors and a concrete base for a mattress. Here prisoners often spend the night before they are taken out to be charged before a magistrate the following morning. In the morning the narrow tunnel that runs from the cells to the stairs that lead up to the magistrates' court is lined with youths on wooden benches. Many look as if they have been there before. They sit pale in the artificial light, most in jeans and cheap imported shoes, waiting for their names to be called to appear before the well-scrubbed face of British Justice in the courtroom above. Where terrorist offences are concerned, the magistrate who formally charges the prisoner has no power to grant bail. Bail is granted only at the discretion of a High Court judge. Prisoners blink as they enter the court from the gloom of the cells below. Their appearance is brief: the charges a formality. Prisoners are then escorted out and put in a van to be sent up the road to the Crumlin Road prison, where they are automatically medically examined. Here, or at the Maze prison, they wait on remand till their case comes up for trial. Owing to pressure of work on the courts, a prisoner can wait anything from six months to two years on remand. If he's convicted, his remand counts as part of his sentence. If he's acquitted, he has no redress: at least in the eyes of the security forces, some undesirable elements have been off the street for anything up to two years. Critics of the system understandably see it as a subtle form of internment.

Interrogations at Castlereagh are planned with military precision. Invariably suspects are brought in in 'sweeps', which may be the result of a particular incident or a prolonged investigation by one of the Regional Crime Squads. Surprise is all-important. Castlereagh has thirty-eight cells and twenty-one interview rooms – some of them the old rooms with the pegboard walls that survived the Provisionals' bomb attack. On any day, suspects, connected with three separate investigations can be interrogated under the same roof. Each group is questioned by a team of detectives, usually from HQ Crime Squad, Belfast Regional Crime Squad and Belfast Divisional CID, although the other two Crime Squads use Castlereagh too. Crime Squad detectives are almost all full-time interrogators. Most of the interrogators were young and of Detective Constable rank, which simply mirrored the constitution of the RUC in 1977, two thirds of whose members were under twenty-four.

A team often consists of over two dozen detectives, who usually work in interchangeable pairs. The operation is planned and directed from the administrative section in the Portakabins that stand alongside the new two-storeyed cell block. Before interrogations begin, each team is briefed by the senior detective in charge in an oblong room with orange tiles on the floor and a desk at one end. A couple of dozen chairs line the walls. When the pressure is really on, detectives told me that they sometimes saw the file on a suspect only minutes before the interrogation began.

When I visited Castlereagh, three separate investigations were in progress. One involved the Provisional IRA, a second the Irish National Liberation Army (INLA) and the third the Protestant Ulster Volunteer Force (UVF). Each set of interrogations was being directed from a different room. An intelligence collator, often a Woman Police Constable, monitors the progress of the interviews. On the wall of each collator's office is a huge chart. Down the left-hand side are written the names of the detectives who work on the team and against them the code numbers they are given to ease collation. There were twenty-seven detectives involved in investigations on the INLA swoop. Alongside the detectives' names are listed the names of the suspects. The times and duration of each interview are then entered in a square. On the basis of information received from each interview, further permutations of detectives and suspects are worked out, which are likely to yield the best results from the next session.

The other chart on the wall is the scoreboard. In the INLA investigation, one suspect had confessed to fifteen offences. The general strategy is to break down one suspect and use his admissions to prise statements out of the rest: the police say that even strong wills crack when they hear that their associates have confessed, and most suspects crack in the first two days. Detectives told me that Castlereagh had such a bad reputation that it often did the job for them. Some said that suspects often came into the interview room ready to 'sing' before anything happened.

Officially, detectives at Castlereagh told me that there was no substance to the allegations and said that the Judges Rules were always applied whenever evidence was being obtained. They said that suspects were trained how to resist interrogation and they had captured documents and cassette tapes to prove it: notes of debriefings by IRA Intelligence Officers had also been seized, and none of them made any reference to ill-treatment. The allegations were, they assured me, part of a skilfully orchestrated propaganda campaign to discredit and undermine the police. They agreed that the bad publicity that surrounded Castlereagh had actually helped them, and most suspects were only too anxious to unburden themselves. Violence against a suspect, they argued, was counter-productive. The art of interrogation was to create an atmosphere in which the suspect would confide in his interviewer. It was this rapport, they insisted, that produced results. I asked them what happened if a man whom they knew to be a senior Provisional sat for seven days and said not a word. They said they had to let him go: to strike him would be an admission of defeat.

But a different story emerged when I spoke to detectives unofficially. Not all were happy with the methods some of their colleagues were using: they believed it brought the police down to the level of the terrorists they were fighting. They said that it was accepted almost everywhere in the world that beating a suspect was often a quick way of getting him to talk. They told me that the atmosphere in the interview rooms was 'indescribable', and only the Provos knew what it was like, because only they had been through it. They admitted that the allegations they made were sometimes based on first-hand experience and agreed that many of them were true. I asked them if the Judges Rules were applied during interviews. They laughed. I asked them if they had read the Bennett Report. They said they didn't bother with that sort of thing. Nor did they seem worried by the threat of prosecution by the DPP. They said they were getting results and that was the standard by which their work was to be judged. A senior police officer I spoke to confirmed some of what they said. He said that in 1977, for the first time, detectives felt that they were not only stemming the tide, they were actually beginning to turn it back. He admitted that at the time senior officers were more concerned with results than the ways in which they might be being obtained.

Privately I asked these detectives whether ill-treatment was known about at a high level. Of all the questions I asked, this was the one detectives were most reluctant to answer. One of them referred the question back to me. He said that if my editor didn't like what I was writing, he could tell me to stop, and if I didn't stop, then he would come down and break the lead in my pencil. He said they had had no such visit from their 'editors'. I asked them if word had ever come down to 'go easy'. They admitted it had, round about the time of Bennett, but wouldn't say from what level it had come. My information was that Chief Superintendent William Mooney, MBE, the senior detective in charge of all the CID – both Crime Squad and Divisional – defended his interrogators when they came under attack, especially when the heat was on. Chief Superintendent Mooney had been the detective behind the RUC's successful detection and prosecution of the UVF's vicious East Antrim gang. He was an experienced and successful police officer, who naturally stood by his men. Nevertheless, it was an attitude that sometimes infuriated some of his superiors. Although Chief Superintendent Mooney might point to the results his men were achieving, senior officers nevertheless pointed out some of the problems that their success was causing. The RUC later told me that if there were problems in this field, they were due to lack of supervision around this time. I was told that account was taken and supervision was later strengthened and improved.

Some detectives spoke of the long hours, and the dangers of being prime targets. The Provisionals they interviewed knew their identities and they were observed every week by their supporters when they gave evidence in court. Nevertheless, they remained fiercely proud of their Force. They also agreed that the rewards were high and their standard of living – should they live to enjoy it – was good. The overtime was generous, even after it was restricted to a hundred hours a month. On the strength of it, many had bought new cars and houses. Castlereagh paid the mortgage and the bills.

There was an undoubted unease. Some believed that policemen had died because of the activities of some detectives at Castlereagh. One said that the book on Castlereagh could only be opened slowly, as what was inside was political dynamite. He told me that several powder kegs were involved and that now was not the time to take the lid off. Some expressed the fear that one day someone would open the book on Castlereagh and they would all be called to account.

On 2 February 1977 the Provisionals opened up a new front in their campaign when they murdered Geoffrey Agate, the head of the American-owned Dupont factory in Derry, shot dead outside his home. It was the first of a series of attacks on industrialists in an effort to deter the business community in general, and American investors in particular, from supporting Roy Mason's efforts to inject some life into the province's dying economy. The killing of Geoffrey Agate, apart from the revulsion it caused among many Catholics in Derry, who were grateful for Dupont's oasis of employment, struck at the heart of Roy Mason's economic strategy. He believed that unemployment was a major cause of the province's ills. Put crudely, the philosophy was that if jobs were provided a grateful Catholic community, which still bore the brunt of unemployment, would give thanks to a government which tried to find an answer to one of its most pressing problems and, perhaps more significantly, its young men might find the prospect of work more attractive than joining the Provisional IRA. To the Provisionals the government's economic strategy undoubtedly posed a real threat. Just before the murder of Geoffrey Agate, the Secretary of State had made his position clear. Writing in a trades union journal on 17 January 1977, Roy Mason said:

With the increasingly important role of the RUC, supported by the necessary levels of Armed Forces, the forces of law and order are now effectively putting behind bars many of the murderers and terrorists. With more cooperation from those in the Province who are yearning for peace, the RUC will gradually tighten the net around these gangsters. It is this that we must encourage.

Castlereagh was where the effects were felt.

Among the first to be netted following the murder was a nineteen-year-old unemployed Derry youth, John Donnelly, who lived on the edge of the Bogside. Donnelly and several other Derry youths were arrested and taken to Strand Road police station in Derry for interrogation. Donnelly alleged he was beaten and threatened with a session at Castlereagh if he didn't confess to the murder. Donnelly said he knew nothing about it. He was transferred to Castlereagh.

During his interrogation there, Donnelly alleged that he was beaten almost continuously by detectives from the Regional Crime Squad, who tried to get him to confess to the murder of Geoffrey Agate. He refused. He says he was slapped and punched extensively: he had already alleged that his hand and wrist had been hyperflexed at Strand Road, and now said that the detectives at Castlereagh made it worse by making him form a fist with his hand and then squeezing it. Donnelly said his interrogation was interrupted while he was taken to Dundonald Hospital to have his hand X-rayed.

Towards the end of his interviews he said he was seen by Chief Superintendent Mooney,[1] who was in charge of all the R U C's detectives. He alleged the Chief Superintendent kept saying that if he confessed to the murder he would only get twelve years and, as prisoners enjoyed half remission of their sentence,[2] that would only mean six years in all. If he didn't cooperate with the police, he would get a stipulated sentence of thirty-five years. Donnelly did not recollect making any admission. He did remember being told that forensic tests on the swabs had proved positive. He said he wasn't aware he was being charged with the murder until he reached Townhall Street police station.

Before he left Castlereagh, he was examined by a Falls Road G P, Dr Joe Hendron, who was also a prominent member of the SDLP. Dr Hendron said that it was the

1. Chief Inspector Mooney was the detective who masterminded 'A' Squad's successful operation against the U V F's East Antrim Gang.
2. Half remission was offered by Merlyn Rees in March 1976 when he abolished Special Category status. It was meant to sugar the pill.

worst case of assault on a prisoner that he had seen: he did not believe that the injuries could in any way have been self-inflicted. Dr Hendron examined Donnelly in the presence of a Castlereagh Medical Officer.

Donnelly named some of the detectives whom he alleged had introduced themselves to him: among them were detectives from the H Q Crime Squad who had interrogated Robert Barclay in Omagh.

Another doctor examined Donnelly at the request of his solicitor, after he had been charged with the murder and admitted to prison on remand. The doctor recorded patchy hair loss at the front and back of the head; a swelling of the ring finger; three bruises on his left arm; a large bruise 4×3ins at the top of his stomach and an abrasion and bruising on his right knee and leg. There was also extensive bruising along both hip bones and fading bruises on the back of his left thigh.

The doctor concluded that his findings of hair loss and generalized bruising were consistent with what Donnelly alleged had happened to him during his interrogation.

A prisoner cannot be held in custody for more than a fortnight without judicial approval being given for his further imprisonment on remand. As a result, once a week or once a fortnight, all remand prisoners go through the ritual of being formally remanded in custody for a further period of time. They are brought to Crumlin Road prison, if not already resident there, and then led through the tunnel under the road that joins the prison with the Belfast City Commission.[1] Remand hearings are held before a magistrate in a small modern courtroom at the back of the courthouse. The magistrate asks the D PP's representative about the state of the case and the stage the police have reached in their inquiries. The prisoner's solicitor invariably asks for the case to be speeded up. The prisoner is then

1. This is the term by which the building is popularly if inaccurately known. Since the reorganization of the legal system in April 1979, the building's proper title has been the Crown and County Courthouse, Belfast.

formally remanded in custody, usually for another two weeks. The formalities often take seconds rather than minutes.

John Donnelly had been making the regular journey through the tunnel to the magistrates' court for six months. He made it for the last time in August 1977. As he stood in the dock behind the glass screen, he heard the DPP's solicitor inform the magistrate that the Director was withdrawing the charges. John Donnelly was released.

Although the DPP will not comment on individual cases and will not discuss reasons for the decisions he makes, it is possible that one of the reasons for withdrawing the charge against Donnelly was evidence of the medical reports, which may not have withstood the test of Section 6. It is also possible that the police evidence simply wasn't strong enough.

8. In the Public Interest? – The Case of Bernard O'Connor

> 'It is quite clear that there is a renewed and orchestrated campaign to blacken the RUC in the eyes of the local community and the world at large. I believe, however, that a sufficiently large number of people are now wise enough to recognize the terrorist lie and to see the RUC for what it truly is.'
>
> SDCC Harry Baillie, 9 March 1977, following BBC-TV interview with Bernard O'Connor

While John Donnelly was being interrogated at Castlereagh over the weekend of 5 February, in Strasbourg the European Court of Human Rights was reviewing the European Commission's report on the allegations of ill-treatment in 1971. The Dublin government had insisted on taking their case to the highest level of the European Court in the hope that the principles of their case would become enshrined in European law. When the court resumed its hearings at the beginning of the following week, the British Attorney-General, Sam Silkin, QC, gave it an 'unqualified undertaking' from the British government that the 'Five Techniques' would not 'in any circumstances be reintroduced as an aid to interrogation'. Results were now being obtained in other ways.

The following day, Keith Kyle, a well-respected journalist and academic, was reading a report of the Attorney-General's 'unqualified undertaking' in the morning paper in a car on his way to Enniskillen in County Fermanagh. Kyle was planning a film for the BBC's Tonight programme on the way that local government functioned in Northern Ireland. Fermanagh council had agreed to let TV cameras into the council chamber.

During a break in the filming, a local councillor took Keith Kyle to one side and asked him if he would have a word with one of his constituents who had a problem. The constituent was called Bernard O'Connor.

Bernard O'Connor was well known locally. He taught music at the local school and was on the national executive of the Catholic Boy Scouts of Ireland. He told Kyle that a few weeks earlier he had been arrested and taken to Castlereagh for interrogation. He gave a graphic description of what he said had happened to him. Kyle was impressed by O'Connor as a witness: he seemed to have total recall of events and appeared to be an untypical visitor to Castlereagh. Kyle was too experienced to be taken in by unsubstantiated allegations, however credible they might have seemed on the lips of a well-educated, middle-class schoolteacher and scoutmaster. Neither Kyle nor O'Connor discussed the possibility of a television programme at this stage.

Kyle's first reaction was to pass the case on to Amnesty International, who, as it happened, were running a study group based at Chatham House, where Kyle had an office. Among its members were the former Lord Chancellor, Lord Gardiner, and the President of the European Commission, Professor James Fawcett. Kyle mentioned O'Connor's case to Professor Fawcett, who, as President of the Commission, had detailed knowledge of the legal implications of the 1971 allegations. Kyle asked him where he would place the kind of ill-treatment that O'Connor had alleged. The Professor said it would come somewhere 'in the middle range'.

By this time Kyle had also thought in terms of a possible TV programme if, after further research, there appeared to be some credibility in O'Connor's allegations. He mentioned the idea to his producer, who showed moderate interest and agreed that more research should be done.

Kyle and his colleagues dug into O'Connor's background. They confirmed that he was well thought of in Enniskillen, especially for his youth work with the school and Scouts. They also made inquiries about his political activities in the Civil Rights Movement of the late sixties.

They found he had edited a scurrilous local 'Private Eye' in which he had lampooned many of the local dignitaries – including the local police chief. He had been fined £8 for sitting down in a street demonstration in 1972, but that, with the exception of a minor offence at the age of nine, was the extent of his police record. They also ascertained that he crossed the near-by border many times on his Boy Scout business and gave driving lessons after school. In any normal society, neither activity would arouse much suspicion. Nevertheless, the RUC believed – and still believe – that Bernard O'Connor was one of the Provisionals' 'Godfathers'.

After much background research and discussion, a decision was made to film an interview with O'Connor. The interview was viewed by the BBC's senior management, who gave the go-ahead for transmission. The Director-General was involved from the beginning, on the grounds that if there was going to be a crash landing he should at least be in on the take-off.

The BBC alerted the RUC to the programme six days before it was due to be transmitted. The RUC said that they were in no position to comment as they were investigating O'Connor's complaint and the papers would be sent to the DPP. They said the case was *sub judice*. There was some pressure to delay the transmission of the programme which Dick Francis, Controller of the BBC's News and Current Affairs, resisted. He argued that coverage of the unpalatable in Northern Ireland shouldn't be delayed on the grounds that it was untimely, nor should transmission be put off where potentially critical issues were concerned until there was an official response. He said that to act in this way would imply a power of veto. So, on 2 March 1977, the BBC broadcast the interview in which Bernard O'Connor told his story.

O'Connor said that he was awakened at 5.30 on the morning of Thursday, 20 January. Police and army knocked at the door of his elegant Georgian terrace house in

Enniskillen and told him he was being arrested under Section 12 of the Prevention of Terrorism Act, which meant that he could be interrogated for seven days. He was taken to Castlereagh on Thursday morning. The Medical Officer asked him if he wished to be examined. He said he did not as he was perfectly healthy.

During the first day of interrogation – Thursday – O'Connor alleged he was slapped around the head, punched in the stomach and generally abused. On television he gave graphic details. From the description of the room he gave, O'Connor's interrogation was carried out in the old interview rooms with the 'pegboard' walls which had survived the Provisionals' bomb attack. There were no spyholes in the door. He said he heard other prisoners being banged against the walls and shouting and screaming (the old interview rooms are prefabricated and not sound-proofed). He said he was accused of being a murderer and a terrorist who was leading young boys astray: the detectives said they knew he was a leader of the Provisional IRA and he was going to be cracked. O'Connor said he was beaten again and forced to do strenuous exercises, press-ups and sit-ups. His track-suit top was placed over his head and his nose and mouth were blocked off. He alleged a detective said, 'Choke the bastard.' He thought he fainted. He said he was made to strip, put his soiled underpants over his head[1] and run around the room.

On Friday O'Connor alleged the ill-treatment continued: he said he was punched on the back of the head and slapped around the face. The detectives kept trying to get him to make statements. They said he was a 'Godfather' and didn't pull the trigger himself, but got young boys to go out and do the jobs for him. He alleged he was punched in the chest and stomach with stiff, extended fingers.

On Saturday he said a senior detective with a briefcase came into the room. O'Connor alleged that he put the

1. This was the allegation that Paul Duffy made a month later to an Inspector at Omagh, immediately after his interrogation at 4.36 p.m. on 23 February 1977.

briefcase down on the table and said, 'Right now, I want the statements.' O'Connor refused. He then alleged that the detective wrote down a statement admitting involvement in the murder of a police constable. O'Connor said he refused to sign. The detective then wrote out another statement about the murder of another policeman. Again O'Connor refused to sign, as he said he was not involved. He then alleged that the detective asked him to write on the statement that he refused to sign. O'Connor said no. The detective said he would produce it in court and say that they were verbal admissions which he had refused to sign. O'Connor alleged that the senior police officer then asked him if he knew that he would have to do a stipulated sentence of thirty-five years if he didn't help the police. If he did admit his involvement, he would get an ordinary life sentence of about fourteen years; with remissions this meant he would only get five.

At teatime on Saturday, O'Connor was visited by his doctor from Enniskillen. His doctor had been worried about O'Connor and about his wife, who had just gone through a Caesarian birth. He was examined in the presence of a Castlereagh Medical Officer. Dr Mulhearn, who had never been in an Interrogation Centre before, was flabbergasted by O'Connor's appearance. He found him 'untidy, unshaven, sweaty and unwashed'. O'Connor had difficulty in raising his arms to remove his jumper and shirt. Both ears were badly discoloured with blue bruise marks: there was a small bruise at the corner of the left eye and an area of bruising over the left upper chest. His spine was tender and he couldn't flex his head. His abdomen too was 'quite definitely tender', as were his kidneys and the backs of his legs, where he alleged he had been kicked. The doctor concluded:

The clinical findings noted above would in my opinion confirm Mr O'Connor's statement that he had been assaulted while in police custody.

O'Connor said that he did not wish to make a complaint. He said he feared that there might be worse to come.

The interrogations continued through Sunday and Monday, but he alleged no further ill-treatment. O'Connor still refused to sign anything, as he insisted he was innocent. No charges were made and he was released on Monday. Before he left, he was asked by the Medical Officer if he wanted a full medical examination. He said he did not, but he did fill in a Complaint Form.

Amongst the interrogators who apparently interviewed Bernard O'Connor were Crime Squad detectives – in particular from HQ – who had interviewed Robert Barclay, Paul Duffy and John Donnelly.

There was a crash landing. Roy Mason accused the programme of being one-sided: he said that O'Connor's complaint would be investigated through the normal channels and that his interrogation was fully justified in the light of evidence available. Airey Neave, his Conservative opposite number, accused the BBC of losing sight of its responsibilities in Northern Ireland and said that the programme had had the most damaging effect on the morale of the RUC. The BBC replied that it believed the transmission of the interview to have been in the public interest. The Police Authority wrote a letter to Sir Michael Swann, the Chairman of the BBC, expressing 'considerable disquiet' at the impression created by the programme. Sir Michael, no doubt with the recent 'Battle of Culloden' in mind, told the Authority's Chairman, Sir Myles Humphreys, in reply:

The BBC took the view that . . . we are drawing attention to allegations which, had they been suppressed, could easily have damaged the RUC more seriously than their publication.

Not all the BBC's Board of Governors agreed with their Chairman's sentiments: one of them said that even if the allegations were true, the BBC should not have broadcast them.

Some of the RUC's detectives took a more sanguine view of the programme: they remained convinced, as did their most senior officers, that Bernard O'Connor was an IRA 'Godfather'. One interpretation offered was that O'Connor had a special mission to destroy Castlereagh. The basis of this theory was that the Provisionals were worried at Castlereagh's increasing success, which was crippling their organization, and had decided that Castlereagh had to be neutralized. It was suggested that the Provisionals arranged for O'Connor to be lifted – this wasn't too difficult as a well-placed word on the confidential telephone was often enough – and taken to Castlereagh for interrogation. The odds were that he would be beaten up. If he could hold up under pressure he would be released. The media would jump at such an articulate and credible eye-witness. An interview would be broadcast and the resulting outcry would lead to, if not the closing down, at least the blunting of Castlereagh. Even if that were the Provisionals' strategy – and such sophistication was not beyond them – it failed. They had to wait another two years before the Bennett Report blunted Castlereagh. Furthermore, Keith Kyle insists that the idea of a TV interview never at any stage came from O'Connor and that all along he was a reluctant participant.

Although the interview did cause an uproar, it also reflected the anxieties that many Catholics felt who were bitterly opposed to the Provisional IRA. The SDLP expressed some of that concern in the following statement:

Illegal police pressure is undeniably being applied to have statements signed or to obtain information often in RUC barracks often far from the victims' homes so that constraint can be minimized. In itself this provides grounds for believing that this kind of activity is approved at high level and is not the result of individual police malpractice . . . If strong preventative action is not taken at once, licence to continue will be assumed with grave consequences.

With statements like that coming from the SDLP, whose

public support the police desperately needed as a first step to winning support in the areas from which the SDLP drew its political support, the RUC stood no chance of becoming a police force acceptable to both communities. Politically, the interview with Bernard O'Connor marked a turning point. To many Catholics, the RUC now had to do something to show that its senior officers meant what they said when they spoke of enforcing the law within the law. All they got were denials and pleas of *sub judice*. Confidence in the RUC and in the political institutions it represented had to be restored. It was not.

After the initial storm died down, there was little desire on the part of the authorities to pursue the matter further. When the Complaints Committee met and considered Sir Michael Swann's reply to the Police Authority's letter, it was suggested that 'the matter might now be quietly dropped'. Ivor Canavan, the Chairman of the Complaints Committee, was the brother of Michael Canavan, the SDLP's spokesman on law and order, who drafted the SDLP statement. Both brothers shared the same concern, but Ivor didn't believe in rocking the boat. He had already expressed a 'feeling of unease' to SDCC Baillie at the beginning of the year. As he told his Committee after the programme, the issue at stake was whether it should have been shown, given the sensitive situation.

A week after the programme, SDCC Baillie spoke of two terrorist wars: one was a war of death and destruction, the other a propaganda war; one killed people, the other killed truth. He reminded the public that the complaints investigation system was probably the most rigorous in the United Kingdom; that the RUC would enforce the law within the law and that any police officer who acted outside it would find the full rigour of the law applied against him.

The Complaints & Discipline Branch investigated O'Connor's complaint, and sent the papers to the DPP. The DPP directed no prosecution.

The Director of Public Prosecutions is appointed by the Secretary of State but is answerable to the Attorney-

General, the United Kingdom's supreme law officer. The Attorney-General is a political appointment made by the government of the day. He does not have a Cabinet seat, but is invited to all Cabinet meetings that affect the work of his Department. The DPP's relation to the Attorney-General is clearly laid down:

> To discharge his functions under the superintendence of the Attorney-General and to be subject to the direction of the Attorney-General in all matters.[1]

It has been suggested however by some legal experts[2] that, although generally independent, the DPP's accountability to the Attorney-General has raised some doubts as to the impartiality of decisions with regard to the prosecution of some members of the security forces, for example, in the case of the 'Bloody Sunday' shootings. It is customary for the DPP to refer his most difficult and sensitive cases to the Attorney-General but only, it must be added, after he has already reached a decision himself.

It is a matter of record that the Attorney-General has never countermanded any of the DPP's decisions. Nevertheless, given the sensitive nature of Northern Ireland and the fact that allegations of ill-treatment by the security forces are perhaps one of the most sensitive issues of all, there are those who suspect that sometimes political considerations may outweigh the absolute requirements of justice. As evidence they cite the decision of the Attorney-General[3] not to prosecute members of the Parachute Regiment for the killing of thirteen civilians on 'Bloody Sunday', and the immunity from prosecution that was believed to have been given to members of the security

1. The Prosecution of Offences (NI) Order 1972 (No. 538), 3(2).
2. Most notably Professor Kevin Boyle, Dr Tom Hadden, and Paddy Hilliard, *Law and the State. The Case of Northern Ireland.* Martin Robertson, London, 1975, p. 126.
3. Technically the Attorney-General confirmed the decision made by the DPP. *Hansard*, written answer, 1 August 1972.

forces who gave evidence at Strasbourg concerning the allegations made in 1971.

The Bernard O'Connor case was one of those which the DPP referred upwards to the Attorney-General. The Attorney-General, Sam Silkin, was in a difficult position, having just given the 'unqualified undertaking' to the European Court at Strasbourg. The DPP had decided not to prosecute,[1] but, as was his practice, did not give any reason for his decision. One can only guess the reasons: it may have been the usual difficulty of identifying individual detectives and proving in court that they were the ones who had ill-treated O'Connor in the way he alleged – although O'Connor was specific in the descriptions and details he gave; it may have been because he refused a full medical examination when he entered and left Castlereagh – an omission which would allow the defence to suggest that O'Connor might have brought the injuries into Castlereagh with him.

Sam Silkin was not happy with the situation. Privately he agreed that there was no real chance of a successful prosecution in such cases, and indirectly implied that O'Connor should seek redress through a civil action where the standard of proof required was less. The Attorney-General appears to have admitted that it was an unsatisfactory state of affairs.

Bernard O'Connor's complaint of Assault During Interview was one of thirty-six lodged in February 1977. In January there had been thirty-three. In March there were thirty-five. O'Connor sued the Chief Constable for civil damages.

Less than a fortnight after the TV programme was shown, eighteen-year-old Constable David Brown of Strabane was shot dead by the Provisional IRA. Constable Brown was the hundredth and youngest member of the RUC to have been killed since 1969. Inevitably those who had most bitterly criticized the BBC's decision to transmit

1. Parliamentary Question to the Attorney-General by Gerry Fitt, 6 February 1979.

the interview with Bernard O'Connor laid his death at the BBC's door. There were others who blamed Castlereagh and not the BBC for his death.

It was only after three years and many interim delays that Bernard O'Connor's civil action for damages against the Chief Constable, Sir Kenneth Newman, finally came to court. In the High Court in Belfast on 30 June 1980, in a reserved judgement lasting two and a quarter hours, Mr Justice Murray awarded O'Connor £5,000 'exemplary' damages and costs. The hearing had lasted twenty-one days. These 'exemplary' damages meant that O'Connor received more than he normally would have done, the usual settlement figure in such cases being around £1,000, because the court wished to underline its disapproval of the RUC's conduct in this instance. Delivering his judgement, Mr Justice Murray cited a previous case in which Lord Devlin had awarded 'exemplary' damages because of 'oppressive, arbitrary or unconstitutional acts by a servant of the Government'.[1]

Referring to O'Connor's arrest and interrogation, Mr Justice Murray said that he was satisfied that the police were absolutely convinced that O'Connor was an IRA wolf, masquerading in the sheep's clothing of a country schoolmaster; but he noted that it was an undesirable state of affairs that one of the detectives who questioned O'Connor, Constable Latimer, was a friend of the murdered Detective Constable Noel Purvis, one of the matters about which O'Connor was being interviewed. He added that he was satisfied, however, that other senior officers were not aware of this. He said that when faced with repeated denials of any involvement in the crimes being investigated, a particularly intense atmosphere built up in the interview room – an atmosphere in which the detectives were sorely tempted to use physical violence to deal with what appeared to be a wrong.

Mr Justice Murray said that O'Connor had grossly
1. *Rookes* v. *Barnard* 1964 AC 1129.

exaggerated certain incidents and invented certain others and had a political motive for so doing which lay in his strongly held Republican and anti-RUC views. (During the hearing the defence had told the court that O'Connor had said at a meeting words to the effect that the only good policeman was a dead policeman.)

Nevertheless, the judge concluded that O'Connor had been physically ill-treated at one interview and by both of the detectives who were then interviewing him. The ill-treatment was not of a sufficiently severe nature to do him any lasting damage, but in addition to some bruising on his ears, face and chest, and tenderness in various parts of his body, it caused him distress and mental disturbance. The ill-treatment, he said, consisted in his being punched and slapped about the head, face and body, being kicked about the legs (but without sufficient force to cause bruising) and being made to stand in a 'stress' position on the toes, knees bent and arms outstretched, for about fifteen minutes.

Further he said that the interview conducted on Saturday, 22 January 1977, which lasted from 10.50 pm to 5.15 am on Sunday morning was unjustified by the state of the investigation. It constituted a breach of the duty of the police as gaolers to take reasonable care of the safety, health and welfare of their prisoner, a duty which is imposed by the common law.[1] He said that this excessively long interview caused O'Connor substantial mental distress and disturbance. He said, however, that he was satisfied that O'Connor had not suffered any brain damage and described the two Danish doctors from Amnesty International who had examined him as 'enthusiastic amateurs'. Nevertheless, Mr Justice Murray said that he was also satisfied that O'Connor was disturbed for up to a period of two years.

His case finally over, O'Connor said he felt that both he and the BBC had been vindicated in what they had done.

But clearly the complaints investigation system had not

1. *Leigh* v. *Gladstone* 26 TLR 139 and *Ellis* v. *Home Office* 1953 2 AER 148 at 159 E.

been vindicated. The Complaints and Discipline Branch had investigated O'Connor's complaint and submitted the papers to the DPP as was the practice. The DPP directed no prosecution. A week after Bernard O'Connor's BBC interview was transmitted, Senior Deputy Chief Constable Baillie said:

The complaints investigation system, operated from Head-quarters as a special unit, is probably the most rigorous in the United Kingdom police service and it is a guarantee to the public that in dealing with the police they have the full protection of their rights.[1]

In the case of Bernard O'Connor, that guarantee looked hollow in the light of Mr Justice Murray's judgement.

The BBC transmitted its interview with Bernard O'Connor on the Wednesday night of a week in which there was already heightened concern about the allegations. The day before the interview was shown, the Complaints Committee had suggested to SDCC Baillie that interviews might be tape-recorded and Flying Squads set up to do spot checks around the province, in order to cut down on the incidence of complaints. The RUC rejected the suggestions on the grounds that such measures 'might impede the police in the legitimate pursuit of their task of obtaining evidence'. The Committee was particularly anxious that something should be done, in view of the latest incident which had happened only the night before. A suspect was alleged to have thrown himself through a window during his interrogation.

On Monday evening, 28 February, Anne McHardy, the *Guardian*'s correspondent in Belfast, was having dinner at the Lisburn home of a colonel in the Green Howards, who was based at Springfield Road RUC station. Over dinner there was a heated argument in which the army officers present 'ganged up' on Ms McHardy, and attacked the

1. RUC press release. Statement by Senior Deputy Chief Constable Mr H. Baillie, 9 March 1977.

press for unfair reporting in Northern Ireland. They said that they were always open, honest, aboveboard, and never told anything but the truth. Moreover, to prove the point, the colonel said that he would allow Ms McHardy to listen to the routine call he was going to make to his duty officer at Springfield Road. The colonel had a loudspeaker system fitted up to his telephone, so that everyone could hear the conversation when he made the call. He asked his duty officer if there was anything happening. The voice at the other end of the line said that there was something happening but they didn't know what it was. He said that a man had been injured, but the police didn't want RUC Headquarters informed just yet. The colonel took the matter no further, shuffled his feet a little, and told his guest that honesty didn't always pay off. He offered Anne McHardy the phone to make any check calls. She phoned the RUC Press Office and asked if anything was happening. They said no. She then rang the army's press desk and received the same answer. The dinner party was then resumed, until about half an hour later she decided to ring the RUC's Press Office once again. This time she was told that there had been an incident at Springfield Road in which someone had been hurt while being questioned and been taken to hospital.

Anne McHardy already had an appointment to see the Chief Constable the following day. She mentioned the incident of the night before. The Chief Constable told her that the man had tried to escape during an interview and had jumped through a window which had been covered by some kind of blackout material. Anne McHardy was allowed to go to Springfield Road to see for herself. She was shown the interview room and the broken window. There had not been any blackout material round the broken window. There was, however, black paper over the window in the room next door, but the window was intact.

These were the facts of the case. Eddie Rooney had been brought to Springfield Road RUC station for interrogation on Monday evening, following a particularly violent weekend across the Province in which a Justice of the Peace had been assassinated, a civilian murdered while celebrating his wedding anniversary and a police sergeant shot in the head at close range. According to the police version of events, Rooney had jumped from an upper-storey window and fallen twenty-five feet on to a car parked in the yard below. He was then taken to the Royal Victoria Hospital, where he lay unconscious for several days with a suspected fracture of the skull. The police said that Rooney had made no complaint about his treatment, and had been acting normally before the incident. In fact it appears that Rooney could not remember a thing. In an official statement the RUC said that Rooney had taken 'two detectives completely by surprise by leaping from his seat and diving through a glass window'. The statement stressed that 'his action in jumping out of the window was deliberate and not caused in any way by the conduct of the police officers'. The police also said that they intended to charge Rooney with an explosives offence.

Eddie Rooney was charged and remanded in custody to await trial. He was given bail, but never returned to stand trial. Eddie Rooney 'got offside' and is now living in the Republic.

What did happen to Eddie Rooney remains a mystery, and one unlikely ever to be satisfactorily solved, owing to the fact that Rooney appears to be unable to recollect what happened because of the head injuries he received when he fell from the window. But whatever the truth of the matter, in the eyes of the Provisionals and their supporters, his case served to add more fuel to the propaganda campaign which was now raging against the RUC – a campaign which had reached a new height following Bernard O'Connor's television interview.

9. Under the Influence of Anger

> 'When there is such a terrorist campaign, it is unfortunately probably inevitable that on occasions a member, or members, of the security forces, acting under the influence of anger and stress, will ill-treat a suspected terrorist.'
>
> HMG Final Submission to the European Court, 20 April 1977

Strasbourg did not impinge directly on most members of the Police Authority, with the exception of Donal Murphy and Jack Hassard, who was reported to be 'eating the carpet with rage' as reports of Strasbourg and reports of the new allegations came in together. But there were civil servants at a high level who watched the proceedings and listened to HMG's assurances with some trepidation. They saw the dangers – as was their job – which the new wave of allegations raised for a government still trying to defend its security forces at an international level from allegations now six years old. A few felt that, in the circumstances, there was now no room for error and the government could not afford even a hint of ill-treatment with Strasbourg looming in the background. Some civil servants warned that the way things were going in the spring of 1977 it was a racing certainty that Amnesty would be over to investigate.

In March 1977, while the British advocates at Strasbourg were trying to convince the seventeen European judges of the human frailties of the security forces, the Police Surgeons back home were growing increasingly worried. The signs that some had noticed towards the end of 1976 were now becoming more obvious. Doctors who examined prisoners after interrogation now noticed 'a significant change in the condition of the people they were being asked to examine at various police centres throughout the province'. The Police Surgeons stated their case in a memorandum from their Association.

Early in 1977 there was a large increase in persons having significant bruising, contusions and abrasions of recent origin especially of the epigastrium and rib-cage areas. There was evidence of hyper-extension and hyper-flexion of joints, especially of the wrist; of tenderness associated with hair-pulling and persistent jabbing. There was evidence of rupture of eardrums and other injuries. At the same time, there was evidence of increased mental agitation and excessive anxiety states.

The memorandum made it clear that the police surgeons were not being misled by Provisional I R A propaganda: they recognized the I R A's vested interest in discrediting the police and their capacity to fabricate stories and self-inflict injuries in order to do so. The Association believed it had two functions: to protect suspects from ill-treatment and to defend the police against unfounded allegations. Nevertheless, it believed that 'a significant amount of ill-treatment of a non-self-inflicted kind occurred in a number of police centres throughout the province'. The Police Surgeons also expressed frustration at the investigation machinery, which they said was 'cumbersome, protracted and obstructive'. They believed it was cumbersome because it was impossible to have a quick but thorough investigation made of cases where ill-treatment was strongly suspected; it was protracted because some cases took over a year to run their course; it was obstructive because they found it impossible to have a semi-official discussion within the system about individual cases until they had been totally and finally completed. The memorandum concluded:

It would be impossible for anyone who has witnessed some of the savageries of the paramilitary organizations in Northern Ireland over the past ten years and the exemplary discipline of both the army and the police not to find his basic sympathy lying wholeheartedly on the side of the forces of law and order. They have carried out a magnificent job in the defence of the decent people of Northern Ireland. At the same time, doctors have to uphold their medical positions as neutrals. That is the role which their profession demands. It is also the role which following the Strasbourg hearings the doctors should carry out to the letter.

The memorandum was intended for the authorities, not the public. Like the Police Authority, the Police Surgeons kept a low profile. As one observer remarked, the Police Surgeons 'backed into the limelight'.

In the first three months of 1977, there was a marked increase in complaints of Assault During Interview. In December 1976, there had been twenty-eight; in January 1977, thirty-three; in February, thirty-six; in March, thirty-five. It was in March that the Police Surgeons first formally expressed their concern to their employer, the Police Authority. The Authority then notified the Chief Constable of the Surgeons' concern, orally, not in writing. In April there was a decrease in complaints of Assault During Interview from thirty-five to twenty-two, the lowest figure of the year, with the exception of December, the month of the Amnesty visit. Dr Irwin was still not happy. His own experience was not limited to what he saw at Townhall Street – he also worked at the Crumlin Road prison, where prisoners were received on remand from all over the province, and he saw the condition in which some of them arrived. Dr Irwin shared the view of most of his colleagues that it was their duty to report their concern to the appropriate authorities and it was then up to them to do something about it. On 14 April 1977, Dr Irwin went a step further and sent a letter to Dr Terence Baird, the Chief Medical Officer at the D H S S. He wrote:

I wish to bring to your attention a matter that is giving great concern to Police Surgeons, namely: an increasing number of detained persons who allege that they have been assaulted by the police while in their custody, and clinical examination confirms the presence of various degrees of injuries, namely bruises and contusions. The number appears to have increased over the past nine months, and is not confined to the Belfast area but comes from various other centres throughout Northern Ireland.

Two aspects of this worry me: first, when a Police Surgeon makes out his Report and summarizes the various injuries observed and sends his Report to the appropriate Police Station for attachment to the prisoner's file, no senior officer has ever seen fit to ring up or see me, or my colleagues about the injuries noted. Second: the second cause for worry is that there is a universal unacceptance of the RUC amongst the people of the ghettoes (such as the New Lodge area in which I work).

When these sort of assaults are made, or alleged to have been made . . . the present set-up will never be accepted and hence peace will be further postponed.

Another main reason for writing to you in this vein is that the Police Surgeons may be called upon at some future date, in some future place, to explain what representations they made about assaults that they have observed – hence this letter.

Police Surgeons condemn terrorism more heartily than the average citizen, because they see it in all its horrors close at hand; but they cannot condone or accept assaults made upon detained persons, as this defeats the justice that we all seek.

Dr Irwin concluded by asking the Chief Medical Officer to bring his views to the attention of those in authority and to inform them that such methods as he had indicated were counter-productive. At this stage, Dr Baird thought it a matter for the RUC, not the DHSS.

In May 1977, events took a dramatic new turn. A new Loyalist coalition led by the Rev. Ian Paisley and backed by Protestant paramilitary groups was threatening to bring the Province to a standstill with a general strike unless the government took tougher action against the Provisional IRA. Dr Paisley and his allies hoped to repeat the successful strike of 1974, when the Ulster Workers Council destroyed the power-sharing executive which it had taken the British government nearly two years to glue together. The strategy failed. Three years on, the climate was different. The 1974 strike had been fuelled by a gut issue – the back-door threat of Irish unity. The 1977 strike was about security. While most Protestants shared Dr Paisley's concern, not all were prepared to heed his call to stop work in support. Furthermore, this time the British government was ready. Whereas in 1974 the dilatory action of government and security forces had persuaded many that it made sense to join the strikers, the situation in 1977 was different. From the beginning Roy Mason made it clear he was standing no nonsense from Ian Paisley. A thousand extra troops were drafted into the province on the eve of the strike to keep the essential services going. But the real difference between 1974 and 1977 was the role of the RUC. In 1974 the police played a secondary role to the army. In 1977 the roles were reversed. The police force that faced the strikers was a very different body in terms of equipment, training and morale from the police who were forced to stand by and watch while the army did nothing in 1974. The strike was the first public test of 'Primacy of the Police' and the RUC passed with flying colours.

Even the more cynical members of the Catholic community were impressed at the way the RUC set about Protestant paramilitary demonstrators in their stronghold of East Belfast. TV pictures of the police taking down Protestant barricades and standing up to the paramilitary leaders outside their Headquarters were dramatic evidence that there was substance to the Chief Constable's claim that the RUC was an impartial force dedicated to uphold the law in the face of all those who sought to break it, whatever their religion. During the ten-day strike, the RUC cleared over 700 road blocks and charged 124 persons, including eleven with murder and attempted murder and thirty-five with intimidation. It was the 'new' RUC's finest hour. All that Kenneth Newman had worked for since he became Chief Constable a year earlier seemed to be reaching fruition. In May 1977 the RUC was as 'acceptable' as it had ever been.

But if Bernard O'Connor was the first turning point, the

strike was the second. There may have been a miscalcula-
tion. In the post-strike euphoria, some may have felt that
because the police had got tough with the Protestants they
could now go after the hard men on the Republican side
with renewed vigour and without too many protests from
the Catholics. In May and June 1977, complaints of Assault
During Interview shot to a record high – fifty-four in May
(more than double those in April) and fifty-two in June.
They were the highest levels in any month during the whole
three-year period.

Paisley's defeat was only temporary. A few weeks later
the measure of support for the message he preached was
evident in the district council elections, where his Democratic Unionist Party (DUP) made unprecedented gains.
The results clearly showed that Ian Paisley may have been
defeated in the strike, but not at the polls. Security was the
theme he hammered. The strike was barely over when Roy
Mason announced a new package of security measures that
included an increase in SAS activity. The government
seemed to be giving the green light to go after the
Provisionals.

But the RUC kept up the pressure on the Protestant
paramilitaries too. Now for the first time Protestants began
to allege ill-treatment at Castlereagh. Although their
members had long been pursued and interrogated by the
RUC – their most successful catch to date had been the
UVF's East Antrim gang – the numbers remained small
compared to the Provisionals, who were, after all, the
source of most of the violence. Hitherto most Loyalist
paramilitaries had refrained from raising the issue of ill-
treatment publicly, lest they appeared to be helping their
enemy by adding their voice to the Provisionals' allegations. They judged it better to suffer in silence as long as
the results were damaging the Provisionals' organization
more than their own.

Whatever the climate of opinion following the strike,
there were other reasons for increasing the pressure on the
Provisionals. The Labour government needed the contin-

ued support of the Ulster Unionist MPs at Westminster, in particular those who had ignored Paisley's strike call and stood by the government. There were political debts to be paid and tougher security was the price. It was Jubilee year, and a royal visit to Northern Ireland was to be the climax of the Queen's tour of her kingdom. Already the Provisionals were making threats: the security forces had to make sure that they were in no position to carry them out. Lastly and most urgently, the Provisionals had promised another long hot summer. Events in June proved that it was no idle threat. On 3 June, three RUC men were shot dead when their unmarked car was ambushed in County Tyrone; on 8 June, a part-time UDR man was murdered as he left the Royal Victoria Hospital in Belfast; on 30 June, two young soldiers were ambushed and killed while travelling in a convoy along the Falls Road. One of them, a young soldier on his first tour of duty, had been in Northern Ireland less than twenty-four hours.

At 6.10 am on Tuesday, 31 May, eighteen-year-old Gerard Murray was arrested at his home in Killclogher, a village a few miles outside Omagh on the road to Cookstown. Murray's family was inevitably under suspicion as his brother had been the victim of what the security forces call an 'own goal': he had been blown up by his own bomb. The Provisional IRA gave him a military funeral.

Omagh High Street had suffered heavily during the campaign. The clock face on the courthouse had got off lightly compared with the shops and businesses it looked down on. Incendiary bombs were just one of the menaces they faced. The small devices, consisting of a watch, a battery and a small amount of explosive packed inside a cassette case, were easily transportable, hard to detect and capable of inflicting thousands of pounds worth of damage on the premises in which they were placed. Incendiary bombs were less spectacular than the car bombs the Provisionals used in earlier years – now more difficult to use anyway, as most town centres, including Omagh's, were sealed off – but capable of producing devastating results.

Gerard Murray was brought to Omagh RUC station by detectives of South Regional Crime Squad. He was subsequently charged with membership of an illegal organization and possession of explosives. His case came to trial a year later, on 5 June 1978, before His Honour Judge McGrath.

In court the defence argued that Murray's statement had been taken in contravention of Section 6. They cited the evidence of the medical reports which showed him entering Omagh Police Station unmarked and in reasonable health, and departing with signs of injury which were consistent with the allegations he made of ill-treatment during his stay in police custody. The court heard that the only sign of injury on initial examination was a previous injury to a finger which the doctor arranged to be X-rayed and treated at the local hospital.

Giving evidence in court, Murray said that during his first interview on Tuesday, 31 May, he was made to stand against a filing cabinet and was slapped and punched. He said he was later taken to another room where he was pulled by the hair, and slapped and punched around the back of the head and neck. He said that one detective sat on a chair and made him lie under it and lift both chair and detective off the ground. Murray said he had only signed statements because he couldn't stand the beatings any more. The court was told that Murray subsequently signed two statements: the first at 8.55 pm on the evening of 31 May, in which he admitted membership of the junior wing of the IRA: the second at 9.40 pm on the same evening, in which he admitted planting fire bombs in Omagh.

Continuing his evidence, Murray said that the beatings continued on the Wednesday, the day after he signed the statements. This time he said he was made to stand against the wall until his sprained finger became like a balloon. The court was told that Murray was examined around 5 o'clock on Wednesday afternoon by Dr Frazier on behalf of the police. Several abnormalities were noted: his scalp was generally swollen and tender; there was a V-shaped red mark at the back of his neck, about five inches long; a small red mark, one and a half inches long, on his shoulder blade; and generalized tenderness of the abdomen. Dr Frazier also noted the swollen finger. But Murray made no complaint of ill-treatment. The court also heard that Murray was examined again at 2.10 pm on Thursday afternoon by the Omagh GP, Dr O'Neill, who found him reluctant to talk or make complaints. In court, Murray said he was reluctant to complain as he feared repercussions if he did. He said he finally did tell Dr O'Neill what had happened to him. The court was told that Dr O'Neill found Murray mentally and physically exhausted. The doctor also recorded tenderness at the back of the neck and signs of early bruising.

In court the police referred to another statement which Murray had made which they said explained some of his injuries. In it Murray had said that he'd felt sick one morning in his cell, got up to vomit, and struck his head on the wall. Murray also said in the statement that when he was being interviewed he kept dozing off and one of the detectives gave him a couple of slight slaps on the head to wake him up. Otherwise he said he was treated very well.

The court also heard evidence concerning the findings of Dr J. D. Watson, Senior Medical Officer at Crumlin Road prison, where Murray was remanded to await trial. Dr Watson found three bruises, yellowish black in colour; one on the shoulder, three inches long; two on the back of the head, one four inches long and the other one and a half inches long. He also noted that the back of Murray's skull was red and tender.

In court the police denied that Murray had been ill-treated and said that the statement he had made to the Station Inspector explained how his injuries had been received. The judge said that this statement was a remarkable document and went on to reject Murray's statements on the grounds that they had been obtained as a result of inhuman and degrading conduct. After nearly a year on remand, Gerard Murray was released.

There were anxieties too in another part of County Tyrone, in particular around the Dungannon–Coalisland–Cookstown triangle, where James Rafferty and Paul Duffy had come from. The unease which many local people had felt over the past six months – by no means all of them supporters of the Provisional IRA – came to a head in June 1977 over the case of a Coalisland man, Peter McGrath. Most of the suspects who were detained and interrogated were young men in their teens and twenties. Peter McGrath was sixty-four.

McGrath was arrested at his home on Monday, 6 June, three days after the killing of three RUC men near Coalisland in an ambush. Other arrests were made around the same time and men were charged with the murders. Peter McGrath was taken to Castlereagh for interrogation. He said nothing. This is what he alleged happened to him.

The detectives were sitting on each side of a table. I was seated. They insulted me immediately. I denied their insults. After a few questions, the door burst open and this fellow burst in and the light was switched off. He hit me a crack with his fist on the top of my head and he lifted me by the lapels of my coat – and another pulled a handful of hair out of my head – this pain helped me to recover from the blow. He held me against the wall in darkness for a few seconds. He let me down on my feet and the light came back on. I could see him standing on the right hand side of me at the corner. I hit him a box on the mouth with my right hand; I got my fingers in his mouth – like the way you drench a calf. The other stood up and took my arm away. He drew up and took a swipe. I ducked, knowing it was coming. I got hit from behind by the third boy and hit the floor.[1]

Peter McGrath was taken to Dungannon RUC station

1. From *The Castlereagh Allegations*, Frs Denis Faul and Raymond Murray.

to face a charge of withholding information about the murder of the three policemen. He was medically examined and sent to hospital. On 16 June the RUC issued a statement saying that Mr McGrath was admitted to hospital not because he was suffering any injury, but because he was unwell: he had made no complaint and had at all times been treated with proper care and consideration. Peter McGrath was admitted to the military wing of Musgrave Park Hospital in Belfast and kept under guard in a hospital bed until he was fit enough to be charged. There he was visited by his solicitor, who found him unmarked but in a stupor. The RUC's statement did little to reassure local people. On Sunday, 19 June, priests in the five churches of the two parishes of Coalisland and Clonoe read a statement condemning the ill-treatment of their parishioners in police custody. They made special reference to the case of Peter McGrath, who was still in hospital. The RUC refused to release him.

On Monday, 20 June, Peter McGrath's solicitor applied for a writ of habeas corpus. The Lord Chief Justice Sir Robert Lowry gave an order directing the Chief Constable to appear before him to show cause why Peter McGrath could not be released. The embarrassment was avoided when the patient was transferred to a psychiatric hospital in Omagh on Monday evening, where he was no longer in police custody. When he recovered, Peter McGrath returned home. No charges were brought. On Tuesday, 21 June, his solicitor announced he intended to sue for illegal arrest, assault and battery. At no stage had the solicitor been allowed access to his client.

There was great anger in the area and demands for action. A decision was made to send a deputation to Belfast to see the Chief Constable and the Secretary of State. The deputation was to make three specific requests in addition to expressing its concern: that families should be told the whereabouts of relatives who had been arrested; that General Practitioners be allowed to visit people in custody at the request of family or solicitor – hitherto a suspect could ask to see his doctor but the request wasn't always granted; and that solicitors be given access to their clients while they were being detained.

On 24 June, the deputation left Coalisland for Belfast. It consisted of Canon McGarvey, the parish priest of Coalisland; Father Coyle, the curate of Clonoe; Westminster MP for Tyrone and Fermanagh, Frank Maguire; solicitor Arthur Byrne from Dungannon; and three local councillors, Patrick McGlinchey, Jack Corr and Jim Canning.

Their first appointment was at Stormont Castle where they met Roy Mason's deputy, Don Concannon. Concannon was another blunt Yorkshireman, but nearly twice Roy Mason's size. It was not a happy meeting. The delegates felt that the Minister was very off-hand and showed little concern or understanding of the anxieties of a few people from Coalisland. They felt he didn't want to hear any criticism of the RUC, as there was a war on. They got the impression, although they admitted he didn't say so in so many words, that he believed a tough situation might require tough methods to bring evil men to justice. They felt the meeting was a waste of time and the Minister had shown little appreciation of their difficulties.

They then made the five-minute journey to RUC Headquarters for their meeting with the Chief Constable. They were already running an hour late and arrived to find the Chief Constable gone. He sent his apologies and explained that he had had to go to another appointment. They were left in the hands of his Deputy, Jack Hermon. The delegates were not unhappy at the prospect of dealing with DCC Hermon. Some even preferred to discuss the matter with him rather than the Chief Constable, whom they felt to be distant and remote from the problems they faced in Coalisland. Some knew Jack Hermon personally from the days in the fifties when he had been a young sergeant in Coalisland. It had been a difficult time with the IRA's border campaign just getting under way.

Jack Hermon had come to Coalisland at a sensitive

moment to replace one of the IRA's victims, Sergeant
Ovens, who had been killed in a booby-trap explosion.
Hermon had been respected by the locals as a strict
disciplinarian and was regarded by some of the delegates
as about as impartial as you could get for an RUC man.
At least they felt he knew their district, was familiar with
its problems, and gave them a sympathetic ear.

The delegates got the impression that Hermon was genuinely concerned. Although he never admitted that suspects
were being ill-treated, he seemed to accept that something
was wrong. He said that the systems designed to prevent
abuse were very tight and that it was more than a policeman's
job was worth to step out of line. The delegates warned him
of the dangers: the Provisionals were the ones who benefited
from the allegations and the local police the ones who suffered. DCC Hermon promised to put their proposals to the
Chief Constable and said he would keep them informed. The
delegates left RUC Headquarters in a better frame of mind
than when they had left Stormont Castle.

The following Sunday, congregations in the five churches
of the parishes of Coalisland and Clonoe heard their priests
assure them that action had been promised.

A month later, Jack Hermon wrote to the delegates. He
said that the Chief Constable had agreed to their first two
requests but not the third: solicitors could not be given
access to their clients. He concluded by thanking the
delegation for 'endeavouring to maintain the good name of
the Royal Ulster Constabulary'. Some senior officers of
the RUC regarded the decision to admit family doctors as
a watershed in the light of what subsequently happened:
they believe that some doctors with Republican sympathies
capitalized on the allegations once they were admitted to
Interrogation Centres.

The delegates from County Tyrone weren't the only
visitors to RUC HQ that week. A few days earlier, a
delegation of senior SDLP politicians had met the Chief
Constable in his office. More than any other political party,
the SDLP had reason to worry about the allegations, as

members of their community were the main victims. As the Catholic community's political representatives, the SDLP had to be seen to be doing something: if it didn't, it risked losing the initiative to the Provisionals. The party had already publicly stated that it believed that ill-treatment was approved at a high level and not the result of individual police malpractice – as the British government had argued at Strasbourg with regard to the 1971 allegations. The composition of the SDLP's delegation reflected province-wide concern: Gerry Fitt and Paddy Devlin from Belfast; John Hume and Michael Canavan from Derry; Austin Currie from County Tyrone; and Seamus Mallon and Frank Feeley from County Armagh. These were the leaders of the community whose support the Chief Constable needed if the RUC was to become an acceptable force. These were the politicians who had been impressed by the way the Chief Constable and his men had handled the Loyalist strike a month earlier.

The Chief Constable told them there was no evidence of ill-treatment and certainly no pattern: there were extensive procedures and safeguards designed to prevent it. Some members grew impatient. They felt they had heard it all before. Now they wanted something done. They told the Chief Constable they had one request: to get it stopped.

The path to Kenneth Newman's office was well-trodden. In mid-June the Chairman of the Police Authority, Sir Myles Humphreys, and the Secretary William Baird, met the Chief Constable to discuss their concern. The following month William Baird visited the Chief Constable again, this time accompanied by Ivor Canavan, the Chairman of the Complaints Committee. Around the same time Canavan and Baird also went to see Roy Mason to tell him at first hand of their growing concern. By the early summer of 1977, both the Chief Constable and Secretary of State knew the depth of public feeling as a result of these series of investigations. Further, by the end of July 1977, the Chief Constable should have been informed of the police surgeons' growing concern. On 27 July 1977 they wrote a letter to their employer, the Police Authority, in which, amongst other things, they reiterated their concern and requested a meeting with the Chief Constable to discuss their anxieties with him. For reasons unclear, the Chief Constable did not receive notification of the police surgeons' request for a meeting until around two months later, at the beginning of October. The letter was sent by the Police Authority to an Assistant Chief Constable, but what happened to it in the intervening period remains uncertain.

The Chief Constable had to do something. On 24 June – the day the delegates from County Tyrone visited Jack Hermon – Kenneth Newman issued a statement which crystallized his position on the issue. It was uncompromising. He said the RUC had predicted some months ago that the propaganda campaign would increase: it was a sign of police success, not police misconduct. He warned that the campaign would be intensified still more; the terrorists were seeking to discredit and destroy the police; the allegations were tying up valuable police officers who should be fighting terrorism, not investigating complaints. He spelled out the additional reasons why the terrorists alleged police brutality: they wanted to get their statements rejected in court and sought to square themselves when they returned to the ranks to face 'kangaroo inquisitions' with regard to the information they had given. He said there was clear evidence that allegations were not only being manufactured but prisoners were going to extreme lengths to self-inflict injuries[1]. Finally he said that the

1. Although serious cases of self-inflicted injuries may have been the exception rather than the rule, there was one notable, well-documented case.

On 23 April 1977, seventy-one-year-old Patrick Devlin was murdered at the Legahory Inn in Craigavon. Albert McCann was detained and questioned at Castlereagh four days later in connection with the murder and made statements admitting his guilt. On 29 April he was examined by a police doctor and alleged that he had been beaten with a stick during his interrogation. The doctor found marks on his body which were consistent with the allegation. On 25 November 1977, McCann was released following the DPP's withdrawal of the charges – presumably

RUC would not be intimidated or deterred from doing its duty and gave a warning:

> People who recklessly engage in purveying serious and unproven allegations against the RUC are playing a dangerous game with policemen's lives. It has already proved fatal for some officers. A heavy responsibility rests on all those who publicly discuss this subject to measure their words and consider the possible consequences.

But concern was also expressed with the RUC's own ranks, albeit with great caution and care. Warnings were given but ignored. Senior police officers who may have questioned the methods were promptly reminded of the results. There was, in the words of one senior officer, 'a lack of sensitivity at the time'. The RUC thought it was winning the battle: only a few officers realized it was losing the war.

---

because of the medical evidence. On 22 December, McCann was detained under the Prevention of Terrorism Act by the Liverpool police. While being questioned, he admitted that during his detention at Castlereagh earlier in the year, he had self-inflicted his injuries with a square-handled lavatory brush when he had gone to the toilet. McCann later argued that he had made the admission under duress after the Liverpool police had burned him with cigarettes. The doctor who examined him did find forty-five burn marks on his body. The Liverpool police said they were self-administered as they had allowed him to smoke in the cell unsupervised.

McCann was returned to Belfast for trial. On 15 June 1978, Lord Justice O'Donnell sentenced him to life imprisonment for murder.

10. A Problem of Success

> 'By any standards it was an eventful and remarkable year in the history of the force. Greater progress than ever before was made in combating terrorist crimes. It was, comparatively, the least violent year since the early 1970s, and side by side with this achievement, a record number of terrorists were brought to justice.'
>
> Kenneth Newman, 1977 Annual Report

The summer of 1977 marked the pinnacle of the RUC's success. In the words of one of its senior officers, 'tails were up, the scent was clear and we were heading for home'. After years of being kicked around and criticized, the RUC had now established itself as the most sophisticated and professional police force in the country. It was almost entirely due to Kenneth Newman. These successes were the result of seeds that had been sown long before. The problem became one of success. Intelligence was so good, a senior officer claimed, that a detective didn't *think* the suspect he was going to interview had committed a crime, he *knew* it. He told me that it reached the stage where terrorists were 'vomiting confessions all over the place' and when detectives were debriefed after interrogating a suspect 'it was like emptying buckets'. Success bred success. Complaints of ill-treatment seemed an irritating distraction. It was only natural that most people not in the know would assume that the Provisionals fabricated the allegations to take off the pressure as the net closed round them. The problem was not to convince people that the allegations weren't true, but to convince them that they were. With the benefit of hindsight, a senior officer remarked that the RUC's senior management at the time was guilty of 'narrow professionalism' in failing to heed the warning signs.

By the summer of 1977, it was Castlereagh that was producing the results. In the preceding winter most complaints of assault and what the Complaints & Discipline Branch referred to as 'Irregularities During Interview'[1] came from places other than Castlereagh.[2] In spring they were about evenly balanced. By summer there were twice as many at Castlereagh as anywhere else.

In the welter of vomited confessions and bucketfuls of intelligence were details of crimes committed months and often years before. Once a suspect started talking, there was no telling where he would stop. RUC jargon called it 'laxity of tongue control'. As Kenneth Newman told the Police Authority, 'the long arm of the law' was reaching far back. The Regional Crime Squads were the arm. In 1977, 1,308 terrorist suspects were charged, almost a thousand of them by members of the four Regional Crime Squads. Again Headquarters Crime Squad, now closely followed by Belfast – whose own HQ was at Castlereagh – had most success. They interviewed 1,106 suspects and charged 354; Belfast Crime Squad interviewed 684 suspects and charged 343; South Regional Crime Squad interviewed 319 and charged 125; North Regional Crime Squad interviewed 241 and charged 117. The Chief Constable remarked:

The picture for 1977 has been one of sustained and expanded effort by Crime Squad personnel and divisional police, resulting in the removal from circulation, through skilful investigation and successful prosecution, of many active and dangerous criminals. Among those charged was a considerable number of prominent and high-ranking members of the Provisional IRA who had been on the run from the beginning of the present terrorist campaign. However, success cannot be measured in mere statistics, nor do they adequately reflect the tremendous effort, patience and

1. This category, IPC (irregularities re persons in custody), included threats, exercises, long stands and statements made under duress.
2. From July 1976 to 7 November 1979, 5,067 suspects were questioned at Castlereagh. Of this number, 1,964 have been charged and 3,103 released. At Gough, a total of 897 persons were interviewed between 28 October 1977 and 31 October 1979. Of this number, 197 were charged and 700 released.

perseverance involved in the detailed investigation of crime and in the painstaking interview of suspects. It is nevertheless rewarding that outrages perpetrated several years ago are still being cleared up and the offenders finally brought to justice.[1]

'Bloody Friday' was one of the incidents to which the long arm of the Crime Squads reached back.

Twenty-two-year-old Daniel Jack was arrested at 6 am on 20 June 1977. He was detained at Castlereagh for four days, and after interrogation was charged with conspiracy to cause an explosion in connection with the 'Bloody Friday' bombings on 21 July 1972. On 'Bloody Friday', eighteen people died, most of them civilians. It was one of the most horrific days in Northern Ireland's ten years of violence. Twenty-two bombs – most of them car bombs – exploded within a mile radius of Belfast city centre. No warnings were given, although the Provisionals subsequently maintained that they were, but not passed on. The worst explosion was in the Oxford Street bus station, where four civilians – two of them youths of fifteen and eighteen – and two soldiers were blown to pieces. On the Cavehill Road, three more civilians died – one of them a boy of fourteen. Television pictures of soldiers picking their way through the debris and dropping bits of human bodies into plastic bags brought home to people on the mainland the horrors behind the daily statistics of violence – horrors to which the people of Northern Ireland were now accustomed and their fellow citizens on the mainland now sadly inured.

The court heard that Daniel Jack had admitted hijacking one of the cars which was subsequently used in the Bloody Friday bombings. He had been seventeen at the time and sickened by what had happened. He told the police that at a meeting following the explosions, someone had said that the whole operation was a fuck-up and should never have happened. Others, he said, laughed and said it would 'toughen the bastards up'. Jack told the police that there was drink on the go but he didn't have any.

1. Chief Constable's Annual Report, 1977.

In court Jack's defence argued that he had signed the statement as a result of the beatings he said he had received at Castlereagh. The court heard the medical evidence which his GP, Dr Joe Hendron, had found and which he believed was consistent with the allegations which Jack had made. Jack had told Dr Hendron he had been assaulted on two of the four days he had spent in custody and been threatened with 'the bully boys' if he didn't sign statements. The court was told that, on examination, Dr Hendron had found three large bruises and concluded that Jack had been ill-treated at Castlereagh. Daniel Jack was given a suspended sentence and released.

In the early summer months the Secretary of the Police Authority and the Secretary of the Police Surgeons had remained in touch. William Baird was anxious to keep abreast of the doctors' mood and did not wish to see them become the 'fall guys', while Dr Irwin was anxious to have the situation brought under control. Dr Irwin reasoned that his members were employed by the Police Authority and it was their duty to take action. William Baird mentioned his discussions with Dr Irwin to Ivor Canavan who, as Chairman of the Complaints Committee, was best placed to discuss the matter with senior RUC officers. Both were astute enough to know that the Police Surgeons were a time-bomb under Castlereagh, and were concerned to avoid an explosion that might have, in the light of Strasbourg, incalculable political repercussions. Their aim was 'to dry the problems up at source'.

Again, the chronology is unclear, as such informal discussions tended to happen on an *ad hoc* basis, but it appears that some time in June the three men met. Dr Irwin showed William Baird and Ivor Canavan the kind of cases that he and his colleagues were now seeing and which were causing them such concern. Dr Irwin stressed that, despite the Chief Constable's assurances, he believed that most of the injuries the Police Surgeons were seeing were not self-inflicted. Where an injury was self-inflicted the prisoner would often say so: his explanation was invariably that he had tried to stop the 'torture' by slashing his wrist with a comb or the plastic knife that came with the food served in the cell. The doctors believed that most self-inflicted injuries, even if prisoners did not admit to them, were often obvious. The police said that the injuries may have been self-inflicted in the van on the journey to Townhall Street: the doctors argued that the kind of bruising they were seeing must have been caused before then as bruises took time to develop and could roughly be dated by their colour.

Informal contacts appear to have been made with the Chief Constable to ask for explanations of the injuries in some of the cases that Dr Irwin mentioned. The approach seems to have produced no information apart from the fact that the cases were now *sub judice*. In other words, they could not be discussed.

Another meeting was sought with Dr Irwin. On 5 July Dr Irwin was getting ready to go off to Portugal on holiday. He was ready for the break. He was due to take the shuttle to Heathrow, pick up relations and catch a plane from Gatwick to Faro. His schedule was very tight. The phone rang. William Baird asked if he could come to River House urgently that evening to go over the problem again with himself and Ivor Canavan. Irwin said it was impossible as he had to catch the 6.30 shuttle. Baird stressed the urgency of the meeting and offered to run him up to the airport afterwards. Dr Irwin agreed.

The three men discussed again the cases that Dr Irwin had brought to their attention and the fact that they had received little joy from the Chief Constable. Baird and Canavan told Irwin that they shared his concern and planned to write to the Chief Constable officially as their previous informal approaches had not got them very far.

But the Police Authority was alerted not only by the representations they had received from the doctors, but by a series of judgements in the courts that followed one another in a matter of weeks: all had arisen out of incidents of alleged ill-treatment at Castlereagh the previous year. The Authority asked for copies of the judgements to study the small print. The cases included that of Michael McNaught from Derry, whose statement was rejected by Lord Justice McGonigal, using 'judicial discretion', on 19 May; the case of Terry Magill, whose statements were rejected by His Honour Judge McGrath on 15 June, on grounds of inhuman and degrading treatment; and the case of Francis Bannon, whose statement obtained following interrogation at Castlereagh in February 1976 was rejected by Lord Justice Jones on 17 June 1977. In his judgement Lord Justice Jones said:

The police conduct, and consequential injuries, as alleged by Bannon did not in my view constitute torture or inhuman conduct. In my opinion, to subject a person under interrogation to slapping, poking or punching, hair pulling in the context here alleged, or to make him stand and hold his arms out or to knock his forehead against the wall, is to subject him, in the context of this case as described by the accused, to degrading treatment.

There was growing concern too at a high level of the judiciary, although it was only expressed in the most guarded terms. I was not discouraged by the judiciary during my own early inquiries in 1977. At one clandestine meeting my colleague Alan Stewart and I held with a judge, he expressed distaste at some of the methods he believed were being used to extract statements from suspects and had no doubt that there was ill-treatment. He reminded us that judges were impartial but essentially were on the side of law and order. It was the hypocrisy of the system that annoyed him. He had no time for terrorists and no illusions about their ruthlessness or their ability to fabricate allegations. But he said that if the authorities wanted to run things like this, they would have to change the law. What angered him most was that because innocence or guilt was not a relevant consideration in assessing the admissibility of a statement, there was a danger that guilty men might sometimes go free.

These were concerns shared by many members of the Bar, but only expressed in private. One senior Q C said it was a choice between law or order: most people preferred order; he preferred law. Barristers fought to stay on top in an unequal struggle. The pressures on the judicial system were intolerable. Justice had a deadline. Some Q Cs found themselves reading a brief on a murder case for the first time the night before they went into court. There simply weren't enough criminal lawyers to go round.

Some suspects, however, who appeared before the Diplock courts had greater resources to draw on than others. Two S A S men were acquitted for the murder of John Boyle, a young Catholic who had informed the R U C about an arms cache in a graveyard and then been shot by the S A S when he returned to see if the arms were still there. The defence case was meticulously prepared, even to the extent of video-taping a reconstruction of the shooting in the graveyard in the early hours of the morning – the time the incident had happened.

August was a triumph for the Chief Constable and the Secretary of State. The defeat of the Loyalist strike in May had been the reorganized R U C's first public success: the Queen's visit in August was its second. Her Majesty's visit to one of her oldest and most troublesome provinces – Queen Elizabeth I had trouble with Irish guerillas too – gave the beleaguered Protestants a tremendous boost: to them it was confirmation that Northern Ireland was and would remain part of the United Kingdom, despite the continued efforts of the Provisional I R A to destroy the constitutional relationship. Many Catholics, however, regarded the Queen as head of state of a foreign power whose political presence in the North of Ireland they did not recognize. Inevitably there was tension. 30,000 members of the security forces made sure that the Queen emerged unscathed. There was only one narrow escape: a small bomb was discovered at the University of Coleraine just after she had left.

The continuing violence scarcely scratched the surface of the visit. There was rioting on a scale not seen for several years. A British soldier, Pte Lewis Harrison, was shot dead, allegedly in retaliation for the army's shooting of a young suspected petrol bomber a few hundred yards down the road. But the Queen walked in a different world. When she knighted Sir Myles Humphreys, Chairman of the Police Authority and Lord Mayor of Belfast, the Provisional IRA were setting up a roadblock in Ballymurphy to show the world that Her Majesty's control of her province was only nominal.

At the time there was a huge slogan daubed on the wall that runs along the Falls Road – 'Stone Mason will not break us'. It was more wishful thinking than fact. The British had won the latest round of the propaganda war hands down and the world's press had been there to record it. The Provisionals had promised the Queen a visit to remember. The threat proved empty. Castlereagh's gradual erosion of the Provisionals' ranks helped Roy Mason call their bluff.

Many of those detained for questioning were teenagers suspected of being on the fringes of paramilitary organizations. There were several advantages in bringing them in for interrogation: they were generally frightened and likely to tell a lot; although often not deeply involved, they could name names and give information as to which Unit had carried out which operation. Once inside Castlereagh, new Provisional IRA recruits were not likely to get beyond the Fianna. (Fianna Eireann is the junior IRA.)

Pearse Kerr was a student at the local technical college, training to be an electrical engineer. He was seventeen when, on 18 August 1977, he was taken to Castlereagh for interrogation. This is what he told his solicitor:

On the 18 August 1977 at 5.00 am, the RUC came to my house. I was arrested and taken to Castlereagh Police Office. I was put into a cell until 10.00 am. I was given sausages, eggs and soda bread to eat. At 10.00 am I was taken to the interview room. There were three detectives present.

No. 1 was about six foot, light gingerish hair, medium build, wearing blue and white cheese cloth shirt. I subsequently ripped one of the sleeves off.

No. 2 was about five foot eleven inches, well built, dark hair – short back and sides, green sports jacket, shirt and tie, checked trousers (perhaps).

No. 3 was about six foot, brown and beige tweed suit, black hair – short back and sides (side parted), brown shoes, shirt and tie.

Interview No. 1: 10.00 am–12.30 pm
When I arrived in the interview room, I was told to take my shoes off. I cannot remember who told me. I complied with their request. One of them said, 'I will give you five minutes to think over whether to confess'. I said that I did not want to say anything. I asked for a solicitor. Two minutes later No. 2 came up to me and asked me whether I was going to talk. I said 'No'. He slapped me across the face. He said that he could give me worse treatment than this if I did not talk. I decided to say nothing. One of them said 'You think you are tough', I said 'No'. No. 3 said 'You are some O/C, look at the shape of him'. No. 3 said to the others, 'Let me at him I'll make him talk'. I still refused to talk. No. 1 faced me and grabbed me by the throat. No. 2 held my arms down. This treatment was continued for 3–4 minutes. I was nearly unconscious. I managed to break away. My vision was clouded. I stumbled over to the table. It seemed that their voices were distant (blurred). No. 3 left. The choking treatment was continued after an interval. I was punched in the stomach (cannot remember who it was). I was choked twice after this. No. 2 started to bend my right hand back. No. 1 started to bend my left hand back. I was down on my knees at this stage. I noticed that my left hand was swollen. I broke loose and ripped No. 1's shirt at the sleeve (left sleeve). I was sat down. No. 1 started to massage my wrist and told me that it was only fluid. I was strangled once more. Returned to the cell. There were about three or four interviews.

Interview No. 2: 2.00 pm–3.00 pm
No. 1 and No. 2 came in. I was shown statements. Implicated me in
the IRA membership (O/C and Recruiting officer). I saw that my
friends were named in the statement. An Inspector came in and left
and returned. He asked me if I wanted to see a doctor to examine
my wrist. I replied 'No'. I wrote out a statement. I made the
statement because I was afraid of further ill-treatment. In the
statement, I stated that I was a member of the Junior IRA and that
I had joined one month ago. No ill-treatment. Returned to cell.

In his first statement, Kerr admitted that he had been a
member of the Fianna and gave details of five bombings of
business premises which he had planned. He said that he
agreed with the aims of the Republican movement but
didn't agree with what he had to do; as a member of the
junior Provisional IRA, he said he had to do as he was
told.

After making that statement Pearse Kerr was interviewed
again. This is what he told his solicitor:

Interview No. 3: 4.00 pm–6.00 pm
Accused of being a link man between the Provisional IRA and
Junior IRA. I declined to comment. No ill-treatment and no
statements. Returned to cell to 'think about it'.

Interview No. 4: 9.00 pm–10.30 pm
No ill-treatment.
Inspector interviewed me alone. Detectives were walking in
and out. I could hear men getting their heads banged against
walls. I heard screaming. No. 3 entered and said 'You did not
tell us about the gun'. I denied it. He said 'It may have been
a plastic gun'. I described it to him as a black plastic one with
a brown handle. I made a statement to the effect that a fellow
came to me with the imitation firearm and told me to give it
to two fellows who were to petrol bomb a golf club at Oldpark
Terrace. In the statements, I said that I asked the two men to
make sure that no one was inside when they did the petrol
bombing and to make them produce the gun if challenged.
However if they were challenged by the security forces, they

should drop the gun and surrender. The job was carried out that night.

In the second statement Kerr said that he had hidden the toy gun and told petrol bombers where they could find it to frighten anybody who tried to approach them while they were engaged on their mission. He said he had told the men that they were to make sure that there was nobody inside the premises at the time. He added that the attack was never carried out because there were people inside the building at the time.

Kerr alleged that he had had his wrist hyperflexed on the first day of his interrogation. He told his doctor that one detective had held him by the elbow with one hand and extended his hand backwards with the other. That evening Kerr asked to see a doctor. When the medical officer examined him, he sent him to the Ulster Hospital, Dundonald, to have his wrist X-rayed.

Kerr was examined by the casualty officer in the Accident & Emergency Unit. Dr Steele noted that his left wrist was swollen but there was no bruising or obvious deformity. The wrist was X-rayed: there was a suspected fracture.[1] A short-arm plaster of paris cast was applied and Kerr was referred to the fracture clinic the following day for reassessment and treatment.

Pearse Kerr was one of the cases that caused the Police Authority concern, not least because he was found to be an American citizen and representations had already been made to the US consul in Belfast. The Authority made its own inquiries to try to establish what had happened to Kerr. William Baird wrote to SDCC Baillie. They discovered that when Kerr had been admitted to Crumlin Road with his arm in plaster of paris, the prison Medical Officer had tried to find out from the police how the injury had

1. The medical report said: 'Minimal widening of the dorsal aspect of the epiphysical line highly suggestive of minimal separation.'

occurred. The Authority's confidential report on the case said that the doctor's inquiries addressed to the police

failed to establish how the injuries had been received and there was no medical report as to the man's physical condition on leaving Castlereagh Police Office.

On 2 September, the Police Authority asked the RUC to arrange 'an early and detailed examination of Kerr's allegations'.

However, when I interviewed the Chief Constable on ITV's 'This Week' programme on 27 October 1977, in which I referred to Kerr's case, although not by name, the Chief Constable said:

There is mention of the case where a prisoner was said to have had a broken wrist. This is not so. The medical evidence in our possession shows that that man's wrist was not broken. Furthermore, medical evidence in my possession puts forward the opinion that that injury was probably not sustained while the man was in custody at Castlereagh.

At the Authority meeting on 14 February 1978 individual cases, including that of Pearse Kerr, were discussed. Donal Murphy asked the Chief Constable for access to Pearse Kerr's file. The Chief Constable told the meeting that Home Office advice in Great Britain seemed to him to imply that Police Authorities should not interest themselves in particular cases. He believed that the same principles should apply to Northern Ireland: to do otherwise 'could affect the morale of the Force'. The Authority was told that the RUC's investigation of Pearse Kerr's case was complete and the papers had gone to the DPP. Donal Murphy asked to see the doctors' reports. He was told that they were privileged discussions between doctor and patient. Murphy then pointed out that it was the Police Authority who paid the doctors to carry out the examinations.

The Authority never did find out about Pearse Kerr. In November 1977 the DPP withdrew the charges against him and Kerr was released, presumably because of the medical evidence. Some suspected that political pressure from America might also have played its part. On 25 January 1979, the DPP announced that he was not prosecuting any of the detectives who had interviewed Kerr. Pearse Kerr returned to America to await the result of his civil action for damages against the Chief Constable.

By the summer of 1977, the Provisionals were in a desperate position. Castlereagh was beginning to destroy their organization. They had to reorganize to survive. Ever since its creation sixty years earlier, the IRA had adopted the structures of its enemy, the British army. As a secret British army document admitted,[1] the Provisionals prided themselves on being an 'army', with what they regarded as a military code of ethics: they were not 'mindless hooligans drawn from the unemployed and unemployable'. The Irish Republican Army had a GHQ, brigades, battalions and companies. Orders were passed up and down the command structure as they were in the British army. Volunteers in one company knew volunteers in another. They knew the names of their comrades, the names of their officers and often the names of the brigade staff. The problem was that volunteers knew too much. The organization was vulnerable to infiltration and provided ready fodder for Castlereagh.

To halt the dangerous slide, the Provisional leadership decided to change the structure of its operational units – the ASUs. But this reorganization was not only an admission of Castlereagh's success, but a recognition of its own long-term strategy – to dig in for a war of attrition to drive the British out of the North of Ireland, as the Vietcong had driven the Americans out of Vietnam. The ASUs were reorganized into cells. A volunteer would know the identity of the three or four members of his cell, but his knowledge would end there. At best, Castlereagh

1. 'Future Terrorist Trends', December 1978.

could destroy a cell, but not a whole battalion. It made infiltration more difficult too. If information was leaked, it was easier for the leadership to identify the source. Moles had less room to move in.

However, in the eyes of some police officers, the RUC made a fatal mistake when it had the Provisionals on the run. They believed the mistake was to grant GPs access to suspects at the request of persons other than the suspect himself. It had been a concession the Chief Constable had granted as a result of the representations made by the delegation from County Tyrone the previous June. The watershed decision caused a degree of anger and resentment at certain levels of the RUC. As long as medical examinations were carried out by resident Medical Officers at Castlereagh, then by Police Surgeons at Townhall Street, and finally by DHSS Medical Officers at Crumlin Road, there was a reasonable chance that no alarm bells would ring. Telephones might be lifted and letters discreetly written, but the public would remain largely ignorant of the concern of the medical profession. Some detectives loathed 'Republican' doctors as they loathed 'Republican' solicitors: to them the word 'Republican' meant any person who did not actively support the police, especially when his practice or home might be on the Falls Road, where some of his clients might be Republicans of the more active kind. Some detectives believed that by admitting such 'Republican' doctors to Castlereagh, the Chief Constable was opening the door to the enemy, and handing them the weapons to destroy it. Certainly the RUC were aware of the 'official' doctors' concern as they had access to all their medical reports, but they knew they were discreet and would want to handle matters internally when the occasion arose. They were, after all, employees of the state. The crunch came when the 'official' doctors decided there was a conflict between their professional duties and their professional ethics.

When Dr Irwin returned from his holidays he found the situation had got worse not better. The representa-

207 A Problem of Success

tions which he and his colleagues had made to the proper authorities appeared to have been forgotten or ignored.

The Police Authority were becoming increasingly worried, too, not only at the volume of complaints, but at their apparent inability to do anything about them. The medical evidence was accumulating: in many cases the reports of three different doctors would confirm the same findings.

As summer turned to autumn, Castlereagh remained the focus of attention. In August there were thirty complaints at Castlereagh, compared with thirteen elsewhere: in September, thirty-seven compared to eight; and in October, twenty-nine compared to ten. In that three-month period complaints of assault during interview totalled 115.

In the face of such numbers, it was no use the Police Authority talking in generalities. A decision was made to concentrate on a small number of specific cases which had given the doctors particular concern and take them up with the RUC. As it happened, a case for each month was examined. Pearse Kerr had been the case chosen for August. John Fusco was the case chosen for September. In Fusco's case there was medical evidence from three different doctors. Dr Irwin said that Fusco's case was one of the worst he had seen.

John Fusco was a twenty-three-year-old unemployed labourer who lived off the Falls Road in Belfast. His background was typical of many in the area. The family was poor, there were no jobs, and the children were often in trouble. Fusco had, like most youths in the district, been interned. According to the neighbours, the Fusco house, like many over the years, had been searched and 'wrecked' by the army. Fortunately, they said, John was a handyman and could fix up the damage himself. Fusco was married to a girl much older than himself called Greta. They had four children to support, two of them Fusco's own, the other two Greta already had when they were married. John Fusco had been in trouble before. He had served fifty-one days in a training school for an armed robbery he had been involved in, six years earlier. Greta was said to be a difficult girl and suffered from a nervous disorder. She was described as the kind of woman who would hurl abuse at British soldiers and then be charged with disorderly behaviour. In the area where the Fuscos lived, Greta Fusco was in good company. She was also friendly with the wife of Gerard Kelly, one of the Old Bailey bombers. With those kind of credentials, John Fusco was a natural candidate for Castlereagh.

He was arrested at his home by the army at 6.30 am on 3 September 1977. The soldiers searched his house and said they had found ammunition hidden under the floorboards in the bathroom. Fusco was taken to the Henry Taggart Memorial Hall, which was used as the army post, at the top of his road. He was then transferred to Springfield Road to be photographed, and then to Castlereagh to be interrogated. He was examined by the Medical Officer and found to be in good physical condition.

Around noon on Saturday, 3 September, Fusco had his first interview. He said two detectives asked him about the bullets which the army had allegedly found under the floorboards in his bathroom that morning. Fusco denied all knowledge of them and said that the soldiers must have planted them there, as he was not with them when the bullets were found. He also said he would have been stupid to have left anything in the house after a rocket attack on the army which had occurred a few days earlier near his house. Fusco then alleged that he was beaten around the stomach, body and face. He said that two more detectives entered the room and joined in. He was held on the ground, and a detective stood on both his legs; he alleged his left arm was held and his wrist was bent back. He said he was pulled by the hair, punched in the face, grabbed by the throat and throttled. During the alleged beating, he said that his nose started bleeding and a detective went off to get a cloth and towel to wipe his face. Fusco alleged that he was then kneed in the stomach and brought back to his cell.

He asked to see a doctor. He was examined by the same Medical Officer who had seen him when he had come in to Castlereagh earlier the same day. Fusco complained to him about pain in his ear. The doctor sent him off to the Royal Victoria Hospital for an examination. He was seen in casualty, given no treatment, but told to return for further tests. Fusco complained to the doctor at Castlereagh about the beatings he alleged he had received.

At Townhall Street he was charged with possession of ammunition. He was examined late on Saturday night by Dr Irwin, and Dr Maguire on behalf of his own GP. He gave them both an account of what he said had happened to him at Castlereagh. In particular he told Dr Irwin that while he had been held on the floor, his head had been banged and that he had been repeatedly hit on the right ear.

He noted on examination multiple bruising and an injury to the tympanic membrane (eardrum) of Fusco's ear inside which blood was appearing. Dr Irwin was unequivocal in his conclusion:

> The opinion I formed of this man was that he had received a severe beating, and that the injuries indicated could not have been self-inflicted, but had been received while in police custody.

Dr Maguire's findings were similar. He said that at the time there were blood stains on Fusco's trousers and T-shirt. There were areas of widespread bruising. But he said that the most serious injury was to the left ear: blood could be seen on the eardrum, which indicated that it had been damaged. There was also blood in the left nostril.

Fusco was charged and admitted to Crumlin Road prison on remand. On Monday he was examined by the prison Medical Officers. By then the bruising was well developed. They too recorded the injuries on the appropriate chart.

On 16 September the Police Authority sent a copy of Fusco's medical report to SDCC Harry Baillie. They asked, on behalf of the doctor:

that the origin of the injuries should be sought and established: it was in the interests of the RUC and the Police Surgeons, that any seemingly untoward incidents should be probed and examined.

In his reply, SDCC Baillie said that Fusco had made an official complaint, an Investigating Officer had been appointed, and the direction of the DPP would be made known in due course.

John Fusco's case never came to court. The DPP withdrew the charges. Again, the Director never stated a reason. He did have Fusco's medical reports.

Fusco was released. But it was not to be his last experience of Castlereagh.

The third case the Police Authority examined in detail and took up with the RUC was the case of Charles Morgan, an eighteen-year-old unemployed painter from the Falls Road interrogated in October 1977.

Morgan was one of half a dozen persons arrested in connection with the murder of two British soldiers, Ptes Turnbull and Harrison, on 29 June 1977. It had been a carefully planned ambush. The Provisionals took over a council house in the Divis Flats area, at the bottom end of the Falls Road. The house gave a clear view of the Falls Road and the street that turned off it to the army post in North Howard Street.

At 6.20 pm an army Landrover and a four-ton Bedford truck with eight soldiers from the 3rd Battalion Light Infantry in the back turned the corner into North Howard Street. Several high-velocity shots were fired from the landing window of the council house across the road. Two soldiers sitting in the back were hit in the head and neck. One cried out his blood group before he screamed and fell on the floor. The other was killed instantly. The bullet left

a hole the size of a fist in the back of his head. The army
chaplain, travelling in the Landrover at the front of the
convoy, was hit in the back and wounded. The soldiers
fired six shots at the window, but the gunman had gone.

Charles Morgan was arrested two months later at his
sister's house in the Divis Flats. He was taken to Springfield
Road RUC station, where he alleged a detective pulled
his hair and hit him in the back with a baton. He alleged
that one detective said, 'Tell us all we want to know, and
we will call the dogs off. I can arrange to see you in
Castlereagh. Everything you've heard about it is true.'
Morgan said he knew nothing.

He was taken to Castlereagh about the middle of
Monday morning. Dr Page, the Medical Officer, asked him
if he wanted to be examined. Morgan said no. Dr Page
asked him if he wished to make any complaints. Again
Morgan said no. He was interrogated by detectives from
the Belfast Regional Crime Squad who had been investigating the murder of Ptes Turnbull and Harrison. He was
asked what he knew about the ambush. He said he didn't
know anything. During the course of his interviews,
Morgan alleged that he was hit on the head and slapped
about the face; bent backwards over a chair and rocked up
and down and from side to side, which hurt his back; pulled
by the hair and dragged around the floor. He said the
detectives wanted to know the identity of the sniper. He
said he knew nothing. In the end Morgan said he agreed to
sign statements because he was frightened and exhausted.
He kept insisting he knew nothing: the detectives told him
that he was a liar, because the others had told them
everything, including the part that he had played in the
ambush.

Morgan, who couldn't read or write, signed several
statements. In one he admitted keeping 'dick' (look-out)
for a bomb attack that injured a soldier; in another he
admitted joining the Provisionals – D Company of the 2nd
Battalion – and going to a few lectures where the instructor
never turned up. He then allegedly admitted his part in the

ambush of the army convoy. He said that he had entered
the house which had been chosen for the 'snipe' and told
the family that it was being taken over on behalf of the
Provisional IRA. He said a girl had brought in two
Armalites, the sniper had followed, fired at the convoy and
disappeared. He himself then ran off home. Morgan made
the statements during the evening of his first day at
Castlereagh.

On Tuesday afternoon he was offered a final medical
examination by Dr Page at 2.30 pm. Morgan signed the
medical form 38/17(b), and stated that he did not wish to
be medically examined, but was alleging assault. Morgan
later said that he still had two days to go and he didn't
want to complain as he was frightened of what might
happen to him. Dr Page made a note that Morgan 'stated
he was "banged against the wall a few times" ' and that he
was 'told of offer of examination at Townhall Street'.

At Townhall Street Morgan was examined by Dr
McAviney, one of Dr Irwin's Police Surgeon colleagues,
and his own GP, Dr Sloan. Now for the first time he made
detailed allegations. Dr McAviney found abrasions on both
arms, most of them about three inches long, and small
areas of light blue bruising on the lower back. Dr Sloan
found him 'nervous and agitated'. He recorded the linear
abrasions on the arms and also three abrasions on the lower
back above each hip bone. He said that Morgan was also
tender to the touch at the back of the neck, on parts of his
scalp and at the bottom of his back. He also complained of
pain when pressure was applied to the lower part of his
front rib cage.

When he was charged at Townhall Street, Morgan
pleaded not guilty. He was examined at Crumlin Road
prison by Dr Brennan, who noted his injuries and said they
would appear to 'have occurred about the time alleged'.
Morgan was then taken to the prison hospital, where he
was examined by Dr Irwin, who took photographs of his
injuries. He dressed the raw bleeding areas which were
still exposed. But Dr Irwin was uncertain about the injuries:

he admitted they were difficult to explain and could have been self-inflicted with a brush, a nail file or any other hard instrument; on the other hand, he said they could have been caused by being pulled along a rough carpet, as Morgan had described, especially if, as Morgan alleged, a foot was being pressed on the arm as he was being dragged along. Nevertheless, Dr Irwin said that the injuries to the back would have been very difficult to self-inflict.

The Police Authority attempted to follow up the case. On 7 October 1977 a copy of Morgan's medical report was sent to SDCC Baillie who was informed that:

> The doctor is prepared to accept that the injuries (except those to the prisoner's back) may have been self-administered, but he is anxious that the cause of each of the wounds reported should be confirmed.

No confirmation appears to have been given. The police told the Authority that the allegations had been recorded as a complaint, and an Investigating Officer had been appointed. The case was under investigation.

After twenty-one months on remand in the H Blocks of the Maze prison, Charles Morgan's case came to court. Morgan was one of five men and a woman charged with the murder of the two soldiers. It was a marathon case. The trial started on 16 May 1979 and lasted over a month. One man was found guilty of the murder – not for pulling the trigger, but for organizing the operation – and was given a life sentence by Mr Justice Kelly.

The doctors gave evidence in court. Dr Irwin was asked if he thought Morgan's injuries were self-inflicted. He said they displayed 'a typical pattern of self-infliction', but added there were also a couple of injuries that could have occurred in the manner Morgan alleged. On 21 June the case against Morgan was dismissed on the grounds of inhuman and degrading treatment, but he was returned to custody, pending the hearing of the other charges against him which did not relate to the murder of the two soldiers. Shortly afterwards, the DPP withdrew the additional charges. Charles Morgan was released. He had spent nearly two years in prison on remand.

In October the public heard for the first time that the Police Surgeons were worried. Word slipped out when Dr Joe Hendron, the Falls Road GP and SDLP politician who had already expressed his concern in person to the Chief Constable, said publicly on television that the Police Surgeons had made a request to see Kenneth Newman and had received no answer. In a public reply, the Chief Constable said that he had not received any communication from the Police Surgeons.

Dr Irwin and his colleagues were furious. It had been six months since they had first expressed their concern, two months since they had sent their letter of 27 July to the Police Authority requesting a meeting with the Chief Constable. They decided that they had kept their head down long enough and had got no thanks for doing so. A small group held an emergency meeting at the country home of their Chairman, Dr John Stewart, and decided to issue a statement to the press, saying that they *had* asked for a meeting and had been refused. While they were drafting the statement the telephone rang. Dr Irwin was asked to pick up the extension. William Meharg, ACC (Crime), was on the line from RUC Headquarters. He said that the Chief Constable had heard there was going to be a statement, and was inviting the doctors to issue it through the RUC Press Office. Dr Irwin said they would issue it themselves: they were their own masters and not under anybody's control. ACC Meharg pointed out that the Chief Constable was concerned as to what the statement was going to say. Dr Irwin said that that was too bad: if he would care to ring back later, he would read the statement over the phone.

About 10.30 pm the phone rang again. The final statement was read down the line to ACC Meharg. The statement said that the doctors had requested a meeting with the Chief Constable and had, as yet, not had a reply:

they were seeking a meeting with him early the following week. A couple of minutes later, the phone rang again. The Police Surgeons were told that the Chief Constable would like the doctors to omit the section which mentioned their communication and the fact that they had had no reply. Dr Irwin, who suspected that Kenneth Newman was sitting in the same room as ACC Meharg, said they would not.

On 11 October, the Police Surgeons had their long-awaited meeting with the Chief Constable at RUC Head-quarters. Dr Stewart and Dr Irwin were shown into the Chief Constable's office. There was a TV monitor in the corner that read 'All Quiet – 11.05'. The Chief Constable was standing in the middle of the room, neatly dressed in a lounge suit, and behind him, also in a suit, the much larger figure of SDCC Harry Baillie. Kenneth Newman was holding a letter in his hand. He greeted his visitors and apologized. He explained that there had been a 'hiatus' in his department, and that he had only just received the letter. The doctors were not impressed by the explanation.

Dr Irwin, who had waited a long time for the meeting and had seen many cases that distressed him while he was waiting, didn't mince his words. He said that the 'hiatus' could have resulted in the death of one of his members, once the Chief Constable had said publicly that he had received no communication from the Association. The Police Surgeons were not in the pockets of any organiza-tion, neither the RUC nor the paramilitaries. Its members were doctors who carried out their job independently and they gave their opinions without fear or favour.

The Chief Constable was apparently courteous, cold and factual. He said that he believed in justice, and would severely punish any police officer who transgressed the law; his detectives had a difficult job and were in danger twenty-four hours a day. The doctors told the Chief Constable that they were seeing injuries and no explanation was being given for them. The Chief Constable asked for details and said he would investigate: if they saw any cases in the future, they were to ring him or SDCC Baillie direct and action would be taken. He admitted that there had been a lack of communication and suggested that a liaison committee should be set up to iron out any problems. The Chief Constable thanked the doctors for their help in the past, and hoped that it would continue in the future.

Dr Irwin was not impressed. He felt he had heard most of it before. On 20 October, the Police Surgeons met the Chief Constable again. It was formally agreed to set up a liaison committee. Its function was:

> To provide a direct line of communication with Police Headquarters to avoid delay and remove frustrations. Problems identified could be pursued more directly and effectively.

The Committee's full title was: Senior Medical Officers & Forensic Medical Officers Liaison Committee. It consisted of the Medical Officers who worked at Castlereagh and the new Interrogation Centre at Gough Barracks, Armagh, the Police Surgeons, the RUC and the officers – not the members – of the Police Authority. Its Chairman was to be DCC Jack Hermon. The Chief Constable was to be given a report of the discussions and decisions reached at each meeting. It became known as the Hermon Committee. The RUC insisted that the Hermon Committee had no executive power.

11. Overstepping the Mark

> 'There is no policy or toleration of ill-treatment in this Force.'
>
> Kenneth Newman, Thames TV 'This Week', 27 October 1977

During the week that the Police Surgeons met the Chief Constable and the ground was being laid for the Hermon Committee, twenty-five-year-old Thomas McKearney from Moy in County Tyrone was being interrogated at Castlereagh – significantly not at Omagh RUC station, whose function as an Interrogation Centre had long ago been superseded by Castlereagh. The pressure had been on the area since the Provisionals had murdered twenty-four-year-old Margaret Hearst, a part-time member of the UDR, on 8 October 1977 in her caravan in the presence of her three-year-old child. It was a particularly horrific killing that had shocked the province. Four days later a County Tyrone school bus driver was shot dead. The killing was believed to be a mistake: the ambush was intended for the UDR man who normally drove the bus.

McKearney said he was arrested by the army at his home at 3 am on Tuesday, 18 October. He was taken to nearby Dungannon RUC station, where he was given a medical examination. He was then transferred to Castlereagh and was interrogated for seven days.

When Dr Irwin saw him at Townhall Street a week later, he was pale, nervous and exhausted. He had a black eye that looked fairly recent and bruises whose colour suggested they were five to six days old. His forehead was swollen and many of the muscles at the back of his neck, forearm and abdomen were swollen and tender. His fingers were trembling.

At the beginning of his examination, McKearney was reluctant to complain or say anything about his interviews. It was only after Dr Irwin had questioned him about his injuries that he was prepared to admit that he had been assaulted. He alleged that he had been beaten during interviews on the previous Thursday – the day the Police Surgeons had met the Chief Constable for the second time to finalize the Hermon Committee. McKearney alleged that he had been held by the elbow while his wrist was bent; that he had been punched in the stomach, slapped around the face and grabbed around the throat until he nearly passed out; and that his fingers were also bent. The following day, Friday, 21 October, he alleged he was beaten again. He was made to remain in a crouch position for long periods. On Monday, 24 October, he said the beatings started again. (That was the day the Police Authority's Policy Coordinating Committee also went to see the Chief Constable and informed him of growing community concern about police interrogation methods.) McKearney alleged that his head and trunk were covered with a black plastic sack, the type used for laundry and refuse collection. He said that he was beaten around the head while the bag was pulled tight around his throat. He managed to tear a hole in the bag so he could breathe.

When he examined McKearney, Dr Irwin was angry. The prisoner had come from Castlereagh, pale and trembling, with a black eye, bruising and abrasions and no note from the Medical Officer at Castlereagh to explain how the injuries had been received. McKearney told Dr Irwin that he had not been encouraged to have an examination before he left Castlereagh. Dr Irwin believed that the injuries were consistent with the allegations that he had had to drag out of McKearney, and did not think, from the position of some of the bruises, that they were likely to have been self-inflicted. It was exactly the kind of case that Dr Irwin had had in mind when he had discussed his findings with the Chief

Constable earlier in the month. There was a need for explanation. (McKearney was convicted and joined the blanket protest in the H Blocks.)

Despite his frustration, Dr Irwin resolutely refused to say anything to the press after the Association's earlier statement about meeting the Chief Constable. There were no hints, no inside information, no off-the-record conversations. Nothing. The Police Surgeons had made their point to the Chief Constable and had now chosen to remain silent. I was in Belfast at the time with a colleague, Alan Stewart. We were planning to investigate the allegations for ITV's 'This Week' programme. I had first heard of the allegations earlier in the year when making a programme on the Loyalist strike, but had not paid them much attention. However, working in Belfast through much of the summer, I soon realized that the allegations were becoming a matter of concern to many who stood well outside the ranks of the Provisionals.

We first went through files of statements made by suspects to their solicitors following interrogation. There was a pattern. We then talked to GPs, who showed us medical reports that had caused them concern. We talked to solicitors, who showed us cases. Senior members of the legal profession told us that our investigations were not inappropriate. We went to Stormont Castle, where the Northern Ireland Office told us it was a matter for the RUC. We went to RUC HQ and asked for their side of the story. They gave us the statements that SDCC Baillie and Kenneth Newman had made earlier in the year. I requested an interview with the Chief Constable.

I rang Dr Irwin. He wasn't in. I went round to see him at his house. He wasn't at home. I wrote him a long letter and delivered it by hand. I had no reply. I rang Dr Page, who was then the Medical Officer at Castlereagh. He put the phone down on me. Only one doctor was prepared to appear in the TV programme, Dr James O'Rawe, a Catholic doctor whose group practice on the Crumlin

Road drew patients from both communities. He told me that during the summer he had begun to notice injuries on Protestants whom he examined at Castlereagh: previously the injuries he had seen had been almost entirely on Catholic suspects. In fact he told me he had just seen two Protestants who had been interrogated at Castlereagh whom he believed had been ill-treated.

I went to visit one of them, whom Dr O'Rawe had examined on Thursday, 13 October. He alleged he had been assaulted the day before. I interviewed him on Sunday, 16 October. He was at his girlfriend's house and obviously glad to be home. He had been interrogated for three days, had signed no statements and had not been charged. The police had suspected that he was a member of a Loyalist paramilitary organization. He was nervous and reluctant to talk. He said he was frightened he would get picked up again and taken to Castlereagh if the police found that he had been complaining. He said he had been spread-eagled against a wall and beaten; been bent across a chair in a crab position and punched on the stomach; been made to squat with his back to the wall for an hour, as if he were sitting on an imaginary chair; and had his wrists bent and his fingers pulled. He alleged that at one stage a third detective came in, whom his interrogators called 'the boss', and said 'Hit him again'. When he left, he alleged he said, 'Give him a good bash if he does not answer correctly.' He said a couple of detectives introduced themselves as 'Jekyll and Hyde'.

From his description of the interview room, it was clear that he had been interrogated in the old rooms which had been part of the original Castlereagh Holding Centre, distinguishable by the pegboard covering on the wall. There were no spyholes in the doors. He said he had his head banged repeatedly against the wall which was painful, but didn't leave marks, because the pegboard was soft.

When Dr O'Rawe examined him at Castlereagh on the Thursday, he noted a black eye, various bruises, abrasions and areas of tenderness. When I saw him the following

Sunday, the bruises had faded and were, like the once-black eye, a faint yellow colour. But he was clearly still suffering the effects. When I asked him to repeat the 'crab' and 'imaginary chair' positions and hold them for a few minutes, he did so only with considerable difficulty and pain. I had no doubt that the pain was genuine.

The television programme we transmitted was called 'Inhuman and Degrading Treatment'. It consisted of an explanation of the importance of confessions in the framework of the Northern Ireland legal system; an interview with the GP, Dr James O'Rawe; with two men who alleged ill-treatment at Castlereagh; with solicitor Paddy Duffy, who spoke of his experience as a lawyer; with Professor Kevin Boyle, who explained the working of the Diplock courts, the DPP's office, and the complaints system; and an anonymous interview with councillor Jack Hassard of the Police Authority's Complaints Committee, who at that time wished to protect his identity. Hassard accused the RUC of a 'widescale cover-up'. But the basis of the programme was ten cases which we did not name, but whose complaints and medical reports we summarized.

Six days before the programme was due for transmission, I telexed the script of the programme, details of the ten cases and a summary of the interviews, to the RUC's Press Office. The Chief Constable was reserving judgement on whether to participate in the programme. The decision was delayed until the following week. There were high-level discussions between the RUC, the IBA – ITV's governing body – and the senior management of Thames Television, who made the 'This Week' programme. Finally the Producer of 'This Week', David Elstein, was informed by the management that we could transmit the programme only on the condition that we included a televised statement by the Chief Constable. He would not agree to an interview. We were told that if we did not include the statement, there would be no programme. We considered the programme more important than the principle.

On the morning of transmission, 27 October 1977, I flew

to Belfast to film the Chief Constable delivering his prepared statement to camera. On film he restated his by now familiar position:

No Chief Constable in charge of thousands of men can say without doubt that no member of the Force will fall below the high standards set. But, let there be no doubt that the policy in this Force is enforcement of the law within the law. Every member of the Force knows of this policy, which is being widely propagated, and every member of the Force knows that he would offend against that principle at his peril. I do not rule out the possibility that at times a police officer will be tempted to overstep the mark.

Finally let me make it quite clear, there is no policy or toleration of ill-treatment in this Force. Quite the contrary. And this Force is vitally concerned with human rights. In fact, it is very concerned with the most fundamental right of all, the right to live.[1]

A few hours before the programme was shown, the Chief Constable announced that he was placing his men 'on red alert' as he believed the programme was likely to put their lives at risk.

The programme raised a storm of protest, especially at Westminster. Politicians were outraged, not at the possibility that suspects were being ill-treated, but that a programme investigating the allegations had been made and transmitted. The Secretary of State, Roy Mason, accused the programme of being 'insensitive' and 'riddled with unsubstantiated allegations'. He accused us, rather curiously, of 'cheque-book television', and of making a series of programmes that had been unhelpful to the security forces. He also said, rather ominously in view of later events, that he regretted the fact that the IBA had allowed the programme to be transmitted.[2] He wrote a letter of protest to the Chairman of the Authority, and to the Chairman of Thames Television.

1. Thames TV, 'This Week' programme, 'Inhuman and Degrading Treatment', 27 October 1977.
2. *Hansard*, Vol. 939, No. 16, Col. 1734, 24 November 1977.

The reverberations of the programme continued throughout November. There was a burst of activity, with meetings suddenly held all over the place. The day after the programme, the Complaints Committee met the Chairman and Secretary of the Police Surgeons, Dr Stewart and Dr Irwin. They told the members what their Chairman, Ivor Canavan, and Secretary knew already, that they were seeing unexplained injuries on prisoners which were consistent with the allegations. Ivor Canavan assured them that the Committee was 'aware of its responsibilities in the field'. (It was now almost a year since he had first noted the increasing number of complaints.[1])

Having met the Police Surgeons, the Committee asked to talk to the Chief Constable. They met him with his Deputy SDCC Baillie at 5 pm on 28 November 1977. Ivor Canavan told the Chief Constable that his men were doing very good work, but should not come under pressure for results. The Chief Constable replied that he was concentrating on preventative measures. He said the police had intelligence that the IRA were training their members in anti-interrogation techniques designed to divert or nullify the efforts of their interrogators. Whilst not suggesting that the means justified the ends, he reminded the Committee that his detectives were putting their lives at risk for the community.

There were other meetings too. The Complaints Committee met the newly appointed Senior Medical Officers (SMOs) at Castlereagh, and Gough Barracks, Armagh, the new Interrogation Centre which had opened that month. The doctors told them that in future they would send the Police Authority copies of medical reports of cases that caused them concern. They also said they would resign if their concern was 'unrelieved'. The Police Surgeons held another meeting, to which they invited a representative of the 'Moonlighters', the doctors from the local

1. It was at the Complaints & Publicity Committee meeting at police headquarters on 7 January 1977 at 2 pm that Ivor Canavan expressed his concern over the increasing number of allegations.

hospitals who provided night-time cover at Castlereagh when Dr Page was off duty. They said that they too were worried and had met the Chief Constable and told him of their concern.

But the most significant development was that, in the week following the TV programme, Amnesty International announced that it was sending a mission to investigate the allegations. Roy Mason announced that Amnesty would be afforded every facility, but stressed that no individual cases could be discussed as they were *sub judice*.

In such a climate of activity and public concern, one would have expected the numbers of complaints of Assault During Interview in November to drop. They actually increased. In October there had been thirty-seven. In November there were forty-two, the highest number since July 1977.

Exactly a fortnight after the programme was transmitted, thirty-two-year-old Patrick Fullerton was taken to Castlereagh for interrogation. Fullerton was a ruddy-faced farmer who lived in a district with strong Republican traditions, around Maghera. The sympathies of the area were more Official than Provisional, with roots in the IRA's rural campaigns of the fifties and before. Republicans were either 'Hibs' or 'Shinners'.[1] Fullerton came from a family with a long tradition in the priesthood. The wooden ceilinged lounge of the family farmhouse was lined with old books: *The Life, Writings and Times of Edmund Burke*, *A History of the Protestant Reformation*, *The Persecution of Irish Catholics*, *The Cromwellian Settlement of Ireland*, *Spencer's Poetical Works*, and *Irish Rural Priests*.

On arrival at Castlereagh, Fullerton was medically examined. He was questioned about the murder of a policeman a couple of years earlier in Dungiven, a village a few miles over the mountains. Fullerton said he knew nothing. He was interrogated by detectives from HQ

1. 'Hibs', from the Ancient Order of Hibernians. 'Shinners', from Sinn Fein – the political wing of the IRA.

Crime Squad and Strand Road, Derry, the HQ of the North Regional Crime Squad, which covered the area where the policeman had been murdered.

Fullerton alleged that he was assaulted. He said he was bent over a chair in a crab-like position and punched in the stomach; he alleged he was slapped around the face, had his pullover tightened around his throat, and was threatened with a choking. At one stage he was taken to one of the old interview rooms that had the pegboard coverings on the walls and no spyholes in the doors. There he alleged that he was assaulted with a broomstick handle. He said that the head of the brush was placed on the window ledge while he was beaten with the shaft. Fullerton remembered that the shaft was broken. He was made to stand with his arms in the air and was asked questions. After each question, he alleged that a detective rammed the point of the brush shaft into his stomach.

Fullerton was not charged with any offence. He was examined by GP Dr Joe Hendron before he left Castlereagh. Dr Hendron said he found Fullerton 'in a state of absolute fear'. He remembers Fullerton saying to him, 'What's going to happen to me when you leave, doctor. They'll kill me.' Dr Hendron's examination revealed a bruise 3×1 cm down Fullerton's left side and a smaller bruise down the right side. There were also two more bruises on either side of his chest. The rib cage was swollen and discoloured, with an area of bruising 7×4 cm. Dr Hendron concluded, 'I have no doubt at all that Mr Fullerton was beaten in the manner he described at Castlereagh RUC Interrogation Centre.'

Fullerton made an official complaint. The cell in which he alleged the assault with the broomstick handle had taken place was 'sealed off' until the Scenes of Crime Officers arrived. They searched the room and found the shaft of a broomstick behind the radiator. Forensic tests were carried out and fibres were found which matched the fibres on Fullerton's pullover. The RUC told me their examination of Fullerton's complaint was a 'textbook investigation'. The papers were forwarded to the DPP. The DPP directed a prosecution for common assault against some of the detectives who had interrogated Fullerton. They were charged with assault 'contrary to Section 42 of the Offences Against the Person Act 1861'.

Because the detectives faced a summary charge, the case was heard before a magistrate. Nearly a year after Fullerton's interrogation at Castlereagh, the case was heard at Newtonards Magistrates' Court, before the Resident Magistrate, Dan MacLaughlin. Five detectives were charged: D/S McCoubrey and D/C Bohill from RUC HQ; D/S Wilson and D/C Miller from Strand Road, Derry; and another D/C Wilson. The court was packed with detectives. One observer on the police side is said to have remarked that at least one advantage of the trial was that it emptied Castlereagh for the day.

The Resident Magistrate heard the case and retired for several days to consider his judgement. When he returned to the court on 31 October 1978 and saw it full of press men, he tore up his written judgement and said:

Despite certain evasions and bouts of forgetfulness and possibly even some lies, Mr Fullerton's account of what happened has the ring of truth about it. The defence was a complete denial that any assaults took place. I did not find the defence convincing in its evidence. I feel this was one of those occasions when the system of interrogation which was designed to protect both officers and accused broke down completely. As a jury I was faced with the problem of trying to allocate blame for the assaults which I feel took place. If I could have accepted all the evidence given by Fullerton there could be no difficulty whatsoever, but due to the fact that his story contained evasions and lies I found it difficult to accept all that he said. As a jury my duty was to look at the question of doubt and the accused must get that benefit. The guilty escape with the innocent. I cannot allocate any particular incident to any particular person and I therefore dismiss the summons but I do not doubt that this man was assaulted.[1]

1. *Belfast Telegraph*, 31 October 1978.

The five detectives were acquitted. No disciplinary action was taken against them. The RUC insists that it cannot prefer disciplinary charges related to a criminal offence of which an officer has been acquitted in a court of law. I asked a senior police officer what had happened to the five detectives in view of the discovery of the broom handle and the magistrate's finding that Fullerton had been assaulted. He told me they were no longer engaged in interrogation duties.

The Fullerton case illustrates two significant points. First, that despite the uproar over the TV programme, the public concern and the private representations made to the Chief Constable, a suspect was not only beaten a fortnight later in Castlereagh, but beaten in the most blatant manner. His interrogators must have been either unaware of the climate of opinion outside Castlereagh, or contemptuous of it. Secondly, the case illustrates the near impossibility of convicting police officers of assault. The DPP directed a prosecution. The case was carefully prepared. By all accounts Fullerton was impressive in the witness box. There was strong medical evidence. There was rare forensic evidence as a result of the fibres found on the broom handle. Nevertheless, the guilty went free with the innocent.

It was ironic that one of the most crucial and confidential letters of the period was sent while Patrick Fullerton was being interrogated at Castlereagh. It was written by the DPP, Barry Shaw, who had apparently been growing increasingly concerned at the number of complaint files he was receiving from the RUC that appeared to substantiate the complainants' allegation that they had been assaulted. This was not because detectives were admitting the offence but because no alternative explanation was generally offered for the injuries which the medical officers at Castlereagh and the Police Surgeons at Townhall Street noted during their examinations. These confidential medical reports, which were not available to the patient, his GP or his solicitor, were crucial evidence. But it was not the DPP's function to establish whether a suspect had been ill-treated, only whether a police officer could be made amenable for the assault.

In the climate of November 1977, the D P P clearly believed that it was time to put his concern in writing to the Chief Constable. Barry Shaw is a discreet and diplomatic man. On 11 November he wrote a letter to Kenneth Newman. He said he had been concerned at the number of complaints and had conducted a review of all the relevant complaint files from 1 January to 30 September 1977 – the first nine months of the year. They were all complaints alleging assault in police custody. He noted the emergence of a pattern. He gave the Chief Constable the statistics: he had reviewed about 300 files on 300 individuals, all of whom had been charged with scheduled offences.[1] In around 10 per cent of cases (about thirty) there was medical evidence that the complainant had in fact been assaulted; in about half the cases, assault could be ruled out. The remaining 40 per cent could have gone either way in a court of law. The DPP pointed out that in all these cases he had been able to direct only one prosecution against the police. Where there were a number of detectives involved in interrogation, it was virtually impossible to identify the culprits. The Director warned that the number of prosecutions should not be equated with the number of assaults.

Barry Shaw was clearly telling the Chief Constable that a court of law was not the place to resolve allegations of assault.

In his reply the Chief Constable made no denials. He said that it was the first time that such an assessment of the situation had been brought to his attention. He promised he would investigate. He pointed out to the Director that

1. A D I complaints for January–September 1977 total 356. The discrepancy is probably accounted for by the time which often elapses between registration of complaint, investigation and reference to the DPP. By the time the DPP compiled his list, several cases from the period had still to reach him.

it was still a small number of cases, given the total numbers of terrorist suspects interrogated. (In the nine-month period covered by the DPP's review, over 1,500 terrorist suspects had been detained for questioning.) But despite the DPP's letter, the Chief Constable was still telling the Complaints Committee later that month that the best way of dealing with complaints was in court.

The Attorney-General, Sam Silkin, who had earlier in the year given the 'unqualified undertaking' at Strasbourg, was obviously concerned at the Director's identification of a pattern. The word itself was uncomfortably close to the European Commission's definition of administrative practice, the legalistic term for official toleration of ill-treatment. The issue was even more politically sensitive for the Labour government, as the European Court was about to deliver its verdict.

A confidential minute from the Attorney-General addressed to the Prime Minister, James Callaghan, described the DPP's letter to the Chief Constable. He said it had been prompted by the emergence of a pattern in the cases the Director had reviewed during the first nine months of 1977. He repeated the statistics and observations which the DPP had sent to the Chief Constable. He also warned the Prime Minister that the explanation often offered, that the injuries were self-inflicted, should not be exaggerated.

So in November 1977, before the Amnesty mission set foot in the province, the government knew that suspects had been ill-treated during interrogation. Nevertheless, it clung to its insistence that there was no substance to the allegations.

In the House of Commons on 24 November 1977, Labour MP Philip Whitehead asked Roy Mason if he was going to investigate the 'serious allegations' which had been made on the Thames TV programme. The Secretary of State replied:

No. I have not felt that the accusations were strong enough for my Department or myself to intervene. The Thames Television programme on the occasion referred to was riddled with unsubstantiated accusations. I said that it was irresponsible and insensitive and I still believe that it was.

In response to another question he continued:

One reason why I do not intervene at this stage is to prove to the House that the police are not beyond the law. If they are guilty of a criminal offence, they will be treated accordingly.

When I asked the DPP, Barry Shaw, the Attorney-General, Sam Silkin, the Secretary of State, Roy Mason, and the Prime Minister, James Callaghan, if I could discuss the issue with them, all of them declined.

Amnesty International visited Northern Ireland from 28 November to 6 December 1977. To many doctors, the Amnesty visit proved what they had always privately believed, that ill-treatment could be turned on and off like a tap. They had always accepted that allegations would be made even if suspected terrorists were given tea and biscuits at Castlereagh, as it was an essential part of the Provisionals' propaganda war. What had concerned them over the year was the volume of complaints and the number of cases in which they had found medical evidence consistent with the allegations. In December 1977, doctors told me they found scarcely a case that caused them concern. Perhaps the DPP's letter to the Chief Constable and the Attorney-General's minute to the Prime Minister had had some effect. But, perhaps most significantly of all, Amnesty International was in town.

In December there were only eight complaints of Assault During Interview. It was a figure only matched on two other occasions in the period covered by this book: the first, in June 1978, when there were also only eight complaints – the month the Amnesty Report was published; the second was in April 1979 when there were seven – the month following publication of the Bennett Report.

Even allowing for the smaller number of suspects detained in December 1977 – at Castlereagh there were 101 compared to 147 in November – the drop in the number of complaints of assault remains dramatic. Compared with eight in December, there had been thirty-eight in August, forty in September, thirty-seven in October and forty-two in November. (These are province-wide figures.) The other significant factor may have been the appointment of Dr Alexander, with far more detailed terms of reference, as Senior Medical Officer at Castlereagh. He took over on 29 November, the day after Amnesty arrived.

Amnesty's last visit to Belfast had been in December 1971 to investigate the allegations of ill-treatment that followed the introduction of internment. Amnesty had, however, been in Ireland more recently to investigate the allegations of ill-treatment made against detectives of the Guardai[1] and had concluded, to the embarrassment of the Dublin government, which was still pursuing the British government through the legal machinery at Strasbourg, that suspects had been beaten and maltreated in custody. Again, the purpose had been to obtain confessions.[2]

Amnesty's 1971 Commission of Inquiry concluded that persons arrested had been 'subject to brutal treatment by the security forces', in some cases to obtain confessions. Its report was published in 1972 and observed:

While it is encouraging to note that certain techniques of interrogation have been discontinued, the fact remains that brutality of the type confirmed in the present report apparently continues.[3]

In 1971 Amnesty had no cooperation from the then Conservative government. Nor had it been given facilities by the Dublin government during its inquiries in the South.

1. Garda Siochana ('Guardians of the Peace') – the Irish police.
2. The Amnesty report to the Dublin government was delivered on 26 August 1977.
3. Amnesty International, Report of an Inquiry into Allegations of Ill-Treatment in Northern Ireland, 1972, Foreword.

In 1977 Amnesty, which had just been awarded the Nobel Peace Prize, was given considerable assistance by the British government. For the Labour government to have done otherwise, with the decision of the European Court at Strasbourg expected any minute, would have been politically insensitive. But another explanation is also possible: that the government, now in receipt of the Attorney-General's minute, used Amnesty to get itself off the hook.

The Amnesty mission checked in at Belfast's Europa Hotel on 28 November. It consisted of a Dutch lawyer, Douwe Korff; two Danish doctors, Inge Lunde and Jorgen Kelstrup, who had made a study of Chilean torture victims; and Dr John Humphreys of Amnesty's International Secretariat. During its ten-day visit, the mission took evidence from just about everybody, including the Chief Constable and his Deputy, Harry Baillie; the Deputy Secretary of State, Don Concannon; the Director of Public Prosecutions, Barry Shaw; and his Deputy. In addition they met General Practitioners, solicitors, members of the legal profession and complainants. Meetings were arranged in Derry and Dungannon, as well as Belfast. Two of the delegates were given a forty-five-minute tour of Castlereagh.

But the mission was denied access to the most important information of all: the medical reports compiled by the Police Surgeons and the Senior Medical Officers at Castlereagh and Gough. These were the reports that lay behind the DPP's letter to the Chief Constable, three weeks earlier. Technically they were the property of the Police Authority, as the Authority employed all the doctors. The mission asked the Police Authority if it could see the reports. The Authority had its instructions from the Secretary of State not to make them available to the mission. Roy Mason had said that the government would cooperate with Amnesty on condition that individual cases were not discussed. However, when the delegates held their meeting with the Police Surgeons, who informed them of their frustrated efforts to bring their anxieties to the attention of the Chief Constable, they were told that they had no objection to making their medical reports available to the mission. It had been individual cases that they had been concerned about. The delegates went back to the Police Authority and asked them to reconsider, in view of the Police Surgeons' willingness to lift professional objections. The Authority referred the matter back to the Secretary of State. The answer was still the same. Roy Mason said no. Had they been made available, many of them would simply have confirmed the GPs' findings. These 'official' medical reports would have been the most damaging testimony of all.

On 2 December 1977, while Amnesty was taking evidence, the heads of all the churches in Ireland, North and South, Catholic and Protestant, issued an important statement. It was addressed to the authorities on both sides of the border.

STATEMENT ISSUED BY IRISH CHURCH LEADERS ON 2 DECEMBER 1977

We have been disturbed that serious allegations are being made of ill-treatment of suspects and prisoners; though at the same time we recognize that some persons opposed to State authorities can be expected to attack their security forces not only with physical violence but also malicious accusations.

A grave responsibility, therefore, rests on all law-abiding citizens to seek to strengthen the duly constituted forces of law and order both by constructive criticism and personal support, having in mind the following points:

1. It is a basic responsibility of the forces of law and order to seek to protect not only the general public as they go about their lawful business but also persons who may be in custody.

2. Confidence in this protection is vital to a free society; and anything which would undermine it from within those forces is a serious threat just as are attacks from without.

For this reason the declared policies of the Chief Constable and the Government in Northern Ireland, and of the Government of the Republic of Ireland must effectively be implemented and adequate precautions taken against abuse.

Robert G. Livingstone, President of the Methodist Church in Ireland

Tomás Ó'Fiaich, Archbishop of Armagh and Primate of All Ireland (RC)

Thomas A. Patterson, Moderator of the Presbyterian Church in Ireland

George O. Simms, Archbishop of Armagh and Primate of All Ireland (Church of Ireland)

To senior officers of the RUC, the significance of the statement was not only the nature of the sentiments expressed but the fact that one of its four signatories was Tomás Ó'Fiaich, the newly appointed Archbishop of Armagh and Primate of All Ireland. The new Archbishop was a native of the Provisional IRA stronghold of Cross-maglen and a self-confessed Republican. He openly proclaimed his belief in the unity of Ireland, while bitterly condemning the Provisionals, who sought to achieve it by force. Tomás Ó'Fiaich's political and spiritual credentials were impeccable. To most Catholics in the North, including those who might turn a blind eye to the Provisionals, his word was law. For the new Primate to encourage his flock to give their 'personal support' to the forces of law and order, albeit on certain conditions, was something that no Catholic politician had hitherto been prepared to do. To the RUC, it was the much hoped for sign on the long and difficult road to police acceptability.

But the statement was also a warning. The support the RUC was being offered was conditional. At the time the statement was issued, key figures from the Chief Constable to the Prime Minister knew that suspects had been ill-treated in police custody. There were no excuses. But the warning was not heeded, and the conditions were not met.

Part Three

12. Gough Barracks

'The lack of suitable interview facilities in the South Region
was somewhat of a drawback in the earlier part of the year
but this problem was alleviated on 1 November by the
provision of a new Police Office within the Gough Barracks
Complex.'

Chief Constable's Annual Report, 1977

In November 1977 a new Interrogation Centre opened at
Gough Barracks, Armagh. Although there were rumours
as to what the contractors were doing behind the barracks'
thick fortress wall, the quarter of a million pound conver-
sion of one of the blocks into an Interrogation Centre,
modelled on Castlereagh, was a closely guarded secret. The
authorities feared that, should word leak out, the building
contractors would be intimidated and go, leaving them
with an expensive and unfinished Interrogation Centre on
their hands. (It cost £247,000.)

Officially the reason for the opening of Gough was the
lack of suitable interview facilities in South Region, once
the old police station at Lurgan, which had served as the
administrative headquarters for the area, had been blown
up by a Provisional IRA bomb at about the same time as
the Provisionals had blown up Castlereagh. But there was
no doubt that the success of Castlereagh and the fact that
there were limits to its capacity were additional considerations in the decision to build a second Interrogation
Centre at Gough. Gough also served as the headquarters
of the South Regional Crime Squad.

Gough was strategically placed to monitor terrorist
activities in some of the province's worst trouble spots. At
its nearest point, the border with County Monaghan, which
the Provisional IRA use as a haven and base for their
attacks on parts of the North, is only a dozen miles from
Armagh. Its catchment area includes not only South

Armagh and mid-Tyrone, where the Provisionals were particularly active, but the so-called 'murder triangle' around Lurgan, Dungannon and Portadown, which was the hunting ground for Loyalist assassination squads.

The new Interrogation Centre was a self-contained unit built on Castlereagh's lines. The complex is housed in a rectangular sandstone block, overlooking the barracks' vast central parade ground. The windows that look down on to it have been blocked in to deprive prisoners in the cells behind of all natural light – a deliberate part of the interrogation process, to make prisoners lose all sense of time. The block that houses the Interrogation Centre dates back a hundred years to the time when Gladstone was telling his parliamentary colleagues that they would have to do something about Ireland. The barracks itself goes back even further, to the eighteenth century, when it served as a base for earlier British soldiers sent to Ireland to put down the rebels.

Although the police were responsible for the running of Gough – its operation came under the direct control of Castlereagh – the DHSS were responsible for all medical supervision. To the police, Castlereagh had spelt success; but to the DHSS, ever since the Chief Medical Officer, Dr Terence Baird, had received Dr Irwin's letter in April 1977, Castlereagh had been a warning. In view of the increasing allegations and the increasing concern expressed by Police Surgeons, the DHSS realized that, new Interrogation Centre or not, medical supervision of interrogation would have to be strengthened. Hitherto the duties which Dr Page had exercised at Castlereagh had tended to develop on an *ad hoc* basis. The Department now decided that it was time to put them on a proper footing. Two new posts were created, of Senior Medical Officer status, one at Castlereagh and one at Gough. They became operative from 1 November 1977. Dr Page was, to his annoyance, prematurely retired. The new SMO positions were offered to Dr Charles Alexander at Castlereagh and to Dr Denis Elliott at Gough.

When the Chief Medical Officer, Dr Terence Baird, appointed Dr Elliott from his thirty or so Medical Officers, he knew the kind of man he was getting. In his thirty years as a doctor, Denis Elliott had been a Police Surgeon, a coroner and a general practitioner – as well as a Protestant councillor and Justice of the Peace – and he had spent the past five years of his career working as a prison doctor. Dr Elliott had enjoyed the work, and thought highly of the prison medical service. He believed that deprivation of liberty was a prisoner's punishment, and that once he was inside he should be treated in a humanitarian way in accordance with all the rules and international regulations laid down. Dr Elliott played everything strictly by the book, which did not always make him a popular figure.

On one occasion during the summer of 1977, Dr Elliott had caused a row when he had insisted that prisoners be treated properly. He was working at Magilligan prison at the time, an old army base which had served as an internment camp and was now used as a prison. The prisoners lived not in cells but in Second World War type huts. There had been an emergency at the Crumlin Road prison in Belfast, after a prison officer had found gelignite hidden in the centre of a half pound of butter which was cooling in a basin in the corner of a cell. All the cells were searched and enough gelignite was found to reduce the walls of Crumlin Road prison to the level of the walls of Jericho. Immediately orders were given to search all of Northern Ireland's prisons. At Magilligan, all the prisoners were herded into a hut, while their accommodation and belongings were thoroughly searched. It was a very hot day and, as the temperature soared, Dr Elliott, as Medical Officer responsible for the prisoners' welfare, grew anxious for their health. As the Governor of Magilligan was not available at the time, Dr Elliott told those left in charge of his concern. He appears to have been told to mind his own business. It was one of the rare occasions during his work as a prison Medical Officer that Denis Elliott had reason to complain.

He immediately rang the Chief Medical Officer, who rang the Permanent Secretary at the DHSS, who rang the Director of Prisons, who rang Magilligan and told his men that Dr Elliott's orders were to be obeyed. The prisoners were released from the baking hut. Dr Elliott saw to it that the incident was recorded in the prison record book.

Dr Baird and Dr Elliott knew each other well. Both were close to retirement, Dr Baird in less than a year and Dr Elliott in just over two. Dr Baird had already made his retirement plans. He was going to withdraw to his cottage and read the pile of books that awaited him, although, as a member of the General Medical Council in London, he had every intention of keeping in touch with the world of medical politics. Both doctors had served in the Second World War, Dr Baird on board HMS *Victorious* and Dr Elliott as an electronics engineer. Dr Baird still spoke of patriotism and serving his country and referred to his Medical Officers serving under him as his 'boys'. He ran his department rather like a ship and, although his manner and style were not to everyone's liking, he was widely respected. Dr Baird was a Protestant and an Ulsterman too, from Donegal, one of the original nine counties of Ulster before Ulster, like Ireland, was partitioned.

Dr Baird was no stranger to controversy, having already weathered the storm over the use of CS gas earlier in the decade, but as concern over the allegations mounted, he suspected that his last few months as Chief Medical Officer might not be so easy. Dr Elliott's appointment to the new Interrogation Centre at Gough was no accident.

When Dr Elliott was offered the new position, he said he would only accept on two conditions. First, that a suitable job description should be drawn up and agreed by the DHSS, the Police Authority – to whom the two SMOs were seconded – and the RUC, with whom they would have to work. His second condition was that, if things did not work out to his satisfaction, he could request a transfer back to his old job in the Prison Medical Service. The principles were agreed and a meeting was called to discuss the details on 6 September 1977. Dr Weir, now the Chief Medical Officer elect, took the chair. Also present were William Baird, the Secretary of the Police Authority; Tom Cromey, the Secretary of State's representative on the Authority; and ACC William Meharg, of the RUC. In the course of the discussion, Dr Elliott said that he believed that suspects had been ill-treated. ACC Meharg interrupted and reminded Dr Elliott that the ill-treatment was 'alleged'. Dr Elliott said that in his opinion ill-treatment was real, not 'alleged', but for the sake of argument he was prepared to accept the RUC's insistence on the qualification. Dr Elliott made it clear to the meeting that he was not going to be a party to any 'cover-up'. Apparently Tom Cromey, of the Northern Ireland Office, said that a cover-up was the last thing the authorities wanted. But before final agreement was reached, it was decided that Dr Elliott and Dr Alexander should draw up a list of basic principles.

A month later the two new SMOs submitted their proposals to the Chief Medical Officer. They said that their duty was to look after the health and welfare of prisoners and to protect the police against false accusations. In essence they laid down four basic principles:

1. That suspects should be offered a medical examination before interrogation and as soon as possible after they arrived on the premises. The offer should be made by the doctor in the presence of the police. If the prisoner accepted or refused he should be asked to sign with the doctor acting as witness. If the prisoner refused to sign, then his refusal should also be recorded by the doctor and witnessed by the police.

2. Suspects should be offered a medical examination every twenty-four hours during their detention and immediately before they left the premises either to be charged or released.

3. Suspects should have reasonable access to their general practitioner should they ask to see him.

4. General practitioners should have reasonable access to any prisoner should they ask to see him.

These four proposals were hardly revolutionary but, if they were to work effectively, they did presuppose maximum cooperation on the part of the police. But the police were apparently not enthusiastic about the new role that the SMOs were suggesting for themselves. At the Police Authority meeting which had to discuss and ratify the SMOs' proposals, the RUC expressed their misgivings. Traditionally it had always been the police who decided whether a suspect should have an examination during the course of his interrogation, not the prisoner nor the Medical Officer himself. Essentially the police saw the Medical Officers as passive agents, which was in direct conflict to the positive role in which Dr Elliott saw his new job. His interpretation of being responsible for the health and welfare of suspects was much wider than that envisaged by the police. In the end, after much discussion, the four basic principles laid down by the SMOs were agreed by the Police Authority and the RUC. At this stage the agreement was only verbal and it was nearly six months before anything was put in writing. On this basis Dr Elliott finally agreed to accept the new position of Senior Medical Officer at Gough Barracks, Armagh.

There was no fanfare of trumpets when Gough opened on 1 November 1977. Dr Alexander had agreed to cover for the first few weeks while Dr Page wound up his duties at Castlereagh prior to retirement and Dr Elliott finished off his work at Magilligan. Apparently Dr Alexander thought the work at Gough was relatively light, as more than half the prisoners said they did not wish to be examined as there was nothing wrong with them.

In November 1977, in its first month of operation, seventy-seven suspects were interrogated at Gough, compared to 147 at Castlereagh. At Gough there were eight complaints of ill-treatment, while at Castlereagh there were thirty-one. When Dr Elliott arrived at Gough at the end of the month, he found that the RUC had also strengthened their supervision of interrogations by the introduction of a uniformed inspector. Like Dr Elliott, this inspector apparently took the job only on the understanding that he too could ask for a transfer if he wasn't happy. In December, the month of the Amnesty visit, twenty-eight suspects were interrogated at Gough and there was only one complaint of ill-treatment. At Castlereagh 101 suspects were interrogated and there were only four complaints of ill-treatment.

The police at Gough had already heard what to expect from Dr Elliott. They had been warned in advance that if they gave him a salute, called him 'sir' and accorded him the respect due to his civil service rank of Assistant Secretary, they wouldn't have too many problems with the new Senior Medical Officer. They were ill-advised. Immediately he arrived, Dr Elliott set about reorganizing his new medical room which, owing to 'architect error', was not at the end of the cell block as it was at Castlereagh, but at the end of the corridor that contained the interrogation rooms. The rooms were not soundproofed, nor was Dr Elliott's medical room. He could therefore hear some of what went on. He wasn't satisfied with the facilities he was given. He refused to pour urine samples down the sink in which he was supposed to wash his hands. He requisitioned another sink, which was fitted into the wall complete with a ledge on which he could now stand his bottles of urine samples. There was no cupboard in which to place the extensive supplies of pharmaceuticals which had been agreed on as part of the job description. A new large white cupboard was promptly provided and fixed on the wall, next to the examination couch.

After a while he decided that prisoners weren't getting the exercise due to them under the European Convention on the Treatment of Prisoners. At Castlereagh most prisoners would resort to doing press-ups in a cell, but at Gough, thanks to Dr Elliott, they enjoyed a ten-minute stroll round the small compound at the back of the interrogation block, which Dr Elliott designated an exercise yard. He asked at what times prisoners were given their three meals a day and decided that the gap between evening meal and breakfast was too long. He instituted coffee and biscuits at bedtime. When Dr Elliott said he was responsible for the health and welfare of prisoners, he meant it.

The guidelines agreed for the treatment of suspects held in police custody were strict. They stipulated that the prisoners should be examined as soon as possible on arrival; that the doctors should be responsible for their health and welfare; that they should be seen in private once a day by the Medical Officer; that prisoners could see the MO on reasonable request; that the interrogation records should be examined regularly. These were only some of the provisions laid down to safeguard the prisoner from possible abuse and the RUC from the possible calumny of false allegations.

Because Dr Elliott and Dr Alexander had been given assurances that the safeguards which they wished to see introduced would be honoured, they were able to assure the Amnesty mission that they had no cause for further concern. The Police Surgeons had also felt able to give Amnesty a similar assurance, following the establishment of the Hermon Committee. Both the Police Surgeons and the Senior Medical Officers had also been told that they could use the 'hot line' to DCC Hermon should they be concerned about any particular case. The optimism of both sets of doctors was short-lived.

Early on Tuesday morning, 29 November 1977, a twenty-two-year-old Coalisland youth, Michael McGrath, was brought to Gough Barracks for questioning about the murder of a policeman in 1976. The policeman had been ambushed one Saturday evening as he returned to his house after seeing his girlfriend home. Following his interrogation, Michael McGrath was charged with the murder of Constable McCambridge. The case came to trial in May 1979. The court heard Dr Elliott's evidence. He said that he had examined McGrath at 9.30 on Tuesday morning while he was doing his morning rounds. He said he seemed fit and had no complaint to make. (It was Dr Elliott's practice to explain in detail to every suspect the practical advantages of agreeing to an initial medical examination, regardless of how healthy a suspect said he felt. He would point out that should the suspect wish to make a complaint without having had an initial examination, when the case came to court the prosecution would almost certainly make the case that the suspect had already been injured before he was taken into custody. After such an explanation of the advantages, 98 per cent of suspects at Gough Barracks agreed to an initial medical examination. At Castlereagh, where the explanation may not have been as detailed, the figure was only around 50 per cent.)

The court then heard that on Tuesday afternoon McGrath asked to see his own Coalisland G P, who came and examined him at 7 o'clock in Dr Elliott's medical room. His G P said that McGrath had no complaints to make and showed no signs of any injury, but did remark that he couldn't take much more questioning.

The court was then told that at 8.30 the following morning Dr Elliott carried out an intermediate examination, when McGrath told him that the previous evening he had been held by the throat and punched in the stomach with a clenched fist. Dr Elliott said that McGrath did not wish to sign a complaint form or allege ill-treatment. The court heard that when Dr Elliott examined McGrath, he found slightly tender areas around his chest and throat, but didn't think that they were of any great significance.

The court then heard that McGrath asked to see his G P again, just after lunchtime on Wednesday. When the G P arrived he said there was bruising on McGrath's chest, but Dr Elliott disagreed. He also said that McGrath's throat was tender, an observation with which Dr Elliott did agree. Dr Elliott then said he advised the police that there should be no further interrogation until he could obtain a second medical opinion. He explained that an hour and a half later his Senior Deputy Medical Officer examined McGrath and found a fresh perforation of the eardrum. Dr Elliott said that he also examined McGrath and agreed with what his Deputy had just found.

Dr Elliott told the court that he examined McGrath again early the next morning, but this time noticed two small areas of pale brown bruising on his abdomen, in addition to the perforated eardrum.

The court heard that it was Dr Elliott's custom to review each prisoner's medical history at the end of his interrogation. Reviewing McGrath's case, Dr Elliott said that he dismissed McGrath's psychological state, on the grounds that anybody being interviewed about terrorist crimes would be bound to show signs of anxiety and depression. Nor was he convinced that the bruising was the result of any ill-treatment. He told the court he thought it might have been self-inflicted, but nevertheless he did express concern about the perforated eardrum which he thought would have been most difficult to self-inflict. In conclusion Dr Elliott remarked that although he couldn't find any direct evidence of ill-treatment, and he had seen McGrath at regular intervals during his interrogation, he wasn't prepared to rule out the possibility that McGrath had been assaulted. As was common experience in the Diplock courts, many suspects plainly exaggerated their complaints. McGrath was no exception. At one stage he complained that he had had his head banged against the wall for ten minutes, although there was not a scrap of medical evidence to back up such allegations. His defence challenged his statements on the grounds that they had been obtained in contravention of Section 6, but faced with the disparity between some of the more extreme allegations and the medical evidence, they did not succeed.

The judge sentenced Michael McGrath to life, with a

twenty-year recommendation. McGrath was also sentenced to fourteen years for possession of firearms, five years for membership of the Provisional I R A, and ten years for conspiracy to murder. His defence appealed following his conviction. At the time of writing, the appeal has yet to be heard. But the significance of Michael McGrath's case is that for the first time it raised considerable doubt in Dr Elliott's mind.

Through December 1977 and early January 1978, Dr Elliott saw no further cases to give him cause for doubt. Nor did the Police Surgeons in Belfast, who examined Castlereagh cases, see any medical evidence to re-awaken their concern. They were quiet weeks with Amnesty gone. Dr Elliott's only problem was overcoming R U C resistance to the 'positive' side of his role. In particular he found it difficult to obtain access to the interrogation schedules which would tell him the times and duration of interviews. Denis Elliott thought they were a crucial part of his job. Some detectives thought they were none of his business. At one stage it appears that a senior detective came down to Gough to discuss the problems with Dr Elliott and implied that he was interfering with the course of justice.

At the beginning of 1978, the Provisionals, who had spent the last six months reorganizing, launched a New Year offensive. They blitzed the town centres of Dungannon and Cookstown with car bombs. Both towns were in Gough's catchment area and had recently been re-opened to traffic. There were seventy bomb attacks on business premises and ambushes on the security forces in the border areas, which involved remote-controlled landmines and blast bombs.

As one side stepped up the pressure, the other replied. More suspects were detained for questioning – in January, 136 at Castlereagh and fifty-two at Gough. Complaints of ill-treatment slowly started to rise again – thirteen at Castlereagh and three at Gough.

One of the three complaints of assault made at Gough in January 1978 was registered by a man who lived a mile across the border, in the County Monaghan village of Clontibret. Apparently Paedar Mohan had been arrested while crossing the border with suspicious documents in his possession. At 5 o'clock on the morning of 28 January he was brought to Gough Barracks. He had already served a sentence in the Republic for membership of the IRA. Following interrogation, Mohan was charged with membership of the IRA. His case came to court in early 1971. At his trial the court heard that when Mohan was examined around 9 o'clock on the morning of his arrest, he seemed to be in good health and bore no signs of injury or ill-treatment. Nor, the court was told, did Mohan make any complaint or show any signs of injury until the third morning following his arrest. Giving evidence, Mohan said that he had been ill-treated by being beaten around the head and face. He also said that he had been bent over a table in a crab-like position and had made a formal complaint in the presence of Dr Elliott and the Duty Inspector. Dr Elliott told the court that when he examined Mohan he found two abrasions on his lower back, swelling and tenderness around the spine, and a reddening and swelling area on his scalp, around his ear. Dr Elliott said that the injuries had occurred since Mohan's arrival at Gough and appeared to be of recent origin.

The court also heard that Mohan's own family doctor travelled across the border from County Monaghan to Armagh to examine his patient, and that what he found confirmed what Dr Elliott had already noted. Dr Elliott concluded that Paedar Mohan had suffered some physical abuse during interrogation, although he believed that many of his complaints lacked supporting medical evidence. Mohan's defence unsuccessfully contested this statement, and the judge sentenced him to five years' imprisonment.

The doubt which the case of Michael McGrath had raised in Dr Elliott's mind was now confirmed. The lull appeared to be over. It was unfortunate that, only a couple of weeks earlier, the European Court had found Britain guilty of inhuman and degrading treatment of prisoners during interrogation in 1971.

13. The Pattern Recurs

'The question may be posed whether – if we assume that ill-treatment exists – it is a situation in which the Chief Constable is in full control.'

Police Authority draft document for discussion, March 1978

In February 1978 the Provisional I R A kept up the pressure. Firebombs devastated business premises; a bus depot and eighteen buses were destroyed, causing two million pounds worth of damage; attacks on the security forces continued with little regard for civilians. Gunmen fired at police outside a football ground, missed them and killed an old lady of sixty-nine. Two members of the U D R were killed, one of them when a bomb planted under his car exploded, killing him and his ten-year-old daughter as well. A police constable was shot dead in an ambush on a Landrover, and a reserve constable died in a bomb attack on a restaurant.

The reserve constable was one of 300 people enjoying a Friday night out at the La Mon restaurant near Belfast. A car was driven up to the restaurant and parked outside the window of one of the rooms where the function was being held. When the blast incendiary bomb exploded, twelve people were burned alive in the inferno. The Provisionals said the warning had not got through in time and apologized for their mistake.

Again, complaints of Assault During Interview escalated with the violence. In January there had been seventeen. In February there were thirty-seven. Although most of the complaints were coming from Castlereagh, all was not well at Gough.

On 28 February, Dr Elliott was doing his morning cell round at Gough. He opened the door of Hugh Canavan's cell, whom he had examined the day before when he had been brought in for interrogation. There had been nothing wrong with Canavan when Dr Elliott first examined him. Dr Elliott later told colleagues of his shock when he saw Canavan sitting up in bed with a black eye which was obvious, even in the poor light of the cell. Dr Elliott asked Canavan what had happened. Canavan said that he had been assaulted the previous evening. Dr Elliott immediately informed the duty inspector that Canavan had made a complaint and said that he wished to examine him.

Forty minutes later Canavan was brought to the medical room. He told Dr Elliott that he had been slapped around the face, dragged from the chair by the hair, prodded in the stomach, slapped around the ears with an open hand, and had his left arm twisted behind his back. When Dr Elliott examined Canavan he found bruising around his eye, his nose and both ears, and an eardrum that was slightly inflamed and bleeding. There were also abrasions on the back and front of his shoulder, and tiny patches of bleeding on his scalp. Dr Elliott immediately informed the police that Canavan was not fit for further interrogation. The police never suggested that Canavan had self-inflicted his injuries, and Dr Elliott himself apparently believed that they were injuries which would have been difficult to self-inflict. He concluded that Canavan's injuries were the result of considerable force that had been applied repeatedly. He had no doubt that it was a case of inhuman and degrading treatment and described it as 'a case of serious assault'.

Hugh Canavan was charged with possession of explosives, but he never stood trial as the DPP withdrew the charges a few months later.

After examining Canavan, Dr Elliott no longer had any doubts. He was convinced that suspects were being ill-treated at Gough, and he was determined to do something about it. He got in touch with his DHSS colleagues at Crumlin Road prison, who told him that they too were now seeing injuries once again on prisoners arriving at the gaol. He also got in touch with Dr Irwin, who told him that the Police Surgeons were worried once again by what appeared to be a re-emergence of the pattern of injuries they had observed in 1977. Again, prisoners were arriving at Townhall Street from Castlereagh with injuries which were never explained.

The following are just two examples of the kind of cases the Police Surgeons were seeing at Townhall Street in February.

Martin McManus was arrested and taken to Castlereagh on 13 February 1978. He alleged he was punched on the chest and hit on the jaw. The following day he said he was punched and kneed in the stomach and had his wrist and arms twisted. The doctors found abrasions on his eye and neck and bruises on his eye, neck and ribs.

Thomas O'Hare was taken to Castlereagh on 22 February and alleged he was punched in the stomach and slapped around the face: in later interviews he alleged he was 'throttled', punched repeatedly in the stomach, and had his head banged against the wall 'with cardboard-like holes'. When he was examined, the Police Surgeons found abrasions on his spine and lip and bruises on his arm.

The worst case that Dr Irwin saw in February involved the same suspect, ironically, as one of the worst cases which he had seen the previous year. On 28 February, John Fusco was arrested again and taken to Castlereagh, where he alleged he was repeatedly slapped around the face and ears, punched in the stomach, and 'throttled' until he nearly passed out. At one stage he alleged he was grabbed round the throat and had a sock pushed in his mouth, while pressure was applied to his nose and throat. He said he asked to see his GP but the request was refused. He admitted slashing his wrist with a plastic knife, because he felt he was cracking up, and then dropping the bed on his knuckle so he wouldn't have to sign any more statements. While at Castlereagh, Fusco allegedly made three statements. In the first he admitted firing at an army post. In the second he confessed to firing shots at a funeral. In the third he admitted to being a member of the Provisional I R A.

When John Fusco was examined at Townhall Street on 2 March by Dr Irwin and his own G P, several injuries were noted. There were bruises on both sides of his chest, arm and throat. The self-inflicted injuries to his wrist and hand were also observed, as was the fact that Fusco had himself admitted them. Fusco also complained of pain in his left ear. Dr Irwin noticed redness over the eardrum and a small clot of dried blood (Fusco had received an ear injury during his previous interrogation at Castlereagh in September 1977). The same injuries were also noted by the Medical Officers at Crumlin Road prison where Fusco was taken to be remanded in custody.

At the end of his report, Dr Irwin concluded that Fusco had suffered blows to his body which corresponded in time to the colour changes and to the manner in which he alleged he had received them. As he received no other explanation from the R U C as to how the marks had been received, Dr Irwin concluded that they had been inflicted at Castlereagh as Fusco had described.

When Fusco was charged on 3 March, his bail application was refused. However, on 19 April, his application for bail was granted on compassionate grounds. John Fusco 'got offside'. He fled across the border and never returned to stand trial.

The doctors made their renewed concern known to the officers of the Police Authority. On 6 March 1978, a special meeting of the Complaints Committee was called to which the doctors were invited. The meeting was secret. Having assured Amnesty only three months earlier that the new safeguards were adequate, the Police Authority knew that the need for such a meeting was, in the light of all that had happened in 1977, a grave embarrassment.

Dr Irwin told the Committee that at least 50 per cent of suspects passing through Castlereagh were not medically examined. He said that many prisoners whom he examined at Townhall Street or at Crumlin Road prison, where he also worked, had injuries which, in his opinion, could not have been self-inflicted. He said that standards which had improved at the end of 1977 were now slipping seriously once again. He said he couldn't accept the RUC's denials of ill-treatment. He believed it to be a matter of urgent and immediate importance. A long-drawn-out investigation by the Chief Constable wasn't acceptable. He informed the Committee that he had discussed the matter with his Association and it had been decided that, if things didn't improve, they would speak out publicly and refer the matter to the British Medical Association. He also gave a warning that the Police Surgeons might find it necessary to refuse to examine any more terrorist suspects.

Dr Elliott then described, apparently in some graphic detail, his problems at Gough. He said that his medical room was in the centre of the interrogation room corridor and it was often embarrassing, especially in the presence of visiting GPs, to hear detectives shouting and swearing at prisoners, 'If you don't fucking sign that, I'll get you fifteen years', and 'This can get a fucking sight worse', and 'This is only the first fucking day'. He said that when he complained, it was suggested that his examination room might be moved to 'a more suitable area'. He had noticed from the records that the most popular rooms for interrogation were the ones situated furthest from his office. He apparently said it was his impression that certain detectives now thought that, with Amnesty gone, they could return to their old methods. He gave the Committee details of the cases he had seen at Gough. He said he was far from happy with the way things were going and gave a warning that he was considering getting in touch with Amnesty.

Dr Alexander said that he had only come across one case where he doubted the origin of the injuries, and thought that it could be handled by the RUC's Complaints & Discipline Branch. He did agree with what Dr Irwin had said earlier, that only about half the suspects at

Castlereagh consented to medical examination. The meeting over, the Committee knew that they had to act quickly.

What made the problem more sensitive was that it had arisen once again in an atmosphere of continuing violence. In March, while bomb attacks on commercial targets decreased, perhaps owing to the Provisionals' caution after the horror of La Mon, attacks on the security forces increased. Four soldiers were killed: one by a booby trap in Crossmaglen, another in an M60 machine-gun attack in Belfast, and another in a shoot-out with the Provisionals near Maghera. The fourth soldier was killed while on civilian search duty in Belfast city centre. This last murder was one which particularly outraged public opinion, as both the soldier and the civilian searcher with him were shot dead by a Provisional gunman masquerading as an Arab in a student rag-day procession. Attacks on off-duty members of the security forces also continued. A member of the UDR was wounded while driving a school bus and then finished off by his attackers a few miles down the road. A Reserve Constable was killed by a booby-trap bomb outside his home. Sectarian killings also started again. In Portadown, two Roman Catholics were shot dead by men on a motorcycle. There were retaliatory attacks by Protestants.

There was also a parallel escalation in complaints of Assault During Interview. In February there had been thirty-seven; in March there were forty-three. The figure was the highest for any month in 1978 and the highest since July 1977.

The Chief Constable was aware of the conundrum. At the Police Authority's meeting on 14 March, Donal Murphy asked him if there were any conclusions to be drawn from the upsurge in violence. The Chief Constable said that although good progress had been made against the paramilitaries in 1977, the situation in 1978 had deteriorated for several reasons. He said that the Provisionals had regrouped into a tighter cell structure; a new blast incendiary, like the one used at La Mon, had been introduced;

the M60 machine-gun, though of limited use in urban
areas, had affected the public's perception of the situation.
But perhaps most significantly the Chief Constable pointed
out to the Authority that detectives had become over-
cautious and less active as a result of the Amnesty visit and
the preoccupation with the alleged ill-treatment of suspects.

Its anxieties unrelieved, the Police Authority decided to
concentrate the pressure at the highest level, on both the
Chief Constable and the Secretary of State. The strategy
that evolved, although it is unlikely that any one person sat
down and mapped it out, was to persuade the Chief
Constable to meet the Complaints Committee and the
doctors to discuss the problem at ground level while
preparing the political arena for some kind of 'summit'
meeting should all else fail. These negotiations were, of
course, to be conducted in the utmost secrecy with Amnesty
writing its report and the doctors thinking of writing their
resignations.

On 7 March 1978, the day after the Complaints Committee had been given their ultimatum by the doctors, the
wheels were set in motion. The Secretary, William Baird,
wrote to the Chief Constable asking him to meet the
Complaints Committee and the doctors. The Secretary
received a defiant reply. The Chief Constable appears to
have said that he didn't see what role the Police Authority
had in the matter but would, with reluctance, agree to
meet the doctors by himself. The Complaints Committee
found the reply unacceptable. The Chief Constable then
made another offer. He said he would allow his deputy,
Harry Baillie, to meet the Committee provided there were
only three members present – no doubt Jack Hassard
would not have been one – and no individual case which
the Authority had raised with the RUC was to be discussed.
Some members of the Complaints Committee regarded
the Chief Constable's reply as an insult. There were
mutterings about the Authority having the power to fire
the Chief Constable as well as to hire him.

To avoid mutiny in the ranks, the Chairman of the Complaints Committee, Ivor Canavan, appears to have rung the Chief Constable and explained the situation to him. Canavan returned and told the Committee that the Chief Constable had finally agreed to the full meeting with the doctors and the Complaints Committee.

The Secretary of State was also informed by William Baird that the Authority wished to talk. The last thing that Roy Mason wanted was another row and resignations to follow, as Amnesty International was writing its report in London. He asked his junior Minister, James Dunn, to take the political temperature. Administratively, the RUC was Dunn's responsibility.

Dunn was a useful man for the government to have on its Northern Ireland team. He had originally been sent over by Prime Minister James Callaghan to join Merlyn Rees in 1975. Apart from his earthy approach to political problems, Dunn was also a Liverpool MP and a practising Catholic with an Irish wife. He used to say he had to practise because he wasn't much good at it. James Dunn had all the right credentials for the job.

On 8 March the emissaries from the Police Authority, William Baird and Ivor Canavan, met James Dunn in his office at Stormont Castle. They told the Minister of the meeting they had had with the doctors two days earlier, and warned him of the trouble that lay ahead if something wasn't done. They said that the doctors wanted Amnesty informed that ill-treatment had started again and wished to withdraw the assurances they had given to Amnesty the previous December. Dunn was also warned of the possibility of resignations. Baird and Canavan told him of the Police Authority's own frustrations and the difficulties which they had had in making any headway with the Chief Constable and the RUC. Dunn apparently admitted that Kenneth Newman wasn't the easiest man to deal with. He said he appreciated their difficulties but asked them to be patient and he would see what he could do. Dunn knew the situation was explosive and had to be handled with what he called 'great sensitivity'. As a life-long supporter of Amnesty, Dunn was also worried on the non-political level. On 21 March 1978, the meeting between the Chief Constable, the Complaints Committee and the doctors, which had been so difficult to arrange, was finally held. The official record of the meeting says that 'little ground was yielded on either side'. Some of those who attended said there was a blazing row. The Chief Constable said that he couldn't understand why there were so many complaints when he had set up the Hermon Committee to deal with any problems the doctors had. He had understood that the Hermon Committee was working quite well. Dr Elliott said that the minutes tended to create a false impression. The Chief Constable then repeated his position on the allegations. To avoid a stalemate and to keep some kind of dialogue going, Ivor Canavan suggested that the Hermon Committee should try and deal with 'outstanding matters'. The meeting resolved nothing.

The meeting over, the Complaints Committee opened the Police Authority's drinks cupboard for the doctors and the police, in the hope that a dash of alcohol might help thaw the frosty atmosphere that lingered on after the meeting was over. In an attempt to break the ice, Dr Elliott went over to Kenneth Newman to have a chat and tell him a joke. He told him the story of the teacher, the schoolboy and the policeman. One day a teacher asked her class to write a story about the police. One pupil wrote 'All policemen are bastards'. The teacher scolded him and said that it was wrong. To correct any false impressions, the teacher then invited a policeman to talk to her class. The policeman came along, gave a talk, and handed out sweets. The teacher then asked the class to write another essay about the police. She looked again at the same boy's work. This time he had written 'All policemen are cunning bastards'. In the circumstances, Dr Elliott's joke wasn't in the best of taste.

14. Breaking Point

> 'Doctors shall not countenance, condone or participate in
> the practice of torture or other form of cruel, inhuman or
> degrading procedures, whatever the offence of which the
> victim of such procedure is suspected . . . in all situations
> including armed conflict in civil strife.'
>
> World Medical Association Conference in Tokyo, 1975 –
> 'The Tokyo Declaration'

Since Gough Barracks Interrogation Centre had opened in
November 1977, many detectives thought it a waste of time
working there, as they were not given the latitude which
they enjoyed at Castlereagh. At one stage, senior officers
at Castlereagh, who were responsible for the overall
running of Gough, put pressure on the local police to 'ease
off'. For a start they suggested that Dr Elliott's medical
room, which he himself admitted was embarrassingly close
to the interview rooms, should be moved to a more
convenient location. (At Castlereagh Dr Alexander's medical room was in the cell block.) At the beginning of March,
the uniformed inspector in charge of Gough, who had
taken the job only on the condition that he could ask for
a transfer, moved back to his old station in Armagh. He
was replaced by two other inspectors, one from Lisburn,
the other an ex-Detective Sergeant from Castlereagh, who
had now been promoted to a uniformed inspector. In April
complaints at Castlereagh were halved, while at Gough
they almost doubled.

On Easter Sunday 1978, Daniel Hamill, a teenager
from a Catholic housing estate in Portadown, was arrested
and brought to Gough. He was medically examined on
arrival and showed no sign of injury or ill-treatment.
He was suspected of involvement in the bombing of a
Protestant pub in Portadown in retaliation for the sectarian killing of two Roman Catholics by gunmen on a
motorcycle.

On Sunday evening, Hamill, who weighed only seven stone and was of poor physique, having undergone major surgery, complained that he had been ill-treated during interrogation that afternoon. He alleged that he had been slapped around the head, kicked about the legs and been lifted off his feet by fingers being placed under his ears. Dr Elliott examined him two hours after the interview and found reddening and early bruising around the ears. Later the same evening Hamill complained again, and said that in the next interview he had had his arms twisted, his wrists bent, his face slapped and his hair pulled. The medical findings were the same as before.

On Easter Monday, Hamill was examined again on three separate occasions. Each time more bruises appeared, around the eye, the arm, the chest and the ear. By the time Dr Elliott had completed his final examination on Monday evening, some bruises were on their way out while others were on their way in. Dr Elliott concluded that Hamill had suffered considerable physical abuse and that, although the bruises were not at first apparent, they became embarrassingly obvious later. He did not believe that the injuries were self-inflicted.

Hamill was charged with attempted murder and remanded in custody but his case never came to court. Several months later the DPP withdrew the charges. Hamill was released, having spent nearly a year in prison on remand.

Dr Elliott sent copies of his medical report, as he had been asked to do, to the Police Authority and to Dr Weir at the DHSS. He was later angry to learn that the Police Authority had never seen his reports, as they had been kept from its members. Apparently, he subsequently received a letter from the officers of the Police Authority, asking him in future to mark all his reports 'Personal and Confidential'. He was asked to send them to the Secretary of the Authority in order to ensure privacy and get them as quickly as possible to the 'proper authority'. Clearly members of the Police Authority were not to be told specific details of the doctors' concern.

At the end of April 1978, doctors working at Crumlin Road gaol compiled a list of prisoners who had passed through the prison on whom marks had been noted at the time of admission. Most of the prisoners had been interrogated at Castlereagh. The marks the doctors noted were what they regarded as 'significant injuries', that is injuries which they thought were unlikely to have been self-inflicted. The list covered prisoners who had been admitted to the prison from February 1978 until the middle of April that year. These were the three months when the allegations had been running at their new peak. In total forty-four prisoners were named. Each one was listed against his prison number. The list they produced is shown here. It is one of the most important documents of the period.

There were other prisoners too from this period who were marked but who were not included in this list because they had moved on elsewhere. Further, some of the prisoners listed as not having any marks nevertheless showed signs of tenderness in certain areas. Prisoner No. 818, Robert George Fitzsimmons, for example, was tender around the rib cage.

The doctors examined their medical records on a total of forty-four prisoners. Twenty-eight of them were 'marked'. Of the forty-four prisoners examined, twenty-five had been interrogated at Castlereagh. Of these fifteen were 'marked'. So on average two thirds of all the prisoners surveyed bore signs of significant injury on admission to Crumlin Road prison. If the dates of interrogation at Castlereagh are closely examined, a pattern emerges. There are clearly two main waves of injured prisoners coming from Castlereagh, the first around the middle of February and the second around the beginning of March. It was the period of the La Mon bombing.

Where prisoners named on the list had made a complaint,

NO.	NAME	DOB	STATION	HELD	MARKS	
368	James Martin Doherty	1.6.50	Castlereagh	7.2.78 12.2.78	NO	
296	Wesley Joseph Taylor	22.9.47	Castlereagh	31.1.78 4.2.78	NO	
313	Emmanuel A. McGrory	21.5.58	Castlereagh	3.2.78 6.2.78	NO	
325	Thomas A. M. McGorman	14.5.45	Castlereagh	5.2.78 6.2.78	YES	FIRST
350	Mark Vincent	10.4.55	Castlereagh	6.2.78 9.2.78	YES	
396	Martin McManus	7.6.56	Castlereagh	13.2.78 15.2.78	YES	
397	Anthony McAllister	13.11.57	Springfield Rd	13.2.78 16.2.78	YES	WAVE
464	Thomas J. A. McDermott	14.9.59	Castlereagh	19.2.78 20.2.78	YES	
437	Thomas Noel O'Hare	24.12.58	Castlereagh	21.2.78 22.2.78	YES	
402	Henry Smith	13.7.44	Springfield Rd	23.2.78	NO	
464	Martin Rooney	10.11.51	Castlereagh	24.2.78 25.2.78	NO	

No.	Name	D.O.B.	Place	Date(s)		
465	Anthony Natarantonio	28.7.58	Castlereagh	24.2.78 26.2.78	NO	
504	John Joseph Fusco	23.3.54	Castlereagh	28.2.78	YES	
535	Francis Thomas Jones	10.1.60	Castlereagh	3.3.78 1.3.78 6.3.78	YES	
770	Patrick Joseph Bell	10.3.52	Lurgan	3.4.78	YES	SECOND
546	Anthony Rasey	6.1.55	Castlereagh	4.3.78	YES	
567	Walter Sims	26.1.54	Castlereagh	6.3.78 7.3.78	YES	
566	Arthur Beck	19.4.55	Castlereagh	6.3.78 7.3.78	YES	
553	Liam Bleakley	26.6.59	Dunmurry	6.3.78	YES	
582	Joseph Plunkett McIlhatton	28.4.59	Castlereagh	8.3.78 9.3.78	YES	WAVE
585	Martin Christopher Heeney	17.4.59	Portadown	9.3.78 11.3.78	YES	
631	Robert Kerr	9.1.56	Castlereagh	13.3.78 15.3.78	YES	
622	Daniel McGarrigle	5.8.62	Strand Road, Londonderry	14.3.78	NO	
621	Kieran McGillicuddy	3.6.62	Strand Road, Londonderry	14.3.78	NO	

NO.	NAME	DOB	STATION	HELD	MARKS
628	Francis Joseph Gill	11.1.57	Castlereagh	15.3.78 16.3.78	YES
663	David George Warren	9.12.48	Castlereagh	20.3.78	NO
	David Nellins	16.6.60	Castlereagh	20.3.78	NO
715	George Gerard Murtagh	13.11.54	Castlereagh	26.3.78 27.3.78	NO
706	Edward Doherty	4.6.59	Army, L/derry	26.3.78	NO
714	John Patrick Dignam	2.8.59	Gough	22.3.78 29.3.78	YES
720	James Pius Clark	2.9.56	Strand Road, Londonderry	26.3.78	YES
722	Daniel Gerard Bonner	21.2.58	Limavady	27.3.78	YES
718	Daniel Anthony McIntyre	1.1.53	Limavady	27.3.78	YES
732	Kevin Trainor	21.2.56	Gough	29.3.78	YES
737	John Joseph McGoran	24.8.56	Castlereagh	29.3.78 30.3.78	YES
752	Liam McCurdie	23.4.49	Castlereagh	31.3.78 2.4.78	YES
746	John Martin Cory	18.9.50	Gough	31.3.78 2.4.78	NO
743	John Richard Patterson	21.7.51	Castlereagh	31.3.78	NO

713	Daniel Joseph Hamill	12.1.59	Gough	26.3.78 28.3.78	YES
719	John Gerard Sheerin	14.2.59	Limavady	27.3.78	NO
793	Robert Benedict Livingstone	28.9.53	Gough	8.4.78	YES
816	George Taylor McClelland	9.6.50	Gough	10.4.78 11.4.78	YES
822	Allan Clark	6.10.58	Musgrave St	13.4.78	YES
818	Robert George Fitzsimmons	19.5.45	Castlereagh	12.4.78	NO

TOTAL: NO 16   YES 28

Complaints & Discipline investigated and then sent the papers to the DPP. As of 16 September 1979, the DPP had directed a prosecution in only one case, that of prisoner 752, Liam McCurdie. But the prosecution directed by the DPP in Liam McCurdie's case had nothing to do with his interrogation. It was a prosecution directed against a police officer for common assault during arrest. On 16 January 1979 the officer was convicted.

One of the last names on the list was that of prisoner 793, Robert Benedict Livingstone, a twenty-five-year-old former internee from Portadown. Livingstone was interrogated at Gough on 8 April 1978. He was listed as 'marked'. He was a big, strong man who had made his reputation while he was interned as a footballer who used to run through defenders and not round them. When he arrived at Gough on Sunday, 2 April, he was apparently nervous and apprehensive, as he had been interrogated a couple of times previously and alleged that he had been ill-treated. He was examined and his health was found to be satisfactory. Livingstone didn't complain until teatime on Tuesday and requested to be medically examined. He told Dr Elliott that during interrogation on Tuesday afternoon he had been pulled by the hair, punched in the stomach, slapped round the face and ears, been kicked in the groin, caught by the throat in a 'throttling' position and had his wrists bent backwards. Dr Elliott examined him and found bruising around his eye and cheek, redness on his scalp and tenderness around his ribs. He thought that Livingstone's injuries were consistent with the allegations he had made, but were somewhat exaggerated.

Early on Wednesday morning Dr Elliott examined Livingstone once again. He made a further complaint, saying that after he had been examined and made his complaint the night before, he had been taken for further interrogation by the same detectives about whom he had made the complaint. He alleged that they had punched him in the stomach, laid him on the floor, crossed one leg over the other and pressed down on his feet. He said he had tried to cry out in pain, but they had pushed his clothes into his mouth to gag him. He then alleged that they pushed him around, slapped his ears, pulled his hair and grabbed him by the throat. This time, Dr Elliott did not think that Livingstone was exaggerating. Dr Elliott examined him again and found more extensive bruising and swelling.

On Wednesday lunchtime the police said that they wished Livingstone to be examined again, as he had just made an important statement. By this time, it appears, Livingstone was lethargic and depressed. The doctors' findings were the same, except there was now additional bruising on Livingstone's lip. Livingstone asked to see his GP, who came to see him early on Wednesday afternoon. His GP confirmed what the Medical Officers had already established, and said that he didn't think that Livingstone would be fit for further interrogation until the following morning. It was a view with which the doctors agreed.

On Thursday morning Livingstone was examined again and judged fit for limited interrogation. That afternoon the police asked for a further examination, as they said that Livingstone had just made another important statement. Dr Elliott apparently decided that Livingstone was medically unfit for further interrogation that day.

On Friday morning, Dr Elliott again reviewed Livingstone's condition. He had consultations with a senior CID officer and advised him that only limited interrogation should now be allowed. Livingstone asked to see his GP again. His GP said that his patient was unfit for any more interrogation and should be removed from Gough as soon as possible.

On Saturday morning, Livingstone was examined for the last time. Dr Elliott noted that some of the bruises and abrasions were now beginning to fade. Apparently, by this time, Livingstone's evident depression was now mixed with some euphoria at the prospect of getting out of Gough Barracks, albeit for the Crumlin Road prison. Dr Elliott had no doubt that Livingstone had been assaulted on two separate occasions.

A few days after Livingstone had made his complaint, the police suggested to Dr Elliott that his injuries were the result of an incident in the interview room, when detectives had been forced to restrain their prisoner. Dr Elliott said that if such an incident had occurred, it should have been recorded and reported. He pointed out that no such record had been made.

Livingstone was taken from Gough to Portadown to be charged before a Special Court in the police station. His solicitor was surprised to see that his client had a black eye. Livingstone was being accompanied by a detective from Gough. The solicitor asked the detective whether he could see the black eye. He said he couldn't. The solicitor then asked his client to move over to the window, in case the detective was having difficulty with the light. The detective still insisted that he couldn't see anything, even when the solicitor pointed his finger straight at it.

At the Special Court Livingstone was charged with the murder of Thomas Gerald Rafferty, on 7 February 1976 – a young schoolboy who had unwittingly entered a derelict house where a booby-trap bomb had been placed to await the arrival of the security forces. For the rest of the year and the first month of 1979, Livingstone made the journey to Belfast City Commission once a week to be remanded in custody. On 2 February 1979 he made the journey for the last time. When he appeared before the magistrate, he was told that the charges against him had been withdrawn. When his solicitor arrived at the Magistrates' Court and saw his client sitting in the corridor outside, he thought he was seeing a ghost. Livingstone's sudden release was unexpected. His solicitor had not seen the medical report.

The Hermon Committee had been established the previous October to deal with the kind of problems that Dr Elliott, Dr Irwin and their colleagues were now coming across once again. The purpose of the Committee was to help doctors short-circuit the normal procedure of going through the Police Authority, to enable them to approach the RUC directly with their concern. In emergencies, they had been encouraged to use the 'hot line' to DCC Hermon. The problem at about this time was that Jack Hermon wasn't at the end of the 'hot line' to RUC Headquarters, as he had taken some leave to move house once again. Two of his previous homes had already been attacked by both the IRA and the UVF.

Dr Irwin, concerned at the increasing number of unexplained injuries he and his colleagues were now seeing again, decided that it was imperative he should talk to DCC Hermon as soon as possible. Dr Irwin decided to go and see Jack Hermon at his new home.

When he arrived he found the Deputy Chief Constable chopping down a tree in his front garden. Jack Hermon did not expect to see Dr Irwin and invited him in. The Hermons still hadn't completed their move and there were packing cases around the house. Dr Irwin told DCC Hermon that the injuries had started again and had to be stopped. Jack Hermon didn't need reminding that Amnesty International were now back in London writing their report on the events of the previous year. He told Dr Irwin that the problem was one of identification and asked him to assist in future by taking detailed notes of the descriptions of those detectives against whom the allegations were most frequently made. He promised Dr Irwin that he would then make his own inquiries.

Dr Irwin did as DCC Hermon requested. He took notes of the distinguishing features of those detectives whose descriptions seemed to crop up most frequently. Changes in personnel were made. The RUC told me that ten to fifteen detectives were transferred, but stressed that the action taken was the result of 'management sensitivity', not internal inquiries. Senior RUC officers pointed out that it was policy to rotate personnel, especially those involved in the arduous and dangerous business of interrogation. It was certainly true that interrogation, which constituted a key role in the war against the IRA, was not made any easier by the constant scrutiny of the media and unabating campaign of allegations inspired by those whom Castler-aeagh sought to defeat.

The RUC always said that if there was a problem it was the result of the 'bad apple' from which few big organizations were immune. If indeed there were a few 'bad apples' within the RUC, they should be placed in perspective. The RUC's entire detective force consisted of over 600 men, but only a relatively small proportion of them were regularly involved in the daily process of interrogation. As we have seen, in addition to the interrogation duties of Divisional CID detectives, the brunt of interrogation was borne by the four Regional Crime Squads, each of which consisted of around four teams of five detectives. The problem was that when it came to regular interrogation, there weren't that many apples in the barrel to start with.

15. Countdown to Amnesty

> 'It's cheaper than going to Strasbourg again.'
>
> Dr Irwin, on the installation of closed-circuit television at
> meeting with the Chief Constable, 20 April 1978

At the beginning of April 1978, the Police Authority decided it was time to put on the political pressure. On Monday morning, 10 April, Dr Weir, the Chief Medical Officer elect, had a meeting with the Secretary of the Police Authority, William Baird. He told him he had received serious representations from the doctors and something must be done quickly if a crisis was to be avoided. William Baird didn't need reminding, as he, like Dr Weir, had already received copies of Dr Elliott's medical reports and knew how close to resignation some of the Police Surgeons were. William Baird had spent the past month trying to avoid a crisis. The time had now come to get the politicians involved, as pressure on the Chief Constable had produced nothing except references down the line to the Hermon Committee. The Secretary then contacted his Chairman, Sir Myles Humphreys. It was decided that Roy Mason had to be approached. Sir Myles apparently was not anxious to upset the Secretary of State. William Baird drafted a letter to Roy Mason, saying that the Authority was seriously worried about the dangers of the situation and suggested that a summit conference should be held with the Minister, James Dunn, in the chair, in order to try and resolve the crisis. Sir Myles reluctantly signed the letter, which was finally sent off to the Secretary of State.

While the Police Authority was trying to work out what to do next, there was more trouble at Gough Barracks. At

7.30 on Monday, 10 April, Stephen Gilpin, a Protestant from Portadown, was arrested and questioned about a sectarian killing in the town back in 1972. On admission he was examined and no injuries were found.

On Tuesday evening the police asked one of Dr Elliott's deputies to examine Gilpin. They said that he had a 'scratch on the nose'. The 'scratch' turned out to be a deep abrasion, one inch long, which had removed the outer layer of skin. Gilpin told the doctor that he had fallen against the edge of the table in the interview room that afternoon and injured himself. The police apparently later told Dr Elliott that Gilpin had banged his head on the desk while picking up a pen off the floor. The doctor also found fresh abrasions on the cheek, nose and mouth. He decided that Gilpin was not fit for further intensive interrogation.

On Wednesday morning, Dr Elliott examined Gilpin and noted the same injuries as his Deputy. Stephen Gilpin was forty-one, much older than the prisoners who were usually brought to Gough for interrogation. Dr Elliott noted that he was tense, very agitated and even weeping at times. He asked Gilpin if he wished to complain. Gilpin said he did not. Dr Elliott suspected he was frightened to. Gilpin then asked to see his general practitioner from Portadown. By all accounts Gilpin's GP, who was a Protestant, had little time for the allegations of ill-treatment until he arrived at Gough and saw the state of his patient. Gilpin now told him that during interrogation the previous day a detective had hit him on the nose with something. He alleged that the detective told him he had to say that he had accidentally caught his head on the table. Gilpin also alleged that he had been struck repeatedly on the back of the neck and around the ears. He said the detectives had threatened him that 'things would get worse' if he complained. Gilpin said he had been frightened to do so, until he saw his own doctor. Apparently Dr Elliott questioned the detective's explanation of Gilpin's injuries, on the grounds that they were medically unacceptable. He believed that Gilpin had received considerable physical abuse while he was being interrogated at Gough.

Gilpin was charged with a sectarian murder committed in 1972 and remanded weekly in custody until the DPP withdrew the charges against him on 5 January 1979. Stephen Gilpin was released, having spent nearly nine months in prison.

That same week, the Secretary of the Police Authority received two letters from Gough. The first was from Dr Elliott's four deputies, who had decided it was time to put their collective concern in writing. They believed that suspects were being ill-treated at Gough and said that although they thought that some of the allegations were completely unfounded, nevertheless there were some that did cause them concern. Working also as general practitioners in the Gough Barracks catchment area, they said that they found themselves in an embarrassing position and feared that the public might think that they were prepared to sanction a certain degree of ill-treatment at Gough Barracks. They wished to put it on the record that they were not.

The second letter William Baird received from Gough was from Dr Elliott. When he had initially accepted the post, he made it a condition that he could ask for a transfer if at any stage he felt that the situation was not as it should be. Now he said that he wished to take up that option as he didn't wish to be part of an operation that involved the ill-treatment of prisoners. He asked to be transferred to his old job in the prison service.

William Baird also received a third letter. This was sent by the Police Surgeons, who said that they felt it now essential that Amnesty International should be informed about their disquiet, in view of the reassurances which they had given to Amnesty the previous December that they were no longer seeing injuries on prisoners. The Police Surgeons also told William Baird that they felt it was the Police Authority's responsibility, as their employer, to pass on their concern to Amnesty.

By this time the DHSS, now almost besieged by the doctors, and worried by the apparent lack of action, decided to take matters into its own hands. Surprising as it may seem, one of the problems the DHSS faced was that there was no official channel through which it could notify the politicians on the hill at Stormont Castle of the messages being received from its doctors. Apparently, the Chief Medical Officer couldn't just pick up the telephone and tell the politicians what was going on, but had to go through the proper channels. While the Police Authority was still agonizing over which button to press and which finger to use, the DHSS decided to blow the fuses. Dr Baird and his deputy, Dr Weir, had had enough. They told the DHSS Permanent Secretary, Norman Dugdale, that the doctors were on the brink of resignation. Norman Dugdale then informed his Minister, Lord Melchett. Lord Melchett felt that there was little that he could do, as the police were not his responsibility. But by this time he too was worried, as he had seen the medical reports that the doctors were now sending in. He rang James Dunn, the Minister responsible for the police, and warned him that trouble was on the way, and suggested that he talk to Dr Baird and Dr Weir as a matter of urgency.

Dunn realized that the crisis that Ivor Canavan and William Baird had warned him about only a few weeks earlier was now getting worse. He summoned the Chief Medical Officer and his Deputy up to his office at Stormont Castle. Dunn also called in the Deputy Under-Secretary, Jim Hannigan, to act as witness. Dunn told Dr Baird and Dr Weir that he wanted to have a look at the medical reports. They said they couldn't show them to him without their own Minister's permission. Dunn told them bluntly that this was now a police matter and that he was Minister with responsibility for police matters. They showed him a couple of medical reports. It appears that Dunn was horrified at what he read and what he saw marked on the outline drawings of the prisoner's body. He said he had never seen a medical report on a prisoner before, and certainly had never seen the drawings with the injuries marked on them. He claimed he didn't know that such records existed and said that he ought to be sent copies of these reports all the time. Dunn, like most of his political colleagues, had tended to dismiss the allegations as propaganda and the injuries as self-inflicted.

Suddenly, after nearly eighteen months of political indifference, a sense of urgency dawned. The Amnesty Report was only a few weeks away. Dr Baird and Dr Weir warned Dunn that resignations were on the cards. Dunn asked them to be patient and promised that he would do what he could. The Minister managed to buy more time.

By this stage it appears that the government realized that it was too late to defuse the bomb and decided the best they could do was to try to muffle the explosion.

Having notified the Police Authority of his wish for a transfer, Dr Elliott took his letter of resignation up to the DHSS at Dundonald House in order to hand it over in person to Dr Baird. He said his position at Gough was untenable and he wished to be transferred back to his old job in the prison service. Dr Baird knew that if Dr Elliott walked out of Gough, the press would seize the story and destroy any chance the authorities had of stabilizing the situation from within. The problem was that, once Amnesty had left the province, the world outside assumed that all was well. Few outsiders had any idea of the turmoil beneath the surface. Dr Baird wished to steady the boat, to give James Dunn time to take the political action he had promised. He explained the situation to Dr Elliott, warned him of the effect his resignation would have, and told him of the promises that James Dunn had just made. He said that Dunn had told him that action might take time, and went on to warn Dr Elliott that a false move by him might destroy everything. Dr Elliott agreed to bide his time, and stay on at Gough. There was a sigh of relief all round.

It also appears that around this time the DHSS received a copy of the list of marked men that the doctors had compiled at Crumlin Road prison. Again, concern was expressed that medical officers at Crumlin Road prison and Police Surgeons at Townhall Street were seeing unexplained injuries on prisoners arriving from Castlereagh. Shortly afterwards the Police Authority received a letter from Dr Alexander. In that letter he said he was now concerned about the situation at Castlereagh and had just seen a case that had caused him 'serious concern'. Dr Alexander examined the man at the end of March 1978. He was the kind of suspect the police would probably refer to as a 'hard case'. When he was examined at Castlereagh following interrogation, he had two black eyes, a swollen cheek, a swollen nose, a cut lip and several bruises. Apparently his family doctor tried to see him at Castlereagh, but was not admitted. The man made no statement or verbal admission and was released without charge. He did make a complaint. He does not wish to be named.

On the evening of 20 April 1978, the doctors went to RUC Headquarters for an important meeting of the Hermon Committee which was meant to resolve the difficulties which had been left unresolved by their meeting with the Chief Constable and the Complaints Committee the previous month. Before the meeting began, Dr Elliott, Dr Irwin and Dr Alexander were intercepted by a secretary, who said the Chief Constable would like to see them. The secretary escorted them into the Chief Constable's office and the door was closed behind them. The Police Authority officials were left outside in the corridor. Only four people were present at the private meeting: the three doctors and the Chief Constable himself.

The doctors thought that Kenneth Newman seemed unusually affable, more relaxed and informal than usual. He welcomed his visitors and invited them to sit down. He asked what he could do to help them and said that they should feel free to call him any time on his private line. The doctors thanked him and got straight down to business. Dr Elliott said that he didn't wish to carry on working at Gough and had already asked the DHSS for a transfer.

He told the Chief Constable that not only did he feel that ill-treatment was continuing, but he did not detect any real desire on the part of the RUC to stop it. The Chief Constable seemed a little startled and said that he was sorry to hear of Dr Elliott's problem, and implied that this was the first time he had heard of the doctor's request for a transfer. Dr Elliott, who had just examined a further case that morning, Anthony Maguire, said that ill-treatment was still continuing despite repeated warnings from the doctors. He told the Chief Constable that his four Deputies had already written to the Police Authority, making the same complaint. Again, this appeared to be news to Kenneth Newman, and he looked a little taken aback. Dr Irwin then produced the list of marked men from the Crumlin Road prison. He explained that all these were recent cases from the past three months. He pointed out that it wasn't a comprehensive list either, as many other prisoners who had been interrogated during this period had already been transferred to other prisons and therefore were not included in the list. Once again, the Chief Constable appeared to be disturbed. It seemed to be the first time that he had heard of or seen the list. He told the doctors that he couldn't understand how these injuries could occur when interviews were observed and, the moment anything untoward happened, officers from the Scenes of Crime department and Complaints & Discipline branch moved in. Dr Irwin suggested that closed-circuit television might be the answer. The Chief Constable said it would be expensive. Dr Irwin replied that it would be cheaper than going to Strasbourg once again. It appears that at this point Dr Elliott interrupted and asked the Chief Constable what he meant by 'the observation' of interviews. The Chief Constable said that he was referring to the 'spyholes' in the doors of the interview rooms. Dr Elliott said that there weren't any spyholes at Gough. The Chief Constable seemed confused, until Dr Alexander pointed out that there were spyholes in most of the doors, but not in all of them. (The fact was that at Castlereagh there were spyholes only in the doors in the new interrogation blocks. The older interview rooms, with the pegboard walls that so many prisoners had described, had no spyholes. At Gough the cells had spyholes, but not the interview rooms.)

Dr Irwin then asked the Chief Constable about the Scenes of Crime officers, and said that he had never seen any photographs that the police had taken of prisoners' injuries. Dr Elliott pointed out that if the police were going to photograph injuries on a prisoner, they would have to remove some of his clothes, and they couldn't do that unless a Medical Officer were present. He said that he had never seen such a thing happen, nor had any other doctor to the best of his knowledge. Dr Alexander said that he hadn't either. As far as photographing the interview rooms was concerned, Dr Elliott remarked that they would hardly be expected to show signs of assault, unless blood and hair were scattered around the walls. He said that injuries could be serious without being so obvious. He said that in his view the problem was that there was ill-treatment, but no policeman had ever been found guilty of it. He believed that if there was a genuine desire on the part of the RUC to stop it, the system itself would have to be changed. As things stood at the moment, he told the Chief Constable that he didn't think that any policeman would ever be convicted of assaulting a suspect during interview. The Chief Constable by this time appeared to be getting annoyed. He told the doctors most emphatically that he *did* want to stop it and asked them for suggestions. Dr Irwin repeated his proposal for closed-circuit television. Dr Elliott said there should be spyholes in *all* the interview room doors, and that the uniformed inspectors who patrolled the corridors should all be Chief Inspectors. He mentioned the name of the uniformed inspector who had recently asked for a transfer from Gough and said that he was the kind of police officer that he had in mind. The Chief Constable promised to give these points his urgent attention.

The following morning, when Dr Elliott arrived at his

office, he found a workman with a hand-drill boring holes in the doors of the interview rooms. He was fitting spyholes. Dr Elliott asked what was going on. He was told that there had been a hell of a row and that all the spyholes had to be fitted by noon. He also found that the uniformed inspector who had asked for a transfer was now back at Gough, suddenly promoted to the rank of Chief Inspector. Dr Elliott saw no more cases of ill-treatment at Gough Barracks.

Around this time a government Minister was also shown the list of marked men at Crumlin Road prison. He didn't like what he saw and decided to pay Castlereagh a visit. He was given lunch and an official tour. After he had been shown the administrative block and the cells, he was shown round the interview rooms. He was told that proposals were being considered to introduce closed-circuit television. As he was walking down the corridor after seeing one room, he made some remark about the other interview rooms whose doors were closed. His escort told him that all the rooms were the same. On impulse, the Minister opened a door. The room was empty but still warm from a recent interview. The smell of cigarettes still hung in the air. The room was a bit untidy. The Minister looked round and was surprised to see spit on the wall. It was the kind of phlegm you get from trying to clear a blocked throat. The Minister immediately jumped to the conclusion that someone had been 'throttled' and had tried to clear his throat while gasping for breath. He didn't think that detectives spat on walls, but didn't ask any questions. He said he thought he wouldn't have got any answers.

At the regular monthly meeting of the full Police Authority, on 9 May 1978, the Secretary William Baird outlined to members the intricate negotiations that had gone on behind the scenes in April in an attempt to 'dry up' the allegations at source once again and to avert the prospect of mass resignations by the doctors.

Over the previous three months, complaints of assault

during interview had almost reached the pitch of the previous autumn: February, thirty-seven; March, forty-three; April, thirty-two. In May, the month which followed the meetings with James Dunn and the Chief Constable's long interview with the doctors, they fell to twenty-seven.

Much of the meeting at River House was taken up with discussion of the new tide of allegations. Dr Conlon, who was a member of both the Authority and its Complaints Committee, said they were now seeing a pattern similar to the one they had seen in 1977: disquiet expressed by the doctors, followed by the RUC's insistence that there were statutory procedures laid down to deal with complaints and that they were no concern of the Authority's until they had been investigated by the police and, if necessary, the DPP. He reminded the Authority that in 1977 the cause for complaints had dried up when Amnesty arrived, and that they were seeing the same thing now, following the intervention of the Authority, the DHSS and a government Minister.

At such meetings, it was customary for the Chief Constable to give a report on the security situation the preceding month. At the meeting on 9 May, the report was ready by SDCC Harry Baillie, as the Chief Constable had not been able to attend. He said there had been four deaths in April, due to the security situation: one civilian, one UDR, one Reserve Constable, and one Constable. The Constable referred to was Constable Laird Millar McAllister from Lisburn, victim 1834 of the Troubles, murdered in his home at lunchtime on Saturday, 22 April. Constable McAllister was a police photographer and an ardent pigeon-fancier. He wrote a column under the pen-name of 'The Copper' for the *Pigeon Racing News & Gazette*.[1] When a copy of the magazine fell into the hands of the Provisionals, Constable McAllister became a target. A man called at his bungalow in Lisburn and said that his father, a member of the Duncairn Pigeon Racing Club,

1. *Sunday Times*, 23 December 1979.

wanted Constable McAllister to take some photographs of his pigeons. The visitor then pulled out a ·38 revolver and shot Constable McAllister dead.

SDCC Baillie told the Authority that three persons, including one female, had already been charged in connection with the murder of the Constable. What the Authority didn't know was that, while they were listening to SDCC Baillie, a fourth man was being interrogated in connection with the same murder. He was Brian Maguire.

Brian Maguire was a twenty-seven-year-old electronics engineer who worked at the Strathearn Audio plant in Andersonstown. He was an official of his trades union, the AUEW, and thought well of at work. He had just been told of coming promotion. Maguire lived at home with his mother in a mixed neighbourhood where both prison officers and a policeman had homes. Maguire had been in trouble on one previous occasion when he robbed a pub: he had been remanded in custody for ten months and then given a suspended sentence. Mrs Maguire, a widow, was proud of her son. He was an extrovert young man with an obsessional pride in his appearance. In the early seventies he had paid nearly £50 to have his teeth crowned privately. He spent most of his money on clothes. His wardrobe contained twenty shirts, which he was known to change four times a day, as he couldn't stand a dirty collar. The following January he was due to be married to a girl who worked at the local hospital. Mrs Maguire told me that she had heard of Castlereagh but never thought much about it; she had assumed it was just like the local police station at Lisburn. When Brian was arrested at 6 am on Tuesday, 9 May, she asked the policeman if she could make Brian a cup of tea before he left. The police said he would get plenty of tea when he got to Castlereagh.

According to the police, Brian Maguire began his statement at 2.45 pm and finished at 5.40 pm on a Tuesday afternoon. He had been interrogated on Tuesday morning. In the confession he made, he admitted hiding the gun which was assumed to have killed Constable McAllister.

He said that he had been forced to do so after he had been kidnapped the previous day by the I R A, who told him he was going to help them. They threatened him and his girlfriend if he refused, or if he told the police or the 'Brits'. They said a girl would come to his house at lunchtime the following day with a parcel which he was to look after overnight. According to the statement, the plan was carried out. On Saturday lunchtime, a girl came to the door, took a gun out of a bag, wiped it and threw it on the hall floor and said she'd be back the following day to collect it. Maguire said he put the gun under the hedge in the front garden and put a post over it. On the 2 o'clock news he heard that a policeman had been shot dead in Lisburn and said he felt sick as a dog. The next day the girl returned and took the gun away.

Maguire ended his statement by saying that he did not know that he was being involved in the murder of Constable McAllister, and that he had been forced to do it because of threats made against him and his family. In his statement he did not name or describe either his captors or the girl who had twice visited the house.

The police said that at 7.30 the following morning, the Duty Constable brought Brian Maguire's breakfast to his cell, F4. The police knew that Maguire was awake, as he had asked to go down the corridor to the toilet at 7 am, and had returned ten minutes later. At 7.15 am the electric light above the door inside his cell had been turned on by the switch outside. This meant that, with the light now on, Maguire's every movement could be observed through the spyhole in the cell door, whose fish-eye lens makes it virtually impossible for the prisoner to do anything his guards cannot detect. The lens gives a view of most of the cell. When the constable brought Maguire's breakfast at 7.30, he found him hanging from the ventilator grille above the bed opposite the door, with a strip of sheeting tied round his neck. Brian Maguire was dead. This meant that since the light was switched on at 7.15 am and breakfast was brought at 7.30, Brian Maguire must have torn a strip from the sheet of his bed – if he hadn't done so earlier – fastened one end to the ventilation grille, the other round his neck and hanged himself. It was all possible: the sheets were strong enough, the holes in the grille on the wall were big enough to pass two fingers through, and the fixture itself was firm enough to take the weight of Maguire's eleven stones. What was surprising was that Maguire appeared to have done it undetected. Supervision in the corridors was strict, especially in view of the events of the past month.

The post mortem revealed no signs of injury or assault. The only marks on the body, apart from those caused by the hanging, were two purple areas on the back of each calf. The coroner believed they were probably the result of contact with one of the heating pipes that ran along the wall beneath the ventilator grille.

Mrs Maguire had sat up most of the previous night with Brian's girlfriend. The afternoon of Brian's arrest she had telephoned Castlereagh to see how her son was. She said a policeman told her that he had been questioned for four hours and the questioning was now finished. Mrs Maguire assumed that Brian would be coming home and had sat up waiting for him. The following morning Brian's girlfriend heard on the 10 am Downtown Radio news that a man had hanged himself in Castlereagh. A police officer came to break the news to Mrs Maguire. She remembers him saying, 'Brian killed himself, Mrs Maguire. He couldn't face you or his girlfriend, so he killed himself.'

Mrs Maguire admitted that if Brian had been involved it would have destroyed her. But she refused to believe the statement that Brian made and which the police had released to the press as evidence of motive for his 'suicide'. She insisted she had been at home all Saturday lunchtime and had given Brian steak and onions for his meal. Nobody came to the door and if they had she would have heard them. If Brian had hidden the gun under the hedge, the dog would have made off with it. She may well have been covering her son or she may have been telling the truth.

'Brian had too much to live for to commit suicide,' she told me, 'I think they went too far with him.'

The R U C called in a senior police officer from Liverpool to investigate the death of Brian Maguire. His report is believed to have cleared the R U C of any involvement in the incident. At the time of writing, the inquest has still to be held, as Mrs Maguire's solicitors wished to use evidence that had been given in the cases of other suspects who had been interrogated at Castlereagh around the same time, in connection with the same murder. One of them was a young zoology student from Queen's University, Belfast, Phelim Hamill.

Constable McAllister was murdered on 22 April 1978. Phelim Hamill was arrested and interrogated at Castlereagh three days later. He was charged with the murder of Constable McAllister, not on the basis of any statement he had made or signed, but because of a verbal admission he had allegedly made. He was examined by a general practitioner, Dr Maguire, at 5.15 pm on Saturday, 29 April. He alleged that he had been severely beaten during his interrogation in an attempt to get him to sign a statement admitting his involvement in the murder of Constable McAllister. He refused to do so. He said that at the end of his interrogation a doctor asked him if he wished to be examined and make any complaint. Hamill told Dr Maguire that he wasn't convinced that the doctor was a real doctor. Dr Maguire's report continues:

He was informed that it was Dr Alexander who asked him if he had any complaints. Phelim said, 'I had no bruises when I came in, but I have bruises and marks now, but I am making no complaint.'

Dr Maguire marked Hamill's extensive injuries on the outline chart of the human body. Hamill was literally covered in bruises. Amongst them were three on his neck. Dr Maguire's report concluded:

Has many bruises and injuries which are consistent with his allegations of assault and ill-treatment.

The charges against Hamill were subsequently withdrawn and he was released. This is the allegation that he made to Dr Maguire on 29 April 1978, which was of particular concern to those involved in Brian Maguire's case:

He detailed how, on one occasion, someone got a towel and put it round his face, making it difficult for him to breathe. Water was then poured over the mouth and nose area. This was frightening and was repeated on a number of occasions.

In December 1979, after a trial lasting twenty-one days, Mr Justice MacDermott found three men guilty of the murder of Constable McAllister and sentenced them to life imprisonment. They were Harry Murray – a Protestant married to a Catholic girl – who actually pulled the trigger; Michael Culbert, a Provisional IRA Intelligence Officer who apparently singled out Constable McAllister; and John Smyth, who hijacked the car which was used for the murder. The judge recommended that Murray should serve not less than thirty years of his sentence. The fourth accused was twenty-one-year-old Anne Laverty, who disposed of the weapon. The judge sentenced her to three years' imprisonment for her part in the murder. Murray, Culbert and Smyth contested their statements on grounds of duress, not ill-treatment. Mr Justice MacDermott rejected their plea.

By the summer of 1980, the inquest on Brian Maguire had still to be held. As in the case of Eddie Rooney, it is impossible to say with certainty what happened to Brian Maguire at Castlereagh. But in the light of the background to the case, suicide, not murder, is the more likely explanation. But again, as in the case of Eddie Rooney, in the emotionally charged atmosphere of the time truth was not a priority to those who seized such opportunities to discredit the RUC and undermine still further the effectiveness of Castlereagh.

16. The Amnesty Report

> 'Amnesty International believes that maltreatment of sus-
> pected terrorists by the R U C has taken place with sufficient
> frequency to warrant the establishment of a public inquiry
> to investigate it.'
>
> Conclusion, Amnesty Report, June 1978

Amnesty International sent its Report to the Secretary of
State Roy Mason on 2 May 1978. It confirmed what the
doctors had been saying, what the D P P had told the Chief
Constable, and what the Attorney-General had told the
Prime Minister before Amnesty set foot in the province.
The Report recommended that a 'public and impartial
inquiry' be established to investigate the allegations. In
view of what the government already knew, its conclusions
can have come as no surprise.

The Amnesty mission had based its findings on seventy-
eight cases of alleged ill-treatment which it had examined:
thirty-nine cases consisted of interviews with individuals
who had no medical evidence to back up their complaints;
twenty-six cases consisted of medical evidence but no
interviews with the complainants because most were in
gaol; and thirteen cases where the individuals interviewed
by the mission had medical evidence to back up their
allegations. From the seventy-eight cases, five individuals
were selected for further interview and detailed examination by the two Amnesty doctors. The medical evidence
available was invariably that of general practitioners, as
the mission had not been given access to the 'official'
doctors' reports. All the Amnesty cases were anonymous
as the mission had promised confidentiality to all those
who gave evidence.

In Belfast the burst of activity that had marked the
weeks before Amnesty arrived was repeated in the weeks

before its Report was published. The Police Authority grew increasingly frustrated. By now the Chairman, Sir Myles Humphreys, who had entered the fray only with some reluctance, recognized the fact that the many meetings held over the past few months had been inconclusive. He now believed that it was essential that there should be a Code of Practice drawn up for both the R U C's interrogators and the Police Authority's doctors: this was the kind of role for which the Hermon Committee had been designed, but Sir Myles was not optimistic that the Committee, from which members of the Authority were excluded, could handle the situation.

Finally, at the Police Authority meeting on 9 May 1978, it was decided that Ivor Canavan and Donal Murphy should join the Hermon Committee, perhaps for a month, in the hope of achieving a 'break-through'. Their specific task was to see if the Committee could work out a Code of Practice. Sir Myles said he was going to inform the Secretary of State that the Hermon Committee was being 'strengthened by two Authority members' and request him to tell the Chief Constable of the decision and ask for his full cooperation. The Chief Constable proved less than enthusiastic at the idea.

On 11 May William Baird wrote to Jack Hermon to let him know that the Authority wished Canavan and Murphy to join his Committee. D C C Hermon then phoned William Baird to say that he had referred the proposal to the Chief Constable. Baird passed on the message to Ivor Canavan, as the Complaints Committee was meeting that day. The reply from D C C Hermon increased the frustrations the Committee already felt. Canavan said it was for the Complaints Committee to decide whether he and Donal Murphy met the Hermon Committee.

Murphy and Jack Hassard were now at the end of their patience: they had already joined issue with the sentiments expressed in letters exchanged between Sir Myles Humphreys and Roy Mason, in which the Chairman appears to have told the Secretary of State that the complaints from

the doctors had 'ceased'. In turn, Roy Mason appears to
have informed Sir Myles that the 'possibility of precipitate
action by the doctors' – i.e. their resignation – 'had been
removed'. Murphy and Hassard knew that Dr Irwin and
Dr Elliot were far from mollified. Both doctors had now
made it clear that the Authority should inform Amnesty of
their fresh anxieties.

The Complaints Committee decided to invite the doctors
to a Special Meeting. The Authority's officers, if not all its
members, were already familiar with how some of them
felt. Paddy Farrelly, the Authority's Deputy Secretary, had
recently held a meeting with Dr Elliott's four deputies at
Gough. They had told him that they believed that there
had been physical ill-treatment at Gough and their formal
expressions of concern to members of the RUC had been
ineffective. They told Farrelly that they would be in an
awkward position if, as might happen in the cases of seven
individuals interrogated at Gough, their statements were
ruled inadmissible in court. At the time Dr Elliott himself
was out of action. For reasons unknown (there was a
rumour that detectives were in revolt and refused to work
there) the Interrogation Centre at Gough Barracks had
been temporarily shut down and Denis Elliott had been
transferred to the Maze prison. Suspects were being
interviewed in the ancient police station in Dungannon,
next door to Jack Hassard's post office.

On 19 May the Complaints Committee met the doctors
at River House. They arrived in three separate groups.
First the Committee met Dr Alexander, Dr Elliott and
their DHSS chief, Dr Weir. Ivor Canavan told them that,
after the 'peak' in the allegations in 1977, there had been
a second 'peak' at the beginning of 1978, despite agreed
procedures to 'dry up' complaints at source. The Committee was concerned that there should not be a third. Dr
Alexander said that he had no present cause for concern.
Dr Elliott said that he was most concerned that suspects
weren't being interviewed at Gough any more. Dr Weir
accepted that there were differences in the views of the

two SMOs but that was because the circumstances were different. He did agree, however, that there was evidence of persons leaving Castlereagh with marks. He said that his anxiety was that the public should not think that the doctors were covering up: if this was the impression given, he feared that the doctors might be in jeopardy.

The Committee then met the Police Surgeons, Dr Stewart and Dr Irwin. Ivor Canavan asked Dr Irwin if he thought there might be another 'peak'. Dr Irwin said it was almost inevitable as long as specialist Interrogation Centres like Castlereagh and Gough existed. Making the same point in a different way, Dr Stewart pointed out that in the past when there had been 'lifts' of suspected terrorists and they had been interrogated by detectives from the Divisional CID, there had not been any complaints, and most of the suspects had been convicted. His members had examined them and found nothing to cause them concern. Dr Stewart felt that the introduction of Castlereagh was a 'grave error'.

Dr Irwin was then asked what he thought of the Hermon Committee. Ivor Canavan had yet to find out for himself. He said he was thinking of leaving because it had never been acknowledged that anything was wrong. He said that even the minutes weren't accurate. He had already recommended closed-circuit television to both the Hermon Committee and the Chief Constable but nothing had been done. He said that if attention had been paid to what he said, the recent tragedy of Brian Maguire might have been avoided. Ivor Canavan then told the doctors that he and Donal Murphy were hoping to attend the next meeting of the Hermon Committee with a view to getting 'positive, progressive and urgent action'.

Finally the Committee met Dr Russell, who was one of the seven part-time medical officers at Castlereagh. He said that doctors at Castlereagh believed that the complaints were exaggerated and that they had not noticed a 'widespread resurgence'. He said that over the past two years they had seen around 400–500 suspects and about 10 per cent of them said they had been 'pushed around' but would not register a formal complaint. Dr Russell said that when the suspects were asked to define 'pushed around' they would not give detailed descriptions. He added, however, that if he or his colleagues felt a person to be distressed or injured they would note their observations on the medical report, even if they didn't examine him. If, however, there was a spate of complaints of this kind, Dr Russell said they would advise the police in charge. In a number of instances he admitted that they, the doctors, actually stopped interrogation.

Dr Russell's remarks were interesting, in view of what Dr Alexander himself told me on the telephone. I asked to meet him, but he refused. He said that he had been ordered not to talk to me. I asked him about supervision of the interview rooms. He said that 'scarcely a day went by' when he didn't walk down the corridors and look through the spyholes. But he told me that it was not his job to intervene. He said that if he saw a man having his head banged against a wall, he wouldn't open the door to stop it. He would immediately inform the Inspector on duty. I asked him if he had ever seen heads being banged against walls. He said 'No comment'.

Dr Irwin returned home after meeting the Complaints Committee at River House, but didn't get to bed until late the following morning. Just after 11 pm he received a phone call from Townhall Street: a prisoner had just arrived from Castlereagh; could Dr Irwin come and examine him?

The prisoner was Edward Cochrane, from the Lenadoon area on the fringe of Andersonstown. Cochrane had been arrested the previous day and brought to Castlereagh. He told Dr Irwin that he had been examined when he arrived at Castlereagh and when he left. He alleged that he had been assaulted during his second interview the previous afternoon, and that he had been punched around the head and face. When Dr Irwin examined him, he found discolouration around his eyes, a bruise on each cheekbone,

redness of the gums and another bruise inside the mouth.
Dr Irwin's opinion revealed his frustration:

> This man's appearance, coming from Castlereagh with its so-
> called tight security and no explanation of how the injuries
> occurred or when they occurred, would lead one to believe that
> the allegations made are correct.

Cochrane made an official complaint. It was investigated
by the Complaints & Discipline Branch. A Chief Inspector
wrote to Dr Irwin to ask him for his medical report. He
said it would help the DPP and others concerned with the
investigation if Dr Irwin would include in his report an
opinion as to how the injuries occurred and whether they
were consistent with the complainant's allegations. Dr
Irwin obliged and wrote:

> This man was obviously punched about the face and the injuries
> were consistent with that. It would be facetious to suggest that
> the injuries were self-inflicted without some evidence coming
> from Castlereagh to that effect. One is not inclined to believe that
> the continued parade of injuries is anything other than premedi-
> tated and carried out by so-called upholders of the law.

On 26 May 1978, Roy Mason wrote to Amnesty International asking its International Executive to postpone
publication. At the beginning of his letter he told Amnesty
that the British government would not condone ill-treatment and the Chief Constable would deal with any police
officer who stepped outside the law. He said it was
government policy to see that all members of the security
forces abided by the spirit and letter of the law.

The government faced two problems in handling the
Amnesty Report. The first was how to deal with allegations
which Amnesty had found to be substantiated. Ministers
had had plenty of time to think about it. It was now over
six months since the Attorney-General had told the Prime
Minister that the DPP had identified thirty cases in which
the complaints were substantiated, and they covered only

the first nine months of 1977: Amnesty had taken cases from 1976 and from October and November 1977. Amnesty's total number of cases where corroborative medical evidence was available was only nine more than the DPP's.

The government's strategy was to ask Amnesty to identify its seventy-eight cases so they could be investigated. In his letter to Amnesty, the Secretary of State said that 'the ordinary principles of natural justice require that any investigation must be based on identified witnesses'. Roy Mason argued that once the cases had been identified and investigated, they could go to the Director of Public Prosecutions, 'the independent officer of the Crown charged with deciding whether to bring criminal proceedings'. The fact that the Director had told the Chief Constable in November 1977 – a message then relayed by the Attorney-General to the Prime Minister – that it was not his job to decide whether an assault had occurred, and that the number of prosecutions should *not* be equated with the number of assaults, was ignored. Nobody knew that the government knew that the DPP was unhappy with the role he was being asked to play.

The government's second problem was what to do about Amnesty's demand for a public inquiry into the allegations. On the basis of the information the Attorney-General had given the Prime Minister the previous November, and on the evidence of the medical reports which had finally found their way on to Ministers' desks in the spring of 1978, the government realized that any inquiry into the allegations themselves would probably result in a political scandal. The scandal would also have had international repercussions, in view of the recent judgement of the European Court. Another journey to Strasbourg, with the Attorney-General's 'unqualified undertakings' ringing in their ears, was the last thing that British Ministers wanted. An inquiry into the allegations themselves was politically out of the question. A private inquiry, along the lines of the Compton Committee, might wash the government's linen more discreetly, but in the end the stains would still show.

Allegations of ill-treatment raise three questions for any government. Are they true? If so, how are those responsible made amenable? How are future outbreaks to be prevented? In 1971 the Heath government faced all three questions. The Compton Committee investigated the allegations, the Parker Committee reviewed interrogation procedures, and the Attorney-General appears to have given those involved immunity from prosecution when they gave evidence at Strasbourg. Most members of the Labour government felt that the third stage – the prevention of future outbreaks – was the most important, as well as the most politically expedient. An inquiry into procedures had several advantages: it met part of Amnesty's demands; it would result in the tightening of interrogation procedures; it would reduce the likelihood of further recurrence; it meant the government never had to admit that suspects had been ill-treated. So questions were asked – but they were conveniently changed.

There were even problems in asking a different set of questions. As senior civil servants recognized, the Chief Constable had to agree on whatever action the government decided to take. It was not easy. The polical relationship between the Chief Constable and the Secretary of State had always been delicate, with the Chief Constable jealously guarding his political independence and the Secretary of State realizing that the government was ultimately responsible for what he did.

The Deputy Under-Secretary, Jim Hannigan, was charged with the job of drafting the government's reply to Amnesty. Hannigan was familiar with the climate. He had been present at the series of meetings between the various parties in April that had been called to try to stop the doctors handing in their resignations.

Roy Mason was advised in some quarters that if the Chief Constable was responsible, his only redress was to fire. him, but that everybody knew that such a step was impractical. The Secretary of State was told that if abuse occurred, the government had no comeback; the answer therefore was to make sure that abuses did not occur. Effectively the Secretary of State was being told that the Chief Constable was immune and the government had to carry the can. Some Ministers argued that Section 6 lay at the root of the problem: it had given the RUC's interrogators the latitude they had hitherto lacked. The only way to curb excesses was therefore to repeal or amend the section to make it clear that not only torture, inhuman and degrading treatment were unaccepable in obtaining confessions, but violence or the threat of it as well. It was suggested that Section 6 should be redrafted to include the additional words 'violence or the threat of it' – the words which Lord Diplock himself had used in his Report, but which the government had not included when Section 6 was originally drafted. This would have left no room for misunderstanding or misinterpretation. It would have been tantamount to reverting to the common law test of admissibility which still applied throughout the rest of the United Kingdom. But to return to the common law test risked undermining not only Castlereagh, but the very foundation on which the whole legal edifice in Northern Ireland had been built. As Roy Mason's office told the Prime Minister on 31 May 1978, Section 6 was intrinsic to the non-jury Diplock courts. To amend Section 6 would not only imply that the latitude it had given the RUC's interrogators had resulted in abuses, but it would virtually force the government to tear up the policy it had pursued since the ending of internment. The government was trapped in its own policy. It felt it could not afford to neuter Section 6.

The Secretary of State was also advised not to be misguided by explanations that the injuries were self-inflicted, the straw to which, he was told, some of his officials in the Northern Ireland Office still clung. The Attorney-General had sent the government the same message the previous November. Roy Mason was also warned not to assume that the threat of the DPP and the prospect of criminal prosecution would act as a deterrent to the RUC's interrogators.

Another suggestion made to tighten the system against further abuse was that GPs should automatically be given copies of the Police Doctors' reports. Although it was argued that the Chief Constable would never accept such a move, it was pointed out that at the end of the day the government was answerable if the RUC's interrogators overstepped the mark.

While these discussions were being conducted high in the political clouds, on the ground in Belfast the Police Authority were still trying to achieve their 'break-through'. Ivor Canavan and Donal Murphy seemed no nearer meeting the Hermon Committee. While they were hoping to get in, Dr Irwin and Dr Elliott were already thinking of getting out – both found the Committee a waste of time. Dr Elliott thought the 'Hermon hot line' was useless (he had had reason to ring DCC Hermon about one particular detective on three separate occasions. DCC Hermon had promised he would be removed. It was apparently not until Dr Elliott's third 'hot line' call that the promise took effect). Nevertheless, William Baird battled on to try and make the meeting possible. He knew he might have resignations from the Police Authority on his hands if he didn't. A public outcry would almost certainly follow resignations. He already had enough problems with the doctors wanting Amnesty informed of their renewed concern. Neither would do much to help the delicate negotiations between Whitehall, Stormont Castle and RUC HQ over the government's response to the Amnesty Report.

A few days after he had received Dr Irwin's letter, implying that the Authority was honour-bound to convey his concern to Amnesty, William Baird wrote to SDCC Hermon again, having heard nothing for a week. He repeated his original request for the meeting to which

Canavan and Murphy would be invited, and suggested 25 May as a suitable date. The following day, the Chief Constable phoned William Baird and told him he was uneasy about the proposal that contact with the Hermon Committee should be extended to members of the Authority. The Hermon Committee's function was to iron out problems between the doctors and the police. Officially it was no concern of members of the Authority, but its officers were allowed to attend as technically the Authority employed the doctors. After renewed pressure later that day, the Chief Constable finally agreed that Canavan and Murphy should be allowed to attend and the meeting should be held on 25 May.

The Hermon Committee met at 4 pm at RUC Headquarters on 25 May. Ivor Canavan and Donal Murphy were present, but Jack Hermon was not. He was away at the time, and the Chief Constable took the chair.

With the Amnesty Report now in government hands, the deliberations of the Hermon Committee were largely academic. Only the Chief Constable knew what was in the Report, and was aware of the backstage political manoeuvres that were designed to soften its impact. Others at the meeting, the doctors, members and officials of the Authority, remained in the dark. Nevertheless, the meeting went through the motions of discussion. The Chief Constable said that if the doctors were worried they could ring him or his Deputies at any time on the 'hot line'. If they wished to meet and talk, he would agree. With regard to the particular cases the doctors were concerned about, the Chief Constable said he would see that SDCC Baillie pressed the DPP for early decisions. Ivor Canavan asked the Chief Constable for a copy of any further instructions which had been given to interrogators. The Chief Constable said there were none.

Some of those present thought that the Chief Constable looked under pressure. In view of the imminent publication of the Amnesty Report, he was. But there may have been other pressures too. There were rumours that some of his detectives were on the brink of revolt, on the grounds that the Chief Constable had originally told them to get results – which they had done with great success – and they were now being told to go easy. Whereas I was able to substantiate the original meeting at which the Chief Constable told his detectives he wanted results, I was unable to confirm any subsequent meeting at which the detectives were told to ease the pressure. Some detectives told me, however, that at one stage word did come down to 'go easy'. Exactly when the word came and where it came from, they were not prepared to say.

Shortly after Roy Mason had written to Amnesty asking them to delay publication, the Report was leaked. The source of the leak was never identified. Most suspected Amnesty: some suspected a tactical leak by the Northern Ireland Office to lessen the impact of official publication. At the beginning of the week of 5 June, the *Irish Times* carried a brief resume of the Report. The British press picked up the story. On Wednesday, 7 June, BBC-TV's 'Tonight' programme gave details of the Report. Thames Television had obtained a copy at the beginning of the week, and a half-hour 'This Week' programme was planned for transmission on the ITV network on Thursday evening. I flew over to Belfast to film interviews with politicians and interested parties to whom we had previously given copies of the Report. Dr Paisley was one and said he was most concerned by its findings. I also interviewed two people we had included in our original programme the previous October: Dr James O'Rawe, who spoke of recent cases he had seen at Castlereagh, and Jack Hassard, this time speaking openly to the camera, who said that both the Chief Constable and the Secretary of State had known all along what was happening. He called for the clearing out of 'the heavy brigade' in the Regional Crime Squads in order to 'remove the stain on the RUC's fine reputation'.

While I was filming these interviews in Belfast on Wednesday, there was a meeting of the Cabinet's Northern

Ireland Committee – curiously coded IN – in London. The Prime Minister had instructed his Ministers and civil servants to have the government's reply to Amnesty ready by the previous weekend, 4 June. The Prime Minister was particularly anxious to find out what the reaction in Northern Ireland would be. Certainly by the weekend the Report was leaked, the government had already started preparing the ground. On Friday, 2 June, Jim Hannigan gave Sir Myles Humphreys and William Baird an outline of the Report 'in the strictest confidence'. William Baird did not receive an actual copy of the Report until a week later. The Cabinet Committee, usually chaired by the Prime Minister and attended by the Secretary of State and senior Ministers, discussed the reply the government had agreed to make to Amnesty. It already knew the initial reaction, because the Report had been leaked.

The following morning, the eleven lay members who make up the Independent Broadcasting Authority, ITV's governing body, happened to be meeting at the IBA's Headquarters opposite Harrods in Knightsbridge. The programme which 'This Week' was planning to transmit that evening was discussed. Members and some executives of the Authority were not happy. They remembered the political storm over the previous programme – and others too we had made on Northern Ireland – and recollected the strongly worded letter of protest they had received from Roy Mason, who believed that the Authority should never have allowed the programme to be transmitted. In the preceding seven months the Chief Constable had also met Lady Plowden, the Chairman of the IBA, and made his views on the subject known to her. The IBA banned the programme. It was a decision with which not all the officers of the IBA agreed. In a statement, the Authority said:

Discussion of the Report should be postponed until it is public, thereby giving those involved and the general public a chance to study it in detail.

The political pressure had been applied well in advance of the Authority's meeting. Thames TV replied to the IBA's statement by issuing one of its own, which said:

A fair programme in the public interest had been assembled; it was appropriate to show that programme tonight.

Throughout the day, Thames Television made great efforts to persuade the IBA to change its mind, especially after the government announced that it would be making its reply to the Amnesty Report in the House of Commons that evening. The Authority would not change its decision. In a last bid, the Thames Managing Director, Bryan Cowgill, phoned the IBA's Headquarters. Everybody had gone home, except the Director-General of the IBA, Sir Brian Young, who was just about to leave for an evening engagement. He said he could not countermand a decision of the full Authority. The ban remained.

Thames wished to transmit an alternative programme in the 'This Week' slot. Members of the ACTT, the technicians' union, with the support of the NUJ, blacked the screen in protest at the IBA's censorship of the programme.

The following morning I received a phone call from John Stapleton of BBC-TV's 'Nationwide'. He asked if they could show the film that we had not been allowed to transmit. Jeremy Isaacs, the Thames Programme Controller who over the year had defended our Irish coverage in the face of bitter attack, agreed. The film was sent across London in a mini-cab to the BBC.

Shortly before 'Nationwide' was due to go on the air, Howard Thomas, the Chairman of Thames Television, summoned Jeremy Isaacs and ordered him to get the film back from the BBC. Isaacs refused.

At 6.30 on Friday evening, the BBC transmitted extracts from the programme that ITV had not been allowed to show. In an editorial that weekend, the *Sunday Times*[1]

1. *Sunday Times*, 11 June 1978.

called the IBA 'one of the biggest menaces to free communication now at work in this country'.

Question number 213 – the planned question about the Amnesty Report – was asked and answered in the House of Commons a day earlier than planned. At 5.50 pm on 8 June, Roy Mason answered a question from Gerry Fitt, MP for West Belfast. His reply was a more detailed version of his recent letter to Amnesty. He said that the government recognized that terrorism presented a grave dilemma for democratic governments which involved striking a difficult balance between combatting criminal activity and maintaining the civil liberties of a free society: Amnesty's seventy-eight cases were only a fraction of the 3,000-plus individuals interviewed by the RUC during 1977; the mission had not seen 'official papers' (i.e. Police Doctors' Reports) and therefore Amnesty's cases necessarily represented 'incomplete evidence'.

But the government's most difficult problem was to meet Amnesty's demand for a public inquiry. It coped with it skilfully. The government said it had asked Amnesty to follow the normal legal procedures and give details of their cases in confidence to the DPP, but Amnesty had refused. (The fact that the DPP had probably already examined most of the cases was conveniently overlooked.) Thus the government, while appearing willing to investigate the allegations, was able to shift the blame for its inability to do so on to the shoulders of Amnesty. It said that the course it suggested, involving 'full consideration by the DPP', was preferable to any public inquiry.

The Chief Constable followed the government's line. He said there were 'obvious difficulties in commenting on a Report based on the allegations of anonymous informants'. He challenged Amnesty to 'remove the cloak of anonymity' and pass the cases to the DPP.[1]

The Secretary of State then announced that 'following a suggestion by the Chief Constable' there would be 'an independent and impartial' inquiry set up to 'examine

1. Chief Constable's statement, 10 June 1978.

police procedures and practice' in relation to interrogation. There was not a mention of investigating the allegations in the terms of reference.

The Chairman of the inquiry was to be a Crown Court judge, His Honour Judge Harry Bennett. The other two members were named as Professor John Marshall – a Catholic and a 'recipient of papal honours' as the NIO handout said, an ex-officer in the RAMC and a Professor of Clinical Neurology; and Sir James Haughton, the ex-Chief Constable of Merseyside, who had just retired as HM Inspector of Constabulary.

But the government's announcement of the Bennett Inquiry did not allay public anxiety. Many knew the crucial questions weren't being asked. In Northern Ireland the *Belfast Telegraph* said:

We need not only the inquiry we have got but another one – mostly in public, but offering some kind of protection for police witnesses – to provide an opportunity for investigating serious complaints which have already been made. Otherwise we're only trying to get things right in future and doing nothing about the past . . . If we want to get at the truth, and I suspect that a lot of people are prepared to go without, there is no alternative.[1]

In an editorial, the *Guardian* said that Amnesty's call for a public inquiry was 'unanswerable'. Although the inquiries in Northern Ireland over the past decade read like a judicial roll call, the *Guardian* believed:

There is room for another, and definitive inquiry into the non-uniformed branch of the RUC.[2]

Recognizing some of the inadequacies of the Amnesty Report, such as the mission's lack of access to Police Doctors' reports, the editorial concluded:

All the same, there is enough here to raise the old conviction

1. Barry White, *Belfast Telegraph*, 15 June 1978.
2. *Guardian*, 14 June 1978.

302 *Beating the Terrorists?*

that things are going wrong in Northern Ireland and that before there can be a judgement there must be full exposure of the facts.[1]

And the *Observer* stated in a leader headed 'Behind Closed Doors':

In face of these allegations, Roy Mason's announcement of a private inquiry into 'police practice and procedures' and the complaints machinery is not adequate. What is needed is a public inquiry into the specific charges of brutality in the Amnesty Report.

But the exhortations of the leader-writers fell on deaf ears.

1. *Observer*, 11 June 1978.

17. A Positive Obligation

'A doctor has a special duty to individuals which, in this matter, transcends national interest and security. Doctors having knowledge of any activities covered by the Declaration of Tokyo, have a positive obligation to make those activities publicly known.'

BMA Code of Medical Ethics (7.11), 1979.

Many of the individuals and organizations who had given evidence to Amnesty chose not to give evidence to the Bennett Inquiry, on the grounds that the government had refused to address itself to the specific question of ill-treatment. In a way, their boycott was irrelevant, as the Bennett Committee did have access to the 'official papers' – the doctors' reports – without which Roy Mason had said Amnesty's evidence was incomplete. The 'official' doctors' reports, compiled by those who examined suspects at the Interrogation Centres, Townhall Street, and Crumlin Road prison, were the key to the question as to whether ill-treatment had occurred as both Amnesty and the government knew. These were the reports, coming in over the last eighteen months, which had alerted the Police Authority, the DHSS, and ultimately the DPP and the politicians. The RUC had always had access to them. Although events had overtaken the desire of some doctors to inform Amnesty of the injuries they had seen since its visit, they were now able to tell the Bennett Committee the full story. Most important of all, they were able to give the Committee medical reports on the cases which had caused them particular concern.

Much of the evidence that the Bennett Committee took was inevitably a repetition of the evidence which official bodies like the Police Authority, the RUC and the DPP had already given to Amnesty. The Committee had no power to summon witnesses or take evidence under oath.

In addition to written submissions, the Committee took oral evidence from fifty-eight witnesses who came to the empty Parliament Buildings at Stormont, where the Committee sat in session for two weeks. Of the fifty-eight witnesses, nineteen were members of the R U C, ranging from Chief Constable to Detective Constable; ten were 'official' doctors, including Drs Elliott, Alexander, Irwin and Stewart; eleven were members and officers of the Police Authority. The others included the D P P Barry Shaw, Dr Weir, the Chief Medical Officer, D H S S, and Dr J. D. Watson, the S M O at Crumlin Road prison. Amnesty had covered the period 1975–7. Bennett was concerned with more recent events, those of 1977–8. (Much of the evidence in this book is evidence which was given to Bennett but never published. The book also contains additional evidence of which even Bennett was unaware.)

The Police Surgeons made it clear to the Committee that they were not being duped by the terrorists. They said they were fully aware of their training in subversion, and deception, and knew why they made allegations: as doctors they had seen at first hand the carnage the terrorists caused. In his submission one doctor said he had literally picked up the pieces of the carnage. The doctors made it clear they had no sympathies with the terrorists. But they also made it clear that they believed that ill-treatment had been real, not alleged, and that many of the injuries which they had seen had been inflicted by the R U C's detectives, not the suspects themselves. They told the Committee that despite their repeated representations to the Police Authority, the Hermon Committee and the Chief Constable himself, they had failed to get ill-treatment stopped.

Dr Irwin and Dr Stewart gave evidence on behalf of the Forensic Medical Officers Association. Dr Weir had seen their written submission and told them he thought it was both pertinent and objective. When they went up to the Parliament Buildings in August to meet the Committee, Dr Irwin was asked about the pattern and the time scale of the injuries he had seen. He said there were 'peaks' and 'troughs'. He was then asked what state they were in at the moment. He said he thought they were currently in a trough.

The statistics of Assault During Interview for the summer of 1978 confirm Dr Irwin's analysis. In May – the month before the Amnesty Report – there were twenty-seven; in June – the month the Report was published – they fell to eight; in July there were nine and in August fourteen.

In the autumn of 1978, the 'trough' started to fill up again, although it never reached the level of the previous two 'peaks': September, twenty-four; October, nineteen; November, seventeen; December, twenty.

One of the complaints of Assault During Interview made during September 1978 was registered by a Turf Lodge man, Edward Manning Brophy – a thirty-eight-year-old ex-soldier in the Royal Irish Rifles. His is an important case, not just because the six statements that he made during interrogation at Castlereagh were subsequently rejected in court, but because he was the only person ever charged by the RUC in connection with one of the worst civilian atrocities of the decade – the bombing of the La Mon restaurant on 17 February 1978, in which twelve people died, incinerated in a massive fireball, estimated to have been sixty feet in diameter and forty feet in height.

Edward Brophy was arrested at 5.35 am on Monday, 25 September 1978, at his home in Belfast's Turf Lodge district and taken to Castlereagh, where he had ten interviews spread over four days. In court Brophy alleged he was ill-treated at four out of the ten interviews. Following his interrogation, he was charged with causing various explosions at a number of business premises in Belfast between September 1976 and February 1978, which resulted in loss and damage of more than £600,000; the murder of twelve people at the Le Mon restaurant – his part in the operation was said to have been hijacking a vehicle, keeping the bombs in a shed and then handing them over to the bombing team; and membership of the Provisional IRA between 15 August 1976 and 1 March 1978. Brophy's case came to court in February 1980. The trial lasted forty-six days.

In court Brophy's counsel, Mr Richard Ferguson, QC, challenged the admissibility of all the verbal and written confessions Brophy was said to have made during interrogation at Castlereagh. Giving evidence in court, Brophy said he was not ill-treated at every interview, but only at interviews 1 and 3 on 25 September, at interview 5 on 26 September, and at interview 7 on 27 September. He said that at no stage during his interviews was he cautioned – in accordance with the Judges Rules; nor was he allowed access to a solicitor, permission to see his wife or a medical examination when he requested it. He said that the only detectives who revealed their names to him were the two senior officers, Detective Chief Superintendent William Mooney and Detective Superintendent Hyland, who saw him at his last interview on 28 September. Brophy alleged that he had been ill-treated by seven police officers who had *not* made statements for the preliminary inquiry – three of whom he identified among the other detectives who had assembled in court for the *voir dire*. However, on the basis of Brophy's own observations in court, four police officers against whom he alleged ill-treatment remained unidentified.

In his evidence to the court, Brophy detailed the ways in which he said he had been ill-treated.

1. He said he had been physically assaulted – slapped on the face, caught and pulled about by the hair, punched and jabbed in the stomach, struck on the back of the head and neck, hit on the chest, and his head and neck were squeezed in such a manner that he fell to the floor, losing consciousness; he was pushed against the wall, his hands and arms were bent and twisted into his armpits, his feet were stamped upon, and a heel ground on his big toe.

2. He was made to squat in uncomfortable and exhaust-

ing postures and made to do press-ups and on occasions kicked and knocked over while doing them.

3. He was humiliated and degraded. On three occasions he said police officers opened his trousers, exposed his private parts and flicked his penis up and down by hand. He said one officer spat in his face and at one time tried to force him to drink a cup of liquid which he said was 'piss', and not able to do this, he threw it over him, and made him wipe up what was spilt on the floor.

Brophy said that the ill-treatment he suffered left him ill, exhausted, beaten and degraded. He said he was aware that further ill-treatment would continue so long as he refused to sign statements of confession, statements admitting his involvement in the terrorist crimes the police were alleging. He said that it was in this condition that he was induced to sign six statements. Brophy insisted that although he signed the statements, no part of the contents of any of them were dictated by or came from him in any form. He said that they came from the police, from information already in their possession from other sources. He said they were written down as if they were his own dictated statements.

In his summing-up, Mr Justice Kelly asked rhetorically whether there was any truth at all in Brophy's allegations of ill-treatment. He said:

These are allegations commonly picked up in Northern Ireland. No doubt canvassed amongst terrorists, easily made and at times difficult to refute effectively. The courts frequently have found them to be bogus or not proven. The accused has a powerful and obvious motive for concocting them, facing, as he does, twelve charges of murder and, if found guilty, the reprobation of this community as well as severity of punishment in the courts. He had a criminal conviction in June 1973 for uttering false cheques, and he was sentenced to six years' imprisonment. He admits to being an active member of the IRA for a long period from September 1971 until December 1977, and this may support a secondary motive to discredit the RUC. In the witness box he

308 Beating the Terrorists?

expressed his dislike and contempt for detectives engaged in duties at Castlereagh.

I had the opportunity of observing and hearing him in the witness box for ten days. I thought little of him as a man. I think he is of poor moral character – unreliable, untrustworthy, foxy, weak, although he liked to pose, and here the slang is apt, as 'a tough guy' (witness his bellicose threats of what he contemplated against his interrogators – 'I was going to beat the tripe out of Patterson'; 'I was going to thump him back'; 'Usually I'd have thrown one, but I didn't react'; 'I would have torn the throat out of Patterson'; 'I went to dig him for making filthy remarks about my wife'). And although denying in evidence that he was O C of the Turf Lodge I R A and a member of the Brigade Staff of the I R A, his face clearly showed these suggestions flattered him.

What of Brophy as a witness? His evidence, rambling, at times incoherent, difficult to follow and I'm sure difficult to record, nevertheless revealed numerous evasions, many contradictions, at times obvious lies, some admitted lies and much exaggeration. He was at his least credible in explaining where the contents of the verbal and written statements came from. I believe that they came from him and came from him in every case, although I do not think the written statements were dictated in the spontaneous and fluent manner the police evidence implied . . .

The judge then commented on the police witnesses and said:

The Crown called in evidence first those interviewing detectives on record, who had made statements for the preliminary inquiry. They denied all charges of ill-treatment and impropriety, or that any unauthorized policeman had entered Brophy's interview room at any time. They produced their notes of the interviews, their personal journals and much documentary evidence from Castlereagh Police Office to verify the times of interviews, the identity of those present and what went on during their course. These interviewing officers, experienced in giving evidence, accustomed to meeting from time to time allegations of ill-treatment during interrogation, said in effect that Brophy's charges were a tissue of lies. In all material matters, they corroborated each other, on the whole their evidence tallied and their notes showed no significant inconsistencies. I cannot say that these detectives were ever significantly caught out. A few were not impressive on matters to which I shall refer. In the witness box they appeared impassive, controlled, bland. Not surprisingly they have little independent recollection of the events of these interviews and they were compelled to rely almost entirely on their notes of the interviews. Their evidence therefore amounted in most cases to a mere reading of these notes and constant recourse to them when challenged in cross-examination . . . Uniformed police from Castlereagh who were the gaolers responsible for Brophy's safe custody also gave evidence and it was to the effect that they saw or heard nothing improper or even irregular during Brophy's custody in Castlereagh.

And the Crown finally called as witnesses those detectives, not on record, whom Brophy identified as some who had entered his interview room, unauthorized, and ill-treated him. They were Det. Con. Marshall, Special Branch Officer 'C' and Det. Sgt Burnside. I will comment on their evidence and credibility later.

Mr Justice Kelly then reviewed the medical evidence available.

It was only when Brophy was about to leave Castlereagh on 28th and later in prison on 29th that anything was found that might be termed objective signs of ill-treatment – an injury over his left eyebrow and an injury to his right great toe. The Crown's suggestion is that these were self-inflicted . . .

Mr Justice Kelly then summarized a number of points which, he said, the Crown had not 'negatived to a degree of satisfaction'.

1. While I have commented adversely on Brophy's lack of credibility on a number of matters, nevertheless I thought he maintained a remarkable consistency in his evidence about the infliction of ill-treatment during a long and search cross-examination by Mr Appleton [Crown Counsel]. I was very much struck by this, contrasting so vividly, as it did, with the obvious unreliability of other parts of his evidence.

2. There is a reasonable possibility on the evidence of three doctors that Brophy showed some objective signs of ill-treatment referrable to the time when he said they were inflicted, although a considerable amount of the physical assault he described is not supported by the medical findings, but again there must be some allowance made for the technique of striking without marking.

3. Although I think he exaggerated its effects grossly, Brophy did suffer some kind of episode of physical debility during interview 3 on 25th, and two detectives saw and recorded objective signs of it.

4. And now I state what must be the most formidable cluster of points that the Crown faces:

(a) Brophy chooses to accuse two detectives, Det. Con. Patterson and Sgt Clements, of bursting into his interview room on the morning of 25 September 1978 between 10.40 am and 12.30 pm, quite unauthorized, and in the case of the latter, of assaulting him when two detailed police officers were already present. Neither of these detectives was on record in the case as having interviewed Brophy or encountered him or having been in his interview room for any part of that time, and in evidence they denied this unauthorized entry and the assault. Brophy was taking considerable risk in choosing Patterson and Clements as the culprits in all the circumstances, for they might have been well away from Castlereagh Police Office that morning with strong, perhaps unassailable, independent or documentary corroboration of that fact. Yet it transpired that not only was Det. Con. Patterson in Castlereagh at the material time, but he was free then, in the sense that he had no assigned duties. Sgt Clements answered the accusation by producing his personal journal of duties for the day, to suggest, as the journal on its face indicated, he had spent the morning at the Belfast City Commission and did not arrive at Castlereagh until after lunch. But further investigation prompted and made during the course of this trial, revealed that his case at court did not go on or begin and that he was free for the entire morning. He says he spent the morning at home, although he knew that the first briefing of detectives about the question of Brophy and the first interview would be held at Castlereagh that morning and that he would most likely be one of the interviewing teams. I was not impressed.

(b) Brophy goes on to accuse a Det. Con. Marshall, another detective not on record at the preliminary inquiry, of threatening him and discussing army interrogation techniques on the morning of 25th, again some time between 10.40 am and 12.30 pm. He also said this detective assaulted and indecently assaulted him during the afternoon of 26th between 12.50 pm and 5 pm. Brophy described him in evidence as having the name 'Marshall', having a very cultured accent and as one who appeared to be an ex-British officer, presumably because of his appearance, accent and conversation about interrogation techniques. Later during the course of the trial Brophy picked him out in court from among a number of detectives assembled. When Det. Con. Marshall came to give evidence it transpired that he was English and spoke with what I would call a good accent and he had served for eight years in the army before joining the RUC. And it also appeared that he was in Castlereagh Police Office on the morning of 25th and although he attended the briefing on Brophy, he had no detailed duties at the time Brophy alleged he entered and threatened him. Further it transpired that he was in Castlereagh during the afternoon of 26th, although he says he was on detail interviewing until 3.15 pm but not afterwards until 5 pm when he left.

(c) Brophy also alleged a detective entered his interview room on 25 September unauthorized, towards the end of interview 1 (12.50–4.15 pm) and during interview 2 (4.15 pm –6 pm), and threatened and assaulted him. He did not know his name, Brophy said in evidence, but he described him physically and said he had interviewed him previously in Castlereagh in February 1978. Again during the course of the trial Brophy picked out such a person from among a number of detectives in court. This was Special Branch Officer 'C' who had in fact interviewed him in Castlereagh in February 1978 and who was at the time of the alleged assault on 25 September in Castlereagh Police Office; and his journal showed that he was there, free from assigned duties, between 3.45 pm and 5 pm on that day.

(d) Brophy chose still another detective who again was not on record and charged him to be one of his main aggressors at Castlereagh. This turned out to be Det. Sgt Burnside, whom Brophy described in the witness box before he identified him in court. And he said he assaulted him physically and indecently during interview 5 between 12.50 pm and 5 pm on 26th.

The Crown say that Brophy's description was quite inaccurate and his identification in court was only by name. I have some doubts about this but it did transpire that although Sgt Burnside denied he ever interviewed Brophy or was in any room with him at any time, his personal diary contained the following entry for that day, the 26th: 'Reported for duty at CID Office at Oaks and then to Castlereagh Police Office, *and assisted and supervised interview re Brophy.*' Det. Sgt Burnside said that these words were intended to signify duties which he performed outside Brophy's interview room, e.g. ensuring that Brophy's interviewers were present, gathering information from police records of details of crimes Brophy had confessed to. They did not mean or imply that he was ever inside Brophy's interview room or that he had ever questioned or interviewed him. I have considerable reservations about this explanation.

(e) Brophy said Det. Con. Smyth who had interviewed him on 25th, improperly entered his interview room during interview 5 on 26th (12.50 pm–5 pm) and assaulted and indecently assaulted him. In fact Det. Con. Smith was on duty at Castlereagh on 26th and was free from assigned duties from 3.15 pm.

(f) Brophy alleged that Sgt Clements assaulted him over the course of the interview between 12.50 pm and 5 pm on 26th. Sgt Clements denied this and said that he left the interview room at 1.45 pm when Det. Insp. Meeke took over and that he was given the afternoon off duty from about 2 pm. One part of his personal diary showed that he was on duty until 5 pm but this was stroked out and changed to 2 pm. The evidence related by both Det. Insp. Meeke and Det. Sgt Clements as to why and from what time Clements was given the afternoon off, was not at all convincing.

What a number of coincidences, therefore, these selections of

Brophy's revealed, and what chances he was taking in choosing them, choosing all of these detectives as his aggressors and on the days and at the times he said.

It is one thing for a suspect in custody to invent ill-treatment and details of it. This can be done, rehearsed and presented often without too much trouble. But it is a very different and formidable venture to embark on, to choose as the perpetrators of that ill-treatment not one but a number of detectives who are not on record and to commit their ill-treatment to stated days and times when their whereabouts at the time of the ill-treatment alleged are unlikely to be known to the suspect. As I have said this is a strong array of points that the Crown faces in discharging their onus of proof and I do not think the conjectural theories advanced by Mr Appleton by way of answer were adequate about them and their implication.

5. Police experience of Brophy in Castlereagh Police Office in February 1978 when he then made a complaint of ill-treatment, clearly false to them, must have alerted them during his later detention in September 1978 to the type of individual they were dealing with. They believed also that he suffered from some form of heart condition. In these circumstances I should have thought they might have protected their vulnerability by having Brophy medically examined after interview 5 on 26 September 1978 in which he made many verbal admissions about bombings and shootings, or after interview 6, when he enlarged on them and incorporated them into four written statements; or after interview 7 when he made more confessions, including verbal confessions and a written one about his complicity in the La Mon bombing. It was not until 6.30 pm on 28th September when he was leaving Castlereagh that they sought to have him medically examined. It appears it was not the practice at Castlereagh to have a suspect who had made confessions medically examined afterwards as soon as practicable but knowing Brophy's 'form' they must have contemplated that it would have been prudent to do so. That they did not do so tends to add some weight to the defence suggestion that Brophy had been marked as a result of ill-treatment on the afternoon of 26th and he was being kept from medical examination until these marks diminished or disappeared.

314 Beating the Terrorists?

6. Brophy complained from an early stage in Castlereagh of ill-treatment there even before he made any admissions at all and he alleged police ill-treatment to every doctor who examined him in Castlereagh and thereafter to doctors at the Belfast prison, and although there are clear inconsistencies in the detail of his complaints to doctors, and as he retailed the ill-treatment to me, in a broad and general way I find quite significant consistency . . .

Winding up his summary of the evidence, Mr Justice Kelly said that he was led to the conviction that he had not heard all that went on at Castlereagh from the police over the four days in September 1978. He concluded:

Very many aspects of this case and much of its evidence, which I need not set out here, assists the Crown's contention that Brophy has fabricated the defence of ill-treatment. Brophy may well have fabricated ill-treatment but in law I have to be sure that he has not. I am not sure, I am not sure. The ultimate burden of proof is not on Brophy and the standard of proof is not the preponderance of probabilities.

The cumulative effect of all the points I have set out with others, less strong, that I have not, is that the Crown has not discharged the burden of proof which the law imposes in cases of this kind and that I cannot say that I am satisfied beyond reasonable doubt that the verbal and written statements challenged were not induced by torture or inhuman or degrading treatment . . .

Accordingly I rule all the statements challenged to be inadmissible in evidence.

Mr Justice Kelly sentenced Brophy to five years' imprisonment for membership of the Provisional IRA.

I have recorded these court proceedings in considerable detail because of the case's importance, Brophy being the only man to date brought to trial for involvement in La Mon, and because he was interrogated at Castlereagh *after* the storm that surrounded the publication of the Amnesty Report and *while* the Bennett Committee was taking evidence. In this respect, its significance parallels that of the Fullerton case the previous November (see p. 224).

I remember going to see Dr Irwin in the autumn of 1978 with my colleague, Alan Stewart. It was the first time that Dr Irwin had spoken to any journalists, even off the record. He told us of his anxieties of the past eighteen months and his hope that the Bennett Inquiry would not be a 'white-wash', given its limited terms of reference. He said he thought it unlikely, having met the members of the Com-mittee, who had impressed him as men of independence and integrity. Nevertheless, he expressed some unease that the cover-up might continue.

But in the autumn of 1978, Dr Irwin still continued to see evidence of injuries on prisoners arriving at Townhall Street from Castlereagh, although not on the same scale as before. Most of those he examined said they had just been 'messed around a bit' by the detectives. Some said they had refused to be medically examined at Castlereagh, or make a complaint, for fear of further assault. At the beginning of October one case caused Dr Irwin particular concern.

Hugh O'Neill had been taken to Castlereagh on 9 October 1978. He alleged he had been forced to squat against the wall, punched in the stomach and slapped around the ears. He said he had been kneed in the chest while squatting, been hit in the neck, had his leg twisted and his hair pulled.

Dr Irwin found an 8 ins. square of massive bruising around O'Neill's stomach which he thought was caused by a ruptured blood vessel which was still bleeding. He judged the injury to be not more than two days old. There was also bruising on both his arms and ear.

In his conclusion, Dr Irwin noted that O'Neill had received a beating approximately two days before he had been examined. He did not think that either the stomach injury or the other injuries were self-inflicted. Dr Irwin said he was 'horrified' by the case.

*

By autumn 1978 Gough Barracks Interrogation Centre had reopened for business and Dr Elliott had returned to his post as SMO. Although he had not seen any cases to cause him concern since April, he still felt uneasy at the atmosphere. He continued to carry out the spot checks which had made him unpopular with the detectives and were not entirely approved of by his superiors in the DHSS. In June 1978 while patrolling the corridor, he had noticed that a spyhole was blocked. A piece of chewing gum had been stuck over the lens inside the door of the interview room. The detective was angry and apparently told Dr Elliott that he didn't spy on his patients and he shouldn't spy on his interviews. The suspect being interviewed made no complaint.

In early December, on another patrol, Dr Elliott noticed that vision through another spyhole was impaired. He informed the uniformed inspector on duty. The lens appeared to have been scratched. Dr Elliott was suspicious. The lens was sent off for forensic examination. Again, the suspect made no complaint.

Ten days later he found the spyhole on interview room 3 to be blocked. Again Dr Elliott summoned the duty inspector, who had a word with one of the detectives in the room. There was a ripping sound and a piece of paper, the kind that detectives use for interview notes, was torn from the spyhole. Dr Elliott rang DCC Hermon on the 'hot line' to complain. Later in the day, he examined the suspect who had been in the room. He alleged he had been slapped around the face, had his arm twisted and been grabbed by the clothes in an attempt to drag him across the table in the interview room. Dr Elliott found two small patches of bleeding around the mouth, but no other evidence to confirm the allegations.

But although Dr Elliott saw no further injuries, at the beginning of 1979 he was confronted once again with the injuries which he had observed at the beginning of 1978. He was asked to attend a meeting at the DPP's office in the Royal Courts of Justice in Belfast to discuss certain aspects of the prosecution of prisoners whom he had examined at Gough in the spring of 1978. They were some of the cases about which Dr Elliott's four deputies had warned the Police Authority's Paddy Farrelly when they had met him earlier in the year to tell him their anxieties.

On Thursday, 4 January, Dr Elliott went to the DPP's office. Present were senior members of the RUC, and members of the DPP's staff. Among the cases which appear to have been discussed were those of Hamill, Livingstone and Gilpin, three of the most serious cases that Dr Elliott had seen. Each case was individually examined. The DPP's staff would usually have two files before them: one containing the charges the RUC had brought against the suspect; the other containing results of the investigation carried out by the RUC's Complaints & Discipline Branch into the suspect's complaint. In the latter file would be all the relevant medical reports, including those of Dr Elliott, his deputies and General Practitioners, where they too had conducted examinations.

The point of such a meeting was to enable the Director's office to consider the two files and decide whether the statements made by the accused were likely to be accepted or rejected under the terms of Section 6. Medical reports were usually crucial in reaching this decision.

On such occasions where injuries had been noted by the doctors, the police would sometimes offer an explanation of how they had occurred – that, for example, they were self-inflicted or accidental. A suspect might have banged his head on a table, as the police suggested Gilpin had done; or the injuries might have been inflicted after the accused had attacked the detectives – as the police suggested had happened in Livingstone's case. It appears that Dr Elliott was asked for his opinion of such explanations. Apparently he said he didn't accept them.

The day after the meeting at the DPP's office, the charges against Gilpin were withdrawn. The charges against Livingstone were withdrawn a month later, on 2

318 Beating the Terrorists?

February 1979. Those against Hamill were withdrawn six weeks later, on 16 February 1979. Dr Elliott was not a popular figure. I was told that some detectives were bitter at the suspects' release and put it down to Dr Elliott's 'unhelpful' medical reports.

Although Dr Elliott never saw any further evidence of ill-treatment at Gough, Dr Irwin continued to see injuries at Townhall Street in 1979. In January 1979 there were twenty-six complaints of Assault During Interview. A new 'peak' had been reached, albeit much smaller than its two predecessors in 1977 and the spring of 1978.

On 24 January 1979, Dr Irwin examined Daniel McCann, who had been arrested and taken to Castlereagh six days earlier. He alleged he had been punched on the head and stomach, kicked on the thighs and legs, grabbed by the hair, had his head banged against the wall, strangled round the throat with an arm, and punched in the face and chest. He made allegations against several detectives. He said he had made a complaint at Castlereagh and had been examined by his own GP as well as the Medical Officer.

Dr Irwin noted two black eyes, with the bruising extending over the bridge of the nose on to the cheekbones, and bruises on his thighs, knee and back. All the bruises were of recent origin. Dr Irwin concluded that the injuries could have occurred in the manner described by McCann. He added:

No explanation was received from the police as to how these injuries could have occurred and I therefore suspect, since the pattern fits, that they were caused while in police custody in Castlereagh.

It was now nearly two years since Dr Irwin had first informed the Police Authority of his concern and written to the Chief Medical Officer at the DHSS. Since then he and his colleagues had tried to get ill-treatment stopped. There had been meeting after meeting, codes had been revised, more safeguards had been introduced, supervision of interviews had been tightened, records and documentation made more extensive, and the handling of prisoners improved. Most significantly, 'bad apples' were reported to have been moved. And yet, Dr Irwin and his colleagues continued to see unexplained injuries on prisoners.

Dr Irwin had had enough. For nearly two years, through Amnesty and now through Bennett, he had kept his frustrations to himself. I know from my own experience since I had first written to him in the autumn of 1977, and from the several occasions on which I met him a year later, that he was insistent on trying to work things out within the system. Dr Irwin was no keener to rock the boat than anyone else. But, seeing recent cases like O'Neill's, he felt he had been wasting his time. The authorities had listened, but in effect done nothing about it. He knew that the Bennett Inquiry could only reflect the smallest tip of the iceberg given its limited terms of reference. Dr Irwin decided to go public and pre-empt publication of the Report to make sure it was seen in a context which the public might otherwise have ignored.

On Sunday, 11 March 1979, in a television interview with Mary Holland of LWT's 'Weekend World', Dr Irwin spoke out. He said that over the past three years he had seen roughly between 150 and 160 cases in which he was not satisfied that the injuries were self-inflicted. The television programme was followed by the predictable storm of protest. But the headlines quickly changed.

Shortly after the interview, the *Daily Telegraph* was fed a story by a confidential source in Whitehall. The paper was told that Dr Irwin's wife had been raped in 1976 and that Dr Irwin had harboured a grudge against the RUC ever since for failing to catch the assailant. The *Telegraph* was disgusted by the smear, which had not, contrary to popular belief, emanated from the RUC's Press Office. Soon Fleet Street picked up the story and it became front-page news. The aim of the 'leak' was clearly to question Dr Irwin's motives and thereby undermine his damaging accusations. But the 'smear' rebounded on those who sought to destroy Dr Irwin's credibility. Fleet Street accused the government of 'Nixonian tactics'[1] despite its denial of involvement in the 'smear'.

The innuendo was false, but the story was true. Dr Irwin's wife had been raped in 1976, after driving home with her son late one Saturday evening from a friend's house. Dr Irwin had been called out to Townhall Street. Mrs Irwin had been followed to the door by a man 'with an "English" accent'. He had produced a gun, pistol-whipped the boy, and raped Mrs Irwin three times upstairs in the bedroom. After midnight Dr Irwin received a phone call at Townhall Street from his distraught wife. He rushed home to find the police already surrounding the house. Far from blaming the RUC, he had nothing but the highest praise for the way they handled the case. They had showed the family great concern in their distress, and made every effort to find the rapist. In fact, the detectives in charge of the investigation were personal friends of Dr Irwin's, who often accompanied him on his fishing trips. They did everything they could to track down the assailant. There were strong suspicions that he had been a British soldier, involved in undercover operations, who had been based at the army billet in the old Grand Central Hotel in the centre of Belfast. Inquiries were made there, and then switched to the security forces in Armagh. There the trail appears to have gone cold. There were rumours that the man the police were looking for had been spirited back to Germany. The army denied any involvement in the incident.

The Chief Constable replied to Dr Irwin's charges in a legitimate way. The day after the interview, he sent a Chief Superintendent round to Dr Irwin's home to discuss his statistics. The Chief Constable had ordered Complaints & Discipline to carry out an 'exhaustive analysis' of prisoners whom Dr Irwin had examined over the past three years who had made complaints of their treatment in police custody. The Chief Constable concluded that out of the sixty-five cases there were only ten in which Dr Irwin either agreed with the complainant or found injuries which were

1. *Evening Standard* editorial, 'A Maze of Smears', 16 March 1979.

consistent with the allegations. The Chief Constable said that in three of those cases, Dr Irwin 'opined' that the injuries could have been self-inflicted, and in one case he had submitted no report. In other words, the Chief Constable was implying that the 150–160 cases which Dr Irwin had said he had seen over the past three years, effectively came down to six.

Dr Irwin never replied to the Chief Constable's demolition of his statistics. He saw no point in arguing over what the RUC alleged he had seen and what he knew he had seen. I pressed him hard on the discrepancy between the Chief Constable's figures and his own. He produced a pile of typed medical reports in which he had noted injuries. There were several dozen. Not all of them contained the kind of damaging conclusions noted in some of the cases mentioned in this book. Many of them listed injuries without passing judgement, simply recording that the injuries were consistent with the allegations and could have occurred at the time and in the manner alleged.

Dr Irwin stressed that the pile of typed medical reports were only cases which he had submitted to the RUC on request as he typed a copy of his *original* medical notes only if the RUC asked for a copy for their investigation of an official complaint. Nor did he automatically venture an opinion on an individual case, as the RUC didn't always ask for one. Dr Irwin emphasized that the RUC would only have records of cases in which 'official' complaints had been made, which explained the discrepancy between the Chief Constable's sixty-five cases and Dr Irwin's 150–160, to which he had referred on television. Dr Irwin said that many prisoners whom he had seen over the past three years had never made complaints, either because they had been afraid to, or thought it a waste of time or, in cases which Dr Irwin himself would not have seen, were relieved to have got out of Castlereagh without being charged. He said that the figures he had mentioned referred to *all* the cases he had seen, many of which he had never sent to the RUC because he had never been asked to, as no official complaint had been made.

I asked if I could see his original records. At last, after great reluctance on his part and much insistence on mine, he agreed. He produced a slim 8×4 ins. Twinlock loose-leaved notebook from his pocket. He said he always carried it with him and noted every case he examined. He had done so since before 1976, on the advice of a judge who had suggested that he should keep a detailed personal record of every case he saw. When the Twinlock notebook was full, he transferred the notes to another file. If the RUC asked for details of a case, he would go to his file, type up the original notes, and send them off to Complaints & Discipline. I asked if I could see his original notes going back to 1976. Again he was reluctant. He said no one had ever seen them before. I pressed him. Finally he agreed and produced a large cardboard filing box. Inside were hundreds of notes of cases he had seen going back to 1976, all neatly bundled, tied with an elastic band and dated. I asked him why he had never produced the notes before. He said he had vowed that he would only make them public if there were a full-scale, medically approved, sworn inquiry into the allegations. Until then his notes were to remain stored away in his own safekeeping.

I asked him to pick a few random cases from the bundle marked 'May–November '77', the period which had marked the first 'peak' of the allegations. At a guess there were well over a hundred cases in the bundle. I watched him pick five cases at random: two had marks and three had not. I asked him to repeat the exercise with the bundle marked 'January–April '78' – the time of the second 'peak'. The results were more or less the same.

I asked Dr Irwin if he could go through all his original notes for me in detail and single out the exact number of 'significant' cases he had seen. Several weeks later, he sent me details of the breakdown. He said that between June 1976 and February 1979, he had seen 149 cases and he still had a couple of files to go through. The graph below correlates the 'peaks' and 'troughs' of Dr Irwin's observa-

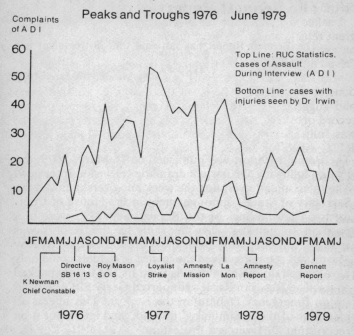

Complaints of A D I

Peaks and Troughs 1976   June 1979

Top Line: RUC Statistics, cases of Assault During Interview (A D I)

Bottom Line: cases with injuries seen by Dr Irwin

J F M A M J J A S O N D J F M A M J J A S O N D J F M A M J J A S O N D J F M A M J

K Newman Chief Constable

Directive SB 16 13

Roy Mason S O S

Loyalist Strike

Amnesty Mission

La Mon

Amnesty Report

Bennett Report

1976   1977   1978   1979

tions and the official R U C statistics of Assault During Interview. Again a pattern emerges.

Following his television interview and the storm over the 'smear', Dr Irwin received a letter from Senator Edward Kennedy which said:

I wanted to send along this note to you and your family in praise of the courage you have shown in the difficult recent days. Few actions speak more loudly in confirmation of your comments on the brutality in Castlereagh than the shameful smear tactics employed in the effort to discredit you.

Nevertheless, Dr Irwin lost more friends than he gained because he had dared to speak out.

18. The Bennett Report

'The Bennett Report has not said that ill-treatment has taken place.'

Roy Mason, 16 March 1979

The Bennett Report was published on 16 March 1979, the Friday following Dr Irwin's dramatic television interview. The rape 'smear' overhung the week and overshadowed the Secretary of State's announcement in the House of Commons on the findings of the Report. Few MPs were in a position to gainsay what he said, as the Report was available for collection from the Vote Office only as Roy Mason was speaking. Even the fastest of readers could only have picked up the bare details from its 143 tightly packed pages. The Rev. Ian Paisley supported Gerry Fitt's demand for an Emergency Debate on the Report. 'This affects all members of the community,' he said, 'and let us put it on record that Dr Irwin is a Protestant.'

The Report was a masterly review, if one limited by its terms of reference, of the climate and structures within which the abuses had taken place. The Report concluded that many of the RUC's interrogators were of junior rank and had no formal training; there were areas of uncertainty as to exactly what treatment would render statements inadmissible; there were uncertainties too over the application of the Judges Rules; no police officer had ever been successfully convicted of ill-treatment, despite successful civil claims against the RUC and out-of-court settlements.

The Report recommended that supervision of interviews should be strengthened; prisoners should be seen by the Medical Officer every twenty-four hours and offered an examination; detectives should be rotated and given other duties from time to time. But most important of all, it recommended that closed-circuit television should be installed in the interview rooms to enable the uniformed branch to monitor interrogations; and that solicitors should be given unconditional access to their clients after twenty-four hours.

The Committee made three points of particular significance. The first concerned the DPP. He should continue to be responsible for the direction of criminal proceedings but should, in cases of public interest where he directed no prosecution, make his reasons for so doing generally known to the Police Authority and other responsible public bodies. (This meant that the public would no longer equate no prosecution with no assault.[1])

The second point concerned the Complaints & Discipline Branch. Although the Committee accepted that investigations into complaints were carried out promptly and painstakingly, and there was no evidence that investigating officers had met a 'wall of silence', nevertheless it noted that the statements obtained from the police did not take the Investigating Officers very far. The Committee had seen the Complaints & Discipline files of investigations. In a paragraph that contained echoes of Strasbourg, the Committee said:

The evidence from police officers seems often to consist of short statements to the effect that the allegations are wholly denied (from detective officers who interrogate prisoners) or that nothing untoward was seen or heard (from uniformed officers). Officers against whom complaints are made are interviewed in accordance with the Judges Rules, and this is generally held to entail that they be cautioned at the beginning of an interview. An experienced detective officer, whether cautioned or not, is not likely to incriminate himself. We have to consider the unwelcome possibility that the questioning by the officers investigating complaints may not be as searching or persistent as it might be.[2]

1. Bennett Report, para. 381, p. 126.
2. ibid., para. 344, p. 115.

The third point concerned the Police Authority. The Committee noted that the Chief Constable's argument that once an investigation into a complaint had begun the matter was *sub judice* was not, strictly speaking, accurate. The Committee said that it was unsatisfactory for the Authority to be informed by the RUC in cases of public concern that the matter was *sub judice* or the file was with the DPP. In order to comply with its statutory obligation to keep itself informed as to the manner in which complaints were dealt with by the Chief Constable, the RUC must provide the Authority with more detailed information.[1] The Committee also encouraged the Authority, perhaps with the Rafferty case in mind, to use its power to institute a tribunal; moreover, it suggested that, should it be felt necessary, the tribunal should be given additional powers to compel the attendance of witnesses and the production of documents. Bennett was not only encouraging the Police Authority to use one of the few weapons it had, but advising it to make the weapon more powerful. Even given its limited terms of reference, the Bennett Report was a damaging document, given the RUC's insistence over the previous two years that the safeguards for persons in custody and the complaints investigation procedures were among the most rigorous in the United Kingdom. Bennett washed such assertions away.

Roy Mason insisted that the Bennett Report did not say that ill-treatment had taken place. The Chief Constable was more guarded in his interpretation. Only in one of the Report's 143 pages did the Committee permit itself to step outside the terms of reference which the Secretary of State had carefully given it. It could hardly have done otherwise, given the weight and force of the evidence, both written and oral, which it had received from 'official' doctors. But even then it trod warily.

The Committee said that in some cases it had been able to compare a prisoner's condition from several sources: from medical reports compiled by the Medical Officer at

1. Bennett Report, para. 389, p. 129.

the Interrogation Centre, the Police Surgeon at the Charge Office, and the Prison Medical Officer who examined the prisoner when he was remanded in custody. The Committee listed the medical evidence it had reviewed: 105 detailed medical reports compiled by Medical Officers at the Interrogation Centres concerning prisoners who complained of ill-treatment in 1978 (the Committee made no mention of 1977, the 'peak' year for complaints); detailed clinical records of twenty-three of those prisoners compiled by the Police Surgeons when they were charged; and a further fifty-two cases of prisoners examined when remanded in custody. In addition they saw twenty-eight reports from one G P and several other reports from other family doctors. As the Committee noted, the medical evidence it had seen was detailed, extensive and from independent sources.

Nevertheless, however extensive and detailed the evidence was, it was of limited use given the Committee's remit. Its real importance as far as its terms of reference were concerned was to show the need for an urgent and drastic review of the R U C's interrogation procedures. It was what the doctors had been saying for nearly three years.

The Committee listed five categories of alleged ill-treatment. The first and largest category involved complaints of the kind of ill-treatment which was unlikely to leave marks and in which the medical evidence was therefore negative. The second category was where the allegations were clearly fabricated, as marks would have been visible had the allegations been true. The third category was where injuries were clearly self-inflicted. The fourth, where the marks noted could have been inflicted by others or could have been self-inflicted. (In some of these cases the Committee noted that the Police Surgeons had concluded from detailed clinical examination that they were not self-inflicted.) The fifth and most important category as far as the Committee was concerned involved evidence which indicated that the injuries sustained during the period of detention in the police office were inflicted by someone other than the prisoner himself. This is indicated beyond all doubt by the nature, severity, sites and number of separate injuries in one person.[1]

Nevertheless, the Committee stressed the word 'indicates', as none of the parties involved had been subject to cross-examination. It concluded:

There can, however, whatever the precise explanation, be no doubt that the injuries in this last class were not self-inflicted and were sustained during the period of detention at a police office.[2]

In a significant addition the Committee said:

What we have found reinforces the concern shown by the Doctors and the Police Authority and demonstrates the need for an improvement in the supervision and control of interrogation. Moreover, we cannot blind ourselves to the possibility that if, as we have found on the basis of the medical evidence, ill-treatment causing injury could occur, so could ill-treatment which leaves no marks.[3]

It was an unspoken hint of the potential scale of the problem.

Such a conclusion, however carefully worded, could scarcely be interpreted as giving the RUC's interrogators 'a clean bill of health', as some MPs tried to argue. As the government itself knew, but had never admitted, the whole premise on which the Committee had been set up was that ill-treatment had taken place. It was also the premise on which the Report was written. The only matter of dispute that remained was the scale on which ill-treatment had existed. There is no doubt that Judge Bennett himself believed that there had been ill-treatment on a disturbing scale and was aware that it had caused the doctors considerable distress, which he hoped would be alleviated

1. Bennett Report, para. 163.
2. ibid.
3. ibid., para. 164.

by the many detailed recommendations his Committee now made.

The ripples of the Bennett Report quickly spread across the Atlantic. In a St Patrick's Day statement issued the week after the Report was published, the four powerful political leaders of the Irish-American community – Senators Edward Kennedy and Daniel Moynihan, Leader of the House of Representatives Tip O'Neill, and Governor of New York Hugh Carey – said:

> If these reports and comments are accurate, the massive scale of the violations, the large number of victims involved and the lengthy period over which the abuses have occurred, make it difficult to believe that such practices could exist without the acquiescence, or at least the negligence of the British government.
>
> In effect it appears that the British government has violated the spirit of its recent pledge to the European Court of Human Rights . . . We urge that a more comprehensive investigation should now be undertaken, including an investigation of specific cases of brutality, the prosecution and punishment of all officials guilty of abuses, and other appropriate steps to see that such abuses will not recur.

In America, the Bennett Report produced more than just words. The Congress placed an embargo on 6,000 ·357 Ruger magnum pistols due to be sent to the RUC. The news came as a shock to people in Britain: it seemed to imply that they were being equated with the repressive regimes of the world with whom the Americans refused to do business under President Carter's Human Rights policy. It was an uncomfortable thought.

The government announced that it fully accepted the recommendations of the Bennett Report. It was left to its Conservative successor to implement them.

The Labour government had been living on a knife edge for months. Now deserted by the Scottish Nationalists and abandoned by the Liberals, who had ended the Lib-Lab pact, the government could no longer command a majority in the House of Commons. The votes of the Ulster Unionists, which the government had cemented by its offer of extra seats for the province, were no longer sufficient to keep the Labour government afloat. Technically the Prime Minister had six months left before he had to go to the country, but by the time the Bennett Report was published in March 1979 he knew he could barely hang on a few weeks, let alone six months. The last thing the government wanted was a spring election, after a winter of strikes which had destroyed the government's claim to have a special working relationship with the trades unions. The memories of that difficult winter were still too fresh to give the government much hope of winning an early election. Autumn looked a much better bet. But in order to scrape through the summer, Prime Minister James Callaghan needed to win a vote of confidence in the House. The motion was tabled for Wednesday, 28 March 1979.

The Labour whips did their sums and realized that the outcome might depend on a single vote. Every effort was made to ensure that every available Labour vote was on hand for the crucial division on the Wednesday evening. On their hair-line mathematics, the whips calculated that two votes were crucial to the government's survival, and both of them rested in the hands of Northern Ireland MPs. One was Frank Maguire, the Independent MP for Tyrone and Fermanagh; the other, Gerry Fitt, SDLP member for West Belfast. Maguire's vote was as unpredictable as Fitt's was reliable. Gerry Fitt had always supported the Labour government during his thirteen years as a Westminster MP, despite his political differences with Roy Mason and Michael Foot, who had offered the Ulster Unionists more seats at Westminster in return for their support. Frank Maguire was an Irish Republican, who did not recognize British sovereignty in the North of Ireland and usually saw no reason to throw a lifebelt to a government he held responsible for 'torture' at Castlereagh and the H Blocks of the Maze prison. But on this crucial division, every vote counted. Before the vote, Roy Mason's deputy, Don

Concannon, who was responsible for prisons in Northern Ireland, called at Maguire's home in Lisnaskea, where he ran a pub. It was said to be a purely 'social' call, as Concannon happened to be in the neighbourhood. It was stressed that there was no talk of the government buying Maguire's vote in return for a deal on the H Blocks. Nevertheless, Maguire flew over to London for the vote which was, in itself, an event.

Gerry Fitt, for the first time in his political career at Westminster, felt unable to give the Labour government his vote. During the debate, he made an impassioned speech from the floor of the House.

I did not make up my mind about how to vote tonight because of devolution in Scotland and Wales. I made up my mind the Friday before last when I read the Bennett Report on police brutality in Northern Ireland . . . That Report was only the tip of the iceberg. We have heard of Watergate and Muldergate and there will be a 'Bennettgate'. When the true story emerges of what has been happening in the Interrogation Centres, the people in the United Kingdom will receive it with shock, horror and resentment. That is why I take this stand.[1]

For Fitt, the Bennett Report had been the last straw. For nearly two years, he and his SDLP colleagues had been telling Roy Mason what they believed the Bennett Report now confirmed, that prisoners were being ill-treated in Northern Ireland's Interrogation Centres. As far as Fitt was concerned, it was families in his constituency who were most affected; it was their sons who were lifted in the early hours of the morning and taken off to Castlereagh for interrogation; it had been GPs in his constituency who had first brought ill-treatment to his notice. The government had denied it then, and continued to deny it even after Bennett. Fitt was furious. He demanded a full inquiry into the allegations which the government had neatly side-stepped when it set up the Bennett Committee. The

1. *Hansard*, 28 March 1979.

government refused. Fitt said that under the circumstances he could not vote for the government.

The Labour government lost the vote of confidence by 311 votes to 310. Maguire and Fitt abstained. Maguire had also said he could not vote for a government which condoned 'torture'. Had Fitt voted for the government, it would have survived with the addition of the Speaker's casting vote. It was a fine irony that the issue the government had consistently refused to face, the ill-treatment of suspects in its custody, was at the end of the day the issue that finally destroyed it.

In the General Election that followed, Mrs Thatcher's Conservatives won a handsome majority, guaranteeing her party a full term of office, and leaving the Labour Party in the political wilderness where, no longer cemented by office, the splits in the party grew wider. Had the government been able to hang on till the autumn, things might have been different.

The day after the government fell, Gerry Fitt and Airey Neave, the Conservative's shadow spokesman on Northern Ireland, shared a taxi together to get to the BBC to take part in the BBC Northern Ireland's 'Spotlight' programme. While travelling across London, they discussed the vote and the Bennett Report. Airey Neave, who had been a prisoner-of-war in Colditz in the Second World War, told Fitt that if and when he became Ulster Secretary, he would institute a full inquiry into the allegations. He said he had been tortured by the Gestapo and it had left its mark.

Airey Neave never lived to see his promise fulfilled. The following afternoon, as he was driving his car out of the House of Commons' underground car park, he was assassinated by a bomb planted under it by the Irish National Liberation Army.

After the Bennett Report was published, complaints of Assault During Interview fell again. In January 1979 there had been twenty-six; February, eighteen; March, eighteen. In April there were eight.

Although Dr Elliott still had no reason to complain of ill-treatment at Gough – he had seen no significant case for nearly a year – he had made complaints to DCC Hermon about what he called the 'lack of discipline' amongst visiting detectives. Visiting detectives were not happy either. They were infuriated by the restrictions they continued to face at Gough that they never faced at Castlereagh. Some of them told me they felt it a waste of time doing interrogations at Gough, as the controls were so tight. Differences of opinion between visiting detectives and the resident Senior Medical Officer were inevitable.

After the publication of Bennett, Dr Elliott felt that this 'indiscipline' grew to an intolerable level because neither the Secretary of State nor the Chief Constable had publicly accepted that prisoners had been ill-treated. He appears to have been particularly incensed by the official line which suggested that ill-treatment would be recognized only when police officers were convicted in court: it was like saying that a house had never been burgled because the burglars had never been caught.

Dr Elliott resigned from Gough Barracks the week after Bennett was published. Two incidents on 21 March 1979 finally exhausted his patience. The incidents involved two suspects from a Catholic housing estate in Portadown, who had been brought to Gough for interrogation. After three days both had been released without charges. One of them, a youth of seventeen whose instability both the police and Dr Elliott had recognized – he had already tried to inflict several minor injuries on himself – threw himself downstairs and had to be taken to hospital for X-rays. Dr Elliott was angry because the incident appeared to cause some detectives considerable amusement. The same afternoon, Dr Elliott advised detectives that the other prisoner, for whom he had already sought psychiatric advice, was only fit for limited interrogation. In addition, he suggested they take a gentle approach as, given the nature of the youth, he felt more information would be obtained that way. Apparently there was a showdown with the Detective Inspector in charge of the case. He told Dr Elliott that it was up to him to decide whether a suspect was mentally fit for interview, on the grounds that a prisoner's mental condition was his concern, not the doctor's. Many words appear to have been spoken in anger.

Although the incidents seemed trivial compared to events of the past – the RUC told me it was 'a family dispute' – coming as they did a week after Bennett, they marked the end of the road for Denis Elliott, who had spent eighteen months fighting for the kind of controls over interrogation which Bennett had finally recommended. Dr Elliott, convinced that Bennett had had no effect on the attitude of some detectives, resigned his post at Gough.

In a letter to the RUC explaining his resignation, he reviewed his experiences since 1977 and said he had been driven to two conclusions: results were expected and were to be obtained even if a certain degree of ill-treatment were necessary, and that a degree of ill-treatment was condoned at a very high level. Dr Elliott concluded that his position was untenable, despite the fact that he had tried everything in his power to ensure maximum safeguards for suspects undergoing interrogation. He clearly felt his efforts had been in vain.

The day before Dr Elliott wrote this letter to the RUC, the Medical Officer at Crumlin Road prison, Dr Brennan, was examining prisoner number 785/79, who had just come in from Castlereagh. The prisoner had been arrested and taken to Castlereagh on 2 April 1979, a fortnight after Bennett had been published.

He alleged that he had been made to stand against a wall with his arms outstretched while he was struck in the stomach with fists and kneed in the groin and thighs; he was made to 'hunker' (squat) against the wall with his arms extended, and was pulled up by the hair when he fell; he was passed around a ring of four detectives 'like a ball', while being slapped around the head and face. Dr Brennan noted extensive bruising of the abdomen. He concluded 'they would appear to have occurred about the time and in the manner alleged'. Even in the wake of the Bennett Report, little appeared to have changed.

On 22 June 1979, the Police Authority issued a statement designed to reassure the public. The Authority reported that it had asked the five doctors it employed to submit medical reports for the period May 1978 to June 1979 – the period between the publication of the Amnesty and Bennett Reports – where medical evidence tended to support allegations of ill-treatment. The Authority said it had received a total of eight cases over the thirteen-month period and concluded that 'the facts indicate that complaints against the RUC which may have substance have been relatively very few indeed in regard to persons interrogated as terrorist suspects and certainly do not warrant criticism on a scale to which the police have been subjected in recent times on this issue'. The RUC also pointed out that by the beginning of 1980 the DPP had not directed a prosecution against a police officer in any of those cases.

However, three points should be made. First, the doctors in fact submitted a list of twenty-nine cases where medical evidence tended to support the allegations. Only eight of them were believed to involve 'scheduled' (terrorist) offences. Second, the list may not have been comprehensive. For example, the prisoner whom Dr Brennan examined at Crumlin Road prison, whose case is detailed above, was not one of the names on the Police Authority's list. Third, the Authority noted privately that only twelve other cases had been submitted to them prior to 1 May 1978, although they admitted that twenty-eight of the forty-four prisoners named on the Crumlin Road prison list of 'Marked Men' bore signs of injury. Fourth, even if the Police Authority's figure of eight cases was definitive for the period between Amnesty and Bennett, given the public outcry at the time, it might have been reasonable to expect that there would not have been any.

19. Epilogue

'It is because this issue is so central both to the fight against terrorism and the maintenance of civilized behaviour by agents of the State that it needs to be cleared up publicly however difficult that may be.'

Observer editorial on the Amnesty Report, 11 June 1978

By the summer of 1979 a bloody and controversial chapter in the province's history was already closing. The leading actors in the drama were already moving on to other things. Roy Mason joined his Labour colleagues in the political wilderness as Shadow Minister of Agriculture. Kenneth Newman, now with a knighthood, was to return to England to take over as head of the police college at Bramshill. Dr Irwin was to resign as Secretary of the Forensic Medical Officers Association. Dr Elliott retired to the country. Both had lost many friends because of the stand they had taken. Jack Hassard and Donal Murphy both resigned from the Police Authority – Hassard still waiting for the resolution of James Rafferty's complaint. William Baird was no longer Secretary to the Police Authority, but had semi-retired to teach music and play golf.

On Monday, 27 August 1979, the chapter was finally closed when the Provisional IRA assassinated Lord Mountbatten and killed eighteen British soldiers at Warrenpoint. The new Prime Minister, Margaret Thatcher, flew to Belfast at once, and, visibly shaken by her visit, was taken under the army's wing. She was told that 'Primacy of the Police' or 'Ulsterization', the policy the British government had followed since 1976, under which the army had played second fiddle to the RUC, had failed. The army told the Prime Minister they had to be brought back into the game. Within weeks, the Prime Minister appointed Sir Maurice Oldfield, the ex-head of MI6, as Security

Coordinator in Northern Ireland. Senior officers of the RUC were bitter and regarded the appointment as an insult. 'Bugger Maurice Oldfield,' one of them remarked. With 'Ulsterization' now buried and the army back on the streets, the wheel appeared to have turned full circle.

One man, Hugh Murphy, a Falls Road taxi-driver, had paid several visits to Castlereagh and always been released without charge. Although, on past occasions, he had alleged ill-treatment, he always refused to sign statements. On 22 November 1979, Murphy was stopped at an army check-point in Turf Lodge. The army claimed that they found ammunition and a magazine inside his cab. Murphy was arrested and after twenty-four hours at Castlereagh was charged with possessing ammunition. When he was formally charged he denied all knowledge of the army's find and said that the ammunition had been planted on him in order to frame him. He was remanded in custody to await trial. This time there was no question of statements. They weren't necessary.

On 1 January 1980, Jack Hermon took over as Chief Constable. To the regret of some, and the relief of many, Castlereagh was now a shadow of its former self. As senior officers admitted, since Bennett it could no longer function effectively. Detectives who worked there said it was a waste of time. Morale was low. Some admitted that the Provisionals were ten times more motivated than they were after all the setbacks they had received from Amnesty, Bennett and everything else. They said they resented being the 'whipping boys', when they had only been trying to do their job.

One of the tasks that faced the new Chief Constable, Jack Hermon, was to restore morale. He was only recognizing the inevitable when he indicated that he wouldn't be relying on confessions any more to defeat the Provisional IRA.

It is also important to note that in the months that followed the publication of the Bennett Report, complaints of assault in police custody dropped sharply. Compared with 267 complaints of Assault During Interview in police custody made in 1978, there were 159 such complaints in 1979 and only fifteen in the first two months of 1980. Up to the time of writing, in 1980, doctors told me that they had seen very little to cause them concern. A year after the publication of the Bennett report, most of the new closed-circuit TV cameras – installed at a cost of £135,000 – were installed and working. By 1980 also, it appeared that the internal wranglings between RUC and army over control and security that had become public knowledge in the summer of 1979, following Warrenpoint and the assassination of Lord Mountbatten, had been finally resolved in favour of the RUC. The new Chief Constable, Jack Hermon, made it clear – and the government supported him – that the RUC would continue as the prime agency of law and order.

But although as far as Castlereagh was concerned there was an important change of emphasis in favour of hard evidence over confessions, the conditions of the hundreds of prisoners who had been convicted on the basis of statements made during it did not. Castlereagh and the Diplock courts had filled Northern Ireland's gaols with prisoners, most of whom would never have been there were it not for the statements they had made in police custody. The Provisionals continued to insist that they were 'special prisoners', and the government continued to deny it, refusing to acknowledge the fact that they had been arrested, detained, interrogated, tried and sentenced under 'special' emergency legislation. Only in prison did they suddenly become 'ordinary' prisoners, sentenced by a due process of law that was anything but 'ordinary'. In defiance of government's continued refusal to grant them 'special' status, the Provisionals escalated their blanket protest by refusing to wash and slop-out, and by covering the walls of their cells with their own excreta. But the government refused to be intimidated and the public refused to care.

Some members of the RUC, who recognized the political nature of the conflict and acknowledged the fact that many suspects had had statements beaten out of them, admitted that one day there would have to be some kind of amnesty. One detective told me that he believed the British government would have to talk to the Provos if ever there was to be a final resolution of the Irish conflict. He said he was tired of walking behind police funerals. With that day in mind, he told me he kept all his interview notes in case there were ever to be, at some distant date, a war crimes tribunal. He also ventured the opinion that 2 per cent of all those sentenced were innocent of the crimes of which they were convicted. Between 1976 and 1979, well over 2,000 suspects were charged. If that detective is right – and he was one of the RUC's interrogators – it would mean that over fifty prisoners in the province's gaols are innocent.

Some of those who knew the story from the inside were amazed that the British government was never taken to Strasbourg again, although they recognized that the Dublin government could hardly be the instigator once it had been found guilty of ill-treating its own prisoners by Amnesty International. However, should the British government be taken to Strasbourg, the same questions would no doubt be asked about Castlereagh as had once been asked about Palace Barracks, and once again the most important question of all would be asked. Did the authorities know of and condone the ill-treatment of prisoners? Was there, in the legal language of Strasbourg, an 'administrative practice'? In order to prove 'administrative practice', two things must be established. First, there has to be 'repetition of acts', that is, a pattern of ill-treatment at a particular place at the hands of a particular agent of the state. Secondly, 'official tolerance' has to be shown, meaning that either direct superiors knew what was going on and did nothing to stop it or punish those responsible, or that those in a higher authority showed indifference to the allegations by refusing to conduct an investigation to establish their truth or falsehood.

On the basis of these tests, both the European Commission and the European Court found the British government guilty of a 'practice' at Palace Barracks, at the beginning of the decade. If those same tests were applied to Castlereagh at the end of the decade, there is perhaps little doubt what the answer would be.

This book has been an attempt to explain why those questions were never asked.

Appendix 1: The East Antrim Gang

In 1975, East Antrim was plagued with a series of murders, robberies, explosions and inter-factional shootings. There was much intimidation and no one was prepared to give evidence against those responsible. The 'A' Squad was headed by Detective Chief Superintendent William Mooney – who was awarded the MBE in 1977 – an experienced interrogator who had investigated over twenty murder cases. The 'A' Squad's break came in August 1975, when a twenty-seven-year-old UVF officer gave himself up to the RUC and told them what he knew of the UVF's operations in the area. He took detectives to the site of the graves of two UDA men, Hugh McVeigh and David Douglas, who had been kidnapped by the UVF while delivering furniture in Belfast the previous April. They had never been seen again. The UVF informer said that he had been present at the graveside execution and gave the names of the others involved. He told the RUC that he was in fear of his life and wanted protection. At the subsequent trial he was referred to as 'Witness A'. On 6 October 1975, in an operation involving 500 uniformed RUC and sixty detectives, the whole area was sealed off and the UVF leadership arrested in the early hours of the morning. Castlereagh was cleared to receive them.

Twenty-eight men were charged with four murders, three attempted murders, six explosions, seven armed robberies and a number of firearms offences.

The trial ended on 11 March 1979 after lasting seventy-six days. It was the longest and costliest trial in Northern Ireland's legal history (the cost was estimated at £2 million). Lord Justice McDermott rejected the defendants' claim that they had been ill-treated at Castlereagh and gave eight of the twenty-eight UVF men life sentences.

The detection and conviction of the East Antrim gang was important for another reason. Like the RUC's equally successful prosecution of the Shankill Butchers – another Loyalist murder squad – it demonstrated the RUC's impartiality in bringing suspected terrorists to justice.

Appendix 2: The Judges Rules and Directive SB 16/13

As the threshold of admissibility was raised there was no corresponding increase in the protection the suspect was afforded. The laws had been changed to suit the security forces, not the civil libertarians. The Judges Rules remained a suspect's only protection in police custody and, as already observed, they were merely guidelines and had no standing in law. To remove the Judges Rules from the process of interrogation was to expose the suspect to a greater possibility of abuse, despite the Codes and Directives that specifically forbade it.

But despite the clear implication of Directive SB 16/13, the application of the Judges Rules to interrogation remains a matter of dispute. Professor Kevin Boyle says the position is unclear with regard to arrests made under Section 10 of the EPA. The Rules

contemplate a specific offence, of which the person being questioned is suspected, whereas under this Section the police may be aware of no such offence and be concerned only to gather intelligence through the interviews.[1]

The Bennett Report concluded that the RUC's own Code seemed

to recognize by implication that the Rules have no application where the questioning is general.

1. *Current Law Statutes 1978*, Sweet & Maxwell Ltd, para. 11.3.

Lord Shackleton, reviewing the workings of the Prevention of Terrorism Act, was more specific:

> The Judges Rules . . . apply to a person detained under the Act as they do to any person arrested under other powers . . . Even where a charge is not in prospect, however, the police are required to follow the practices and procedures laid down in the general orders of the force which will themselves accord with the Rules . . .[1]

Certainly as far as access to solicitors was concerned, a right which the Rules give prisoners 'as long as no unreasonable delay or hindrance is caused', the Rules did not apply either to interview or interrogation. At Castlereagh and Gough solicitors were denied access to their clients as a matter of practice.

The Rules are supposed to be displayed in police stations. On 8 December 1976 the government was asked in the House of Commons if the Judges Rules were 'prominently displayed in RUC stations, as suggested by the Rules themselves'. The question was evaded. The House was informed that 'specially printed notices' had been issued to all police stations in Northern Ireland which dealt with bail, fingerprinting, solicitors and legal aid. In fact the document referred to was the RUC's 'Notice to Persons in Police Custody' – Form FP 3/11. They were not the Judges Rules. During my visits to Castlereagh and Gough I never saw the Judges Rules displayed, although I was shown FP 3/11.

Certainly most police officers I spoke to, including those at the most senior level and members of the Special Branch, said that the Judges Rules applied to *all* forms of police questioning, whether they were interviews or interrogations. Some made the point that during an interrogation a suspect might say something that may lead to a criminal charge and therefore, to cover that possibility, the Judges Rules had to be applied.

1. *Report of the Committee of Inquiry into Police Interrogation Procedures in Northern Ireland*, Cmnd 7497, HMSO, p. 32.

Appendix 3: IRA Reorganization Document

The following are the contents of a document concerning plans for the reorganization of the Provisional IRA found by the Garda Siochana in the flat where former Chief of Staff Seamus Twomey was staying prior to his arrest of 3 December 1977. It was found in a pencil case in a flat in Royal Terrace, Dun Laoghaire.

STAFF REPORT

The three day and seven day detention orders are breaking volunteers, and it is the Republican Army's fault for not indoctrinating volunteers with the psychological strength to resist interrogation.

Coupled with this factor, which is contributing to our defeat, we are burdened with an inefficient infrastructure of commands, brigades, battalions and companies. This old system with which Brits and Branch are familiar has to be changed. We recommend reorganization and remotivation, the building of a new Irish Republican Army.

We emphasize a return to secrecy and strict discipline. Army men must be in total control of all sections of the movement.

1. A new rank of Education Officer must be created. GHQ must have a department of Education Officers available for Lectures and Discussions at Weapons Training Camps. Anti-interrogation Lectures must be given in conjunction with indoctrination lectures. The ideal outcome is that no Volunteer should be charged unless caught red handed.

It should be pointed out to new recruits the failures of our past structures – the number of men who have been arrested and signed their freedom away. The common sense methods of personal security should be thrashed out. Any new recruit mixing with known volunteers should be suspended pending discipline.

We must gear ourselves towards long-term armed struggle based on putting unknown men and new recruits into a new structure. This new structure shall be a cell system.

2. Ideally a cell should consist of four people. Rural areas, we decided, should be treated as separate cases to that of a city and town Brigade/Command area.

For this reason our proposals will effect mainly city and town areas where the majority of our operations are carried out and where the biggest proportion of our support lies anyway.

As we have already said, all new recruits are to be passed into a cell structure.

Existing Battalion and Company Staffs must be dissolved over a period of months with present Brigades then deciding who passes into the (reorganized) cell structure and who goes into the Brigade controlled and departmentalized Civil Administration (explained later).

The cells of four volunteers will be controlled militarily by the Brigade's/Command's Operations Officer and will be advised by Brigade's/Command's Intelligence Officer.

Cells will be financed through their cell leader who will be funded through the O C co-ordinator. That is, for wages, for running costs, financing of operations. (Expenses etc. will be dealt with through the O C.)

Cells must be specialized into I C cells, sniping cells, execution, bombings, robberies etc.

The cell will have no control of weapons or explosives, but should be capable of dumping weapons overnight (in the case of a postponed operation).

The weapons and explosives should be under the complete control of the Brigade's/Command's Q M and E O respectively.

Cells should operate as often as possible outside of their own areas; both to confuse Brit Intelligence (which would thus increase our security) and to expand our operational areas.

Brigades should be made use of in all operations.

The breaking up of present structure into administration sections and operational cells will make for maximum military effectiveness, greater security, a more efficient back up structure to increase support and cater for our people's problems.

Thus our Operations Officer can go straight into an area and deal exclusively with Military Operations and problems.

All present volunteers under old structure must be reeducated and given up-dated lectures in combating new interrogation techniques.[1]

The document concludes with a paragraph on the role of Sinn Fein.

Sinn Fein should come under Army organizers at all levels. Sinn Fein should employ full-time organizers in big Republican areas.

Sinn Fein should be radicalized (under Army direction) and should agitate about social and economic issues which attack the welfare of the people. SF should be directed to infiltrate other organizations to win support for, and sympathy to, the movement. SF should be re-educated and have a big role to play in publicity and propaganda depts., complaints and problems (making no room for RUC opportunism). It gains the respect of the people which in turn leads to increased support for the cell.

1. Author's note: The RUC say that they have obtained documents and material detailing the Provisional IRA's training in anti-interrogation techniques. The RUC will not comment on their contents, but one senior officer who had seen some of the material told me it was concerned with ways of 'hampering' an interrogator. He admitted that there was no mention of self-inflicting injuries.

More About Penguins
And Pelicans

For further information about books available from
Penguins please write to Dept EP, Penguin Books Ltd,
Harmondsworth, Middlesex UB7 0DA.

In the U.S.A.: For a complete list of books available
from Penguins in the United States write to Dept CS,
Penguin Books, 625 Madison Avenue, New York, New
York 10022.

In Canada: For a complete list of books available from
Penguins in Canada write to Penguin Books Canada
Ltd, 2801 John Street, Markham, Ontario L3R 1B4.

In Australia: For a complete list of books available
from Penguins in Australia write to the Marketing
Department, Penguin Books Australia Ltd, P.O. Box
257, Ringwood, Victoria 3134.

Some books on Politics and World Affairs
Published by Penguin Books